HEADWAY

TEACHER'S BOOK **PRE–INTERMEDIATE**

John & Liz Soars

Oxford University Press

Contents

Oxford University Press, Walton Street, Oxford OX2 6DP

Oxford New York
Athens Auckland Bangkok Bombay
Calcutta Cape Town Dar es Salaam Delhi
Florence Hong Kong Istanbul Karachi
Kuala Lumpur Madras Madrid Melbourne
Mexico City Nairobi Paris Singapore
Taipei Tokyo Toronto

and associated companies in
Berlin Ibadan

OXFORD and OXFORD ENGLISH are trade marks of Oxford University Press

ISBN 0 19 433989 0

© Oxford University Press 1991

First published 1991
Seventh impression 1996

Illustrations by Roland Harmer and Raymond Turvey

Set by Tradespools Limited, Frome, Somerset, England

Printed in Hong Kong

Description of the course

Headway Pre-Intermediate is part of the Headway series, a comprehensive course for adults and young adults learning English in their own country and in the United Kingdom. *Headway Intermediate* can be used as a third-year book; *Headway Upper-Intermediate* leads up to the level of the Cambridge First Certificate examination; *Headway Advanced* is a post-First Certificate book which leads up to the level of the Cambridge Proficiency examination. *Headway Pre-Intermediate* precedes the first, and it is expected that students will have completed either one or two course books prior to starting this one.

The aims of the course are to encourage students to analyse the systems of language in use, to expose them to a variety of challenging and interesting text-types in the listening and reading activities, and to stimulate them to give their own opinions and participate in discussions and roleplays.

Headway is a revision and extension course which provides a thorough coverage of the grammatical and lexical systems of English, combined with extensive practice of the four language skills of speaking, listening, reading, and writing.

Headway Pre-Intermediate provides approximately 120 hours' work, that is, eight hours per unit. This has to remain a somewhat artificial calculation, as teachers always expand activities or cut them short to meet the interests and needs of their students, and to fit in with the constrictions imposed by their timetable. The Workbook is an important component for use in the classroom and at home. It contains further practice of the language areas dealt with in the Student's Book, extra related input, and a writing syllabus.

Organization of the Student's Book

Each unit of *Headway Pre-Intermediate* has the following components:

PRESENTATION SECTION

The target language is shown in a natural context.

● Grammar questions

Students are guided to an understanding of the target language, and invited to work rules out for themselves.

PRACTICE

There are speaking, listening, writing, and grammar exercises to consolidate the target language.

● Language review

The essential rules of form and use are given, and students are asked to translate sample sentences. There is a reference to the Grammar section at the back of the book.

SKILLS DEVELOPMENT SECTION

Language is used for real or realistic purposes. The target language of the unit reappears in a broader context.

● Reading and speaking

There is at least one reading text per unit which is integrated with various free speaking activities.

● Listening and speaking

There is at least one listening activity per unit. This is also integrated with free speaking activities.

● Writing

There are suggestions for writing activities in the Student's Book. The writing syllabus is in the Workbook.

● Vocabulary

There is at least one vocabulary exercise per unit.

● Everyday English

This section comes at the end of each unit. Useful everyday language is presented and practised, for example:
– functional areas, such as greetings and requests
– situations such as the airport check-in desk
– saying numbers and dates
– spelling

Key-notes

A course book for teachers

Headway Pre-Intermediate provides teachers with a comprehensive package and a sense of direction, whether their course lasts for several months or an academic year. It aims to reflect the realities of the classroom, and to complement the teacher's task as far as possible. In the Presentation section, students are guided towards an understanding of the target language through texts and explanations, and their understanding is tested and confirmed via grammar questions, exercises, and an invitation to translate sample sentences. In the Skills Development section, texts and topics have been selected primarily for their interest level, but also for the language they exemplify. Finding texts that are both interesting and accessible to pre-intermediate students is very difficult. In their search for suitable material, teachers of this level risk using material that is either childish and has no real content, or they may use authentic material that contains language way above the students' comprehension. A result of this might be that teachers stop attempting fluency-based activities and have only language-oriented lessons, where students have little or no opportunity to behave as real language users.

Reading texts have been selected from newspapers, magazines, short stories, and biographies, and graded where appropriate. Listening texts are based on real interviews with real people, radio programmes, advertisements, and songs. There are pre-comprehension tasks which set up the activity, and motivate students to read or listen; and there are post-comprehension exercises, such as discussions, roleplays, or project work, to exploit the topic further. Speaking activities, controlled, semi-controlled, and free, occur throughout the unit. In the writing syllabus (which is in the Workbook), students are given training in areas such as writing letters, stories, postcards, reviews, descriptions, and form filling. In all the above, it is hoped that less experienced teachers will be able to rely on *Headway Pre-Intermediate* to provide a relevant syllabus and a balanced methodology, whilst experienced teachers can use it as a core course to integrate their own ideas with.

A course book for students

Much has recently been written about the need for students to take responsibility for their own learning, to be involved in the decision-making, and to 'learn how to learn'. *Headway Pre-Intermediate* has been organized so that students can get the maximum benefit from it as a language learning resource. In the Introduction on page 6 of the Student's Book, they are encouraged to reflect on their role in the teaching/learning processes. It is of fundamental importance that they always know *what* they are doing in class and *why*, so that they become aware of what is involved in language learning. The organization of the Student's Book and the Workbook is made clear to them, and the introduction explains how a unit is structured and how the resource material at the back of the book can be used for active study. It is suggested that at the end of every lesson they should ask their teacher two questions:

– *What did we learn in this lesson?*
– *What are we going to learn in the next lesson?*

There are two reasons behind these questions. Firstly, students should be fully aware of their teacher's aims. What a teacher thinks he/she has done in a lesson can be remarkably different from what students think they have done. Secondly, by knowing what is going to happen in the next lesson, students can prepare themselves in advance.

Throughout the book, activities are signposted to let students know exactly what they have to do. The headings at the beginning of each unit tell them the linguistic aims of the unit, and every new stage of a lesson is signalled, so that learners can focus their attention on the task in hand.

There is constant cross-reference to the resource material, which consists of a Grammar section, unit-by-unit vocabulary lists, and three appendices of irregular verbs, dependent prepositions, and verb patterns. These are to be used as checks at relevant moments in the course of a unit, and for reference whenever students need after that.

After every three units in the Workbook, there is a Stop and Check revision section, which encourages students to review what they have been doing and to decide their priorities for future self-study.

Headway Pre-Intermediate is primarily a course book for classroom use, but it also aims to give individual students insights into language learning processes, and ideas for structuring self-directed learning.

Accuracy and fluency

In recent years there has been much research into how learners learn. The results are inconclusive, but it would appear that students learn in many ways. Some of the questions raised are *When do learners learn more? Is it when the focus of a lesson is on a **part** of the language?* (A *part* might be a grammatical area such as the **going to** future, a functional area such as apologizing, a lexical area such as colours, or a phonological area such as sentence stress.) *Or do they learn more when the focus of a lesson is on the language as a whole?* In such activities, students use the language for *real* purposes, and they behave as real language users. They roleplay everyday situations, they read authentic material, and they do project work.

This is the premise of the accuracy-versus-fluency debate, and it is impossible to resolve, because different teaching approaches appeal to different students at different times. It is probably best to see the situation not in terms of accuracy work *or* fluency work, but accuracy work *and* fluency work. It could be argued that a due measure of both at all levels constitutes a reasonable, balanced approach.

In discussions about the debate, there is the assumption that accuracy and fluency-based activities are entirely different. They are seen as divergent influences. In the *Headway* series, the aim has been to make accuracy and fluency cohere, and see them as confluent influences. In Unit 3 of *Headway Pre-Intermediate*, for example, two past tenses are practised in the Presentation section. Students' attention is on a part of the language. In the Skills Development section, they read an extract from a James Bond story, and listen to an interview about the life of the author Ian Fleming. In doing this, students' attention is on the language as a whole, but both texts contain many examples of past tenses, so the items are consolidated by being seen in context. It is possible to have elements of both accuracy and fluency in the same activity if a natural situation for practice can be found. Students will learn language not only by practising being a language user in fluency work, but by acquiring more of the parts in accuracy work.

Accuracy work

The accuracy work in *Headway Pre-Intermediate* appears in the Presentation section, the Vocabulary section, and the Workbook.

Grammatical syllabus
The approach to grammatical items is generally two steps forward, one step back. Students often feel that because they have had a lesson on, say, the Present Perfect, they 'know' the Present Perfect, but this is sadly not the case. Language items are not learned accumulatively, but acquired through a process of exposure, understanding, and practice over a period of time.

Many items that are found in a first-year book are revised and practised in *Headway Pre-Intermediate*, but more information is given, and the practice is more demanding. For example, in Unit 1 question forms are revised (for several reasons – see the Notes on the Language Input for Unit 1). Students see *all* the question words, and examine **what/which** + noun and **how** + adjective or adverb. In Unit 2 **have got** is revised and seen in conjunction with **have** and the **do/does** forms. In Unit 4, expressions of quantity are revised, and the use of articles is practised. In Unit 5, **want** + infinitive and **like** + **-ing** form are revised, but they are seen in the context of the whole area of verb patterns.

Some items present students with few problems, others are difficult to master and need a lot of practice. Examples of the second are the Present Perfect, saying numbers, prepositions, **What ... like?**, future forms, short answers, and question tags. Some items will be genuinely new to your students, such as **used to**, Past Simple versus Past Continuous, the Present Perfect Continuous, conditional sentences, and the Past Perfect.

Students are referred to the Grammar section at the back of the Student's Book, where they will find rules of form and use, common mistakes, and areas that are easily confused. This section can be studied as homework after the presentation, or in class if it is not too long. Occasionally it is suggested that students look at it *before* a presentation if the item is difficult, so that when the lesson begins, they have already begun to consider the area.

Language review and translation
The Language review comes at the end of the Presentation section, and is seen as the 'blackboard stage' of a lesson. The essential rules of form and use are given to serve as a written record of the introduction to the new language.

There is also an invitation to translate sample sentences in the target language. The use of translation is a contentious issue in language teaching these days. There are several reasons for this. It is seen as a retrograde step, going back to the 'bad old days' of Grammar Translation. Some teachers feel that if they allow just a small amount of L1 in the classroom, this will 'open the floodgates', and students will revert to it endlessly. Some teachers in multilingual classes dislike their loss of control, as they have no idea what their students are talking about.

However, it could also be argued that translation, if harnessed, is a potentially very powerful tool for language learning, and to pretend that students don't have a first language is perverse. If, by comparing L1 and L2 language systems, the students' insights into L2 are furthered, so much the better. You might be able to stop students speaking L1, but you can't stop them thinking and writing in it. If a justification for translation were needed, it would be the Eureka cry of *Ah!* that you hear as, for one student in your class, the 'penny finally drops'.

In *Headway*, translation is suggested as a means of checking what students are thinking, not as a medium of instruction, as it is in the Grammar Translation method. The invitation to translate comes at the end of a situational presentation, after students have read the language item, heard it, spoken it, answered grammar questions about it, and read rules about it. It is possible for students to do all these things mechanically, without cognitively considering what the item means. Translating offers a window into their mind.

In fact, what often happens when students are asked to translate is that they argue not about English but about L1. They have learned the English form consciously and analytically, and have a language rule in their mind, but they have very probably never analysed their own language in the same way.

Make sure that students translate for concept, not form. For example, the use of **will** for spontaneous intention is often expressed by a present tense in many languages. So *I'll give you my telephone number* must not be translated into *Je vous donnerai mon numéro de téléphone* (French), but *Je vous donne mon numéro de téléphone*.

If you are teaching in a monolingual situation, it is obviously much easier to ensure that the students' translation is correct. In a multilingual situation, it is more difficult, but far from impossible. Put students into language groups. Don't forget that if necessary, similar language groups can work together. If you have an isolated student, ask him or her to check their translation with a compatriot from a higher class.

Naturally, you might be worried that the activity gets out of control! The worst thing that could happen is that a group of students argue endlessly in L1 about their own grammar. The activity shouldn't go on for more than four or five minutes. Sometimes you will be able to do it in a matter of seconds. When you decide that it is time to stop, exercise Draconian control and shout *Stop!*

Vocabulary syllabus
Vocabulary work is given a very prominent place in *Headway Pre-Intermediate*. There are usually two exercises per unit in the Student's Book and one more in the Workbook. There is a three-pronged approach to vocabulary development:

1 *Teach new words.*
Lexical sets such as fruit and vegetables, clothes, travel by rail and air are introduced. These are important but limited, as there are so many words in the language.

2 *Encourage effective vocabulary learning habits.*
If you can persuade your students that they need to take some responsibility for their own vocabulary acquisition and can equip them to do it, you will have done them a great service. Unfortunately, many students find the effort too much, but this is not a reason for you to stop trying.

In early units, students are helped to use their bilingual dictionary, both L1 to L2, and L2 to L1. There are many exercises in the Student's Book and the Workbook where either they are given a set of pictures (so they know the word in L1) and have to find the right word in English, or they are given the English word and they have to find the equivalent in L1. There are also extracts from *The Oxford Elementary Learner's Dictionary of English*, showing how collocations, doubling of consonants, and word stress are given.

In the Listening exercise in Unit 5, eight learners of English describe how they approach their own vocabulary learning, and you should encourage students as strongly as possible to try some of these.
Vocabulary networks are suggested as a means for students to add to their vocabulary.
The word lists at the back of the book should be filled in regularly with the translation. You might want to do this at the end of every unit, or as you go through a unit, but unless you 'push', students will do nothing with them.

3 *Introduce students to the systems of vocabulary.*
There are patterns to vocabulary just as there are patterns, or structures, to grammar. They can be used as a vehicle for a vocabulary lesson, and if students come to perceive these patterns, they can act as 'pegs for learning'. Examples of these systems are synonyms and antonyms, homonyms, collocation, homophones, **-ed** and **-ing** adjectives, and multi-word verbs.

Don't forget to refer students to the three Appendices at the back of the book. They cover irregular verbs, dependent prepositions, and verb patterns.

The Workbook
The Workbook consists of exercises that practise the items taught in the Presentation section of the Student's Book. They are suitable for use in class or at home. The key to the Workbook exercises is in this Teacher's Book. You may like to photocopy the answers and give them out so that students can practise correcting their own work.

When tenses are practised, exercises that test the form precede those that test meaning. First there are exercises on forming the positive, question, negative, and short answer, then exercises where students have to discriminate. Many of the vocabulary exercises could be done as warmers in class. The writing syllabus is at the end of each unit, and usually consists of text analysis followed by parallel writing. The text analysis part is best done in class.

After every three units there is a Stop and Check section, which revises much of the input of the three previous units. There is a suggested procedure for its exploitation at the end of Unit 3 of the Teacher's Book. Don't forget to recommend a good grammar and practice book (which must, of course, have a key so that learners can use it on their own).

The Pronunciation book
There are references to exercises in the Pronunciation book (*Headway Pre-Intermediate Pronunciation*) in the body of the unit notes, when the exercise directly relates to an activity in the Student's Book. Otherwise, the exercises are listed at the end of the notes in the **Don't forget!** box. So don't forget them! The Pronunciation book contains useful, interesting exercises to be done in class, in the laboratory, or the self-access centre, and they can provide balance and variety in your timetable. Students might want to buy the book and the tapes themselves.

Fluency work

The lower the language level, the harder it is to have genuine fluency-based activities, because students simply do not know enough language, either receptively or productively. Most unadapted authentic reading texts are probably beyond their ability, and using material that is too difficult can leave students frustrated at what they *don't* know rather than confident with what they *do* know.

In *Headway Pre-Intermediate*, there are fluency-based activities for reading, speaking, listening, and writing. If students find these rather daunting at first, don't worry. They might not have been asked to read anything or listen to anything as long before, but the topics have been carefully selected and the tasks graded. In the free speaking activities that precede and follow the comprehension texts, beware of over-correcting, as this is often demotivating and counterproductive. Students will make many mistakes, but they should be allowed to express themselves as best they can. Naturally, you will have to correct if the message is indecipherable!

Topics have been selected to appeal to people of all ages from about fourteen and above, although it is impossible to please everybody all of the time. We have tried to include topics that have a 'timeless' feel to them, about which both young and old should have something to say. Topics included are:
– People, the great communicators
– Living in capital cities
– Relationships between parents and children
– How strict should schools be?
– Favourite shops
– Arranged marriages
– How 'green' are you?
– Traffic in our cities
– The role of men and women in your country
– Dreams

There are some roleplays, but most of the free speaking comes from personalization exercises, where students are asked to give their own thoughts and talk about their own experiences. This should be more interesting than giving imposed information, and is an example of the natural use of language.

There are six jigsaw activities, where the class divides to study different texts, then comes together to share information. Jigsaw listening requires two or more rooms, which may be inconvenient, but jigsaw reading can be done in one room. These activities are very productive for several reasons: they practise more than one language skill (and often all four); they present an automatic information gap, and students must use language to cross that gap; and if the topic is well-chosen, students are genuinely interested to find out the information they don't know. You need to be very careful with your instructions, however. If you and your class like such activities, you could jigsaw other material in the book, for example the listening in Unit 8, where three people give advice about visiting their country for a holiday, and the listening in Unit 13, where two people talk about their experience of being of mixed nationality.

The exercises that aim to teach the writing skill are in the Workbook, but in most units of the Student's Book there is a suggestion for free writing. When you look at this, beware of over-correcting for the same reason as given above. You might choose to see these free writing exercises as process writing, so be sure that your comments relate only to content, not language.

The Video

A video accompanies *Headway Pre-Intermediate*. It consists of six 'situations' and six documentary-style 'reports'. Information is given in the **Don't forget!** boxes.

We hope you enjoy using *Headway Pre-Intermediate!*

INTRODUCTION (SB page 6)

As you begin *Headway Pre-Intermediate*, you are probably starting a new course, possibly with a new group of students, in which case your initial aims will be introduction and orientation. It is essential that the group feels relaxed, and that people think they are at least beginning to get to know each other. Make sure everyone knows each other's name.

The aim of this introduction is to invite students to think a little bit about languages and language learning. It is not intended to be a serious debate on second language acquisition, rather a pre-sessional mental 'warm-up', where students can reflect on the importance of their active role in the classroom. They are introduced to the organization of *Headway Pre-Intermediate* so that they can get the most out of it as a learning resource.

To the student

Welcome to *Headway Pre-Intermediate*!

If possible, do this exercise in the students' first language. You can read a sentence out loud, with students reading, and then you can translate it. Try to ask questions to involve them, but don't be surprised if you get very little comment or feedback. Students might not have been asked to think about their attitudes to learning before.
You can ask questions such as:
– *What do you like doing in an English class?*
– *Do you like speaking?*
– *Is it important to learn vocabulary?*
– *What do you do outside class to help you with your English?*
– *Do you read/listen to tapes/listen to music?*

The Student's Book

After you have shown the class how a unit of the Student's Book is organized, ask them to look at Unit 1 and find the Presentation section, the Practice section, the Language review, the Skills Development section and the Everyday English section. Ask them also to find the Grammar section in blue at the back of the book.

The Workbook

Do the same for the Workbook.

You

Here we suggest that students ask you, the teacher, two questions at the end of every lesson:
What did we learn in this lesson?
What are we going to learn in the next lesson?

The idea is not to force you, the teacher, to plan two lessons at once! We are trying to stress the point made earlier on this page, that students must know *what* they are doing in class and *why*, if they are to gain maximum benefit from the lessons. Perhaps you are in the habit of telling students what they're going to do at the beginning of the lesson, which is fine. But we would like to encourage students to ask you these questions to make sure they know what's happening.

In our experience, students need a lot of reminding and encouraging to keep asking these questions. They forget to ask in their hurry to leave the room, and they may feel that they are questioning your authority. If you like the idea, don't give up on it. Perhaps it can even become a joke – the class can question you in chorus before you/they leave the room!

UNIT 1

Question forms (1) – Present Continuous – Social English

Introduction to the Unit

The title of the unit is 'People'. In the Presentation section, students are asking each other questions to get to know each other, and in the Skills Development section there is the theme of 'People, the great communicators'. Parent/child relationships and the generation gap are explored in the listening.

Notes on the Language Input

Grammar

It is often a good idea to remind yourself of the grammar in each unit before you prepare your lessons. One way you can do this is to read the appropriate Grammar reference section at the back of the Student's Book.

Question forms

Question forms are the main grammatical focus of Unit 1. This is partly so that students can then ask each other questions, and partly for diagnostic reasons. As the teacher, you need to get to know your students both as people and language learners, and you need to know their linguistic strengths and weaknesses. Perhaps you don't know the language areas covered by students in their previous classes, but you can be sure that some work was done on present, past, and future tenses. By working on questions forms, you can do two things:
1 You can find out how much students know about basic tense forms.
2 You can 'get down to work' and help students with a language area that they always find tricky. Questions do not present students with difficulties of concept but of form. They often omit **do/does/did**, or fail to invert the subject and verb, and try to ask a question (as do many Romance languages) by using the same word order as the positive but with a rising intonation.

You want a coffee?

In Unit 1, the main tenses used are Present Simple and Present Continuous, but there are a few occasions when students are asked to use the Past Simple and the **going to** future. This is for the reason mentioned in 1 above, which is to find out how much students know.

Present Continuous

The Present Continuous is dealt with in this unit, but not in great depth. This is because more attention is given to question forms, and because the Present Continuous is far less common than the Present Simple, which is covered in Unit 2. It is presumed that students have a certain familiarity with the forms and uses of the Present Continuous, although naturally mistakes will be made. In the Student's Book, two uses of the Present Continuous are practised:
1 to express an activity happening now.
   Peter's having a bath.
2 to express an activity happening around now.
   I'm working hard these days.
In the Workbook, there is an exercise on the third use of this tense, which is to express a future arrangement.
3 *What are you doing tonight?*
Uses 1 and 3 are often dealt with in first year courses.

Vocabulary

In the Vocabulary section, students are helped to use a bilingual dictionary, both L1 to English and English to L1.

Everyday English

Common greetings and salutations are practised.

Notes on the Unit

PRESENTATION   (SB page 7)

Question forms and the Present Continuous

T.1a and b

Introduction: Ask students to look at the picture of Rob Fellows, and ask some questions:
– *How old is he?* (About nineteen.)
– *Where is he?* (In front of an old building, like a castle.)

– *What does he do?* (Maybe he's a student.)
– *What do you think the buildings are?* (Maybe they're part of a university.)

1 `T.1a` Ask students to read the text about Rob as they listen to the tape. Check any words you think your students might not know. Avoid the temptation to ask questions about Rob, because this would necessitate the use of the third person (*Where does he come from?*). In this first presentation exercise the first and second persons are used, so that when students come to ask each other questions and ask you questions in the Practice exercises on page 8, they are fully prepared.

2 Ask students to look at the picture of Maggie. Ask questions:
– *Where is she?* (At home.)
– *What's she doing?* (She's studying.)
– *How old is she?* (About thirty-five.)
– *Is she studying at university?* (Perhaps. We don't know.)
Ask students to work in pairs to complete the questions about Maggie. Naturally, some students will do well, and others not so well.
Answers
a. Where does she come from?
b. What is she studying?
c. How many languages does she speak?
d. Is she enjoying her course?
e. Where does she live?
f. Who does she live with?
g. When did her course start?
h. What is she going to do after the course?

Possible problems
Students omit **does** and **did** in the Present and Past Simple.
They confuse the Present Continuous and the Present Simple (* What does she studying?).
They treat the modal verb **can** as though it were a full verb (* How many languages does she can speak?)
They forget **is** in the **going to** question. (* What she going to do after the course?)

When students have finished, ask individuals for the completed questions. When each question form has been established, give a model yourself and drill each question, chorally if you like, but certainly individually, for pronunciation. Remember that English uses a wider voice range than many other languages, and question-word questions should start with the voice high and then fall.

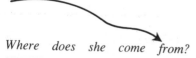

Where does she come from?

3 `T.1b` Students listen to Maggie and, working in pairs, they write the answers to the questions.
Answers
a. She comes from Australia.
b. She's studying art.
c. Two.
d. Yes, she is.

e. She lives near London.
f. She lives with her husband and three children.
g. A year ago.
h. She's going to look for a job as a librarian in a museum.

4 Students work in pairs to complete the questions.
Answers
a. Which university do you go to?
b. Have you got/Do you have a job?
c. When did you come to England?
d. What's your husband's name?
e. What does Dave do?
Again, you could drill these questions around the class.

5 Students work in pairs to match the questions and the answers.
Answers
1 – d.   2 – g.   3 – b.   4 – c.   5 – f.
6 – a.   7 – e.

● Grammar questions (SB page 8)

Ask students to look at the two example sentences, and ask the Grammar questions to the class. Make sure that all the class absorb the information. This is where students are expected to think analytically about the language, so don't rush it. If your students find it easier or more rewarding to answer in L1, let them.
Answers
– The two verb forms are Present Simple and Present Continuous.
– They are formed differently. In the third person of the Present Simple there is **-s** at the end. The Present Continuous uses the verb **to be** and the **-ing** form of the verb.

More importantly, they mean different things. The Present Simple is used to express an action which is always true, or true for a long time. The Present Continuous is used to express an activity happening now, or around now.

PRACTICE (SB page 8)

1 Speaking and listening

1 If you feel your students have enough questions to want to ask each other, ask them immediately to start. If you feel they would like a few minutes first to think of some questions, let them do so. If your students already know each other well, distribute pictures of people cut out of magazines, and they can assume these new identities.
As students are asking and answering questions, monitor the pairs, helping and correcting as necessary.

2 Give students three or four minutes to think of some questions to ask you. If they know you very well already, you could have a picture of someone else. Hold it up and say *This is me. Think of some questions to ask me.*
Correct any mistakes very carefully. You want to have genuine communication at this point, but you also want well formed questions with a good pronunciation.

2 Grammar

Students work in pairs to decide which is the correct verb form. As you get the answers, ask *Why?* each time to reinforce the rules about the Present Simple and the Present Continuous.

Answers

a. comes (because this is a fact which is always true)
b. speaks (same reason)
c. is wearing (because this is an activity happening now)
d. smokes (because this is a habit)
e. isn't smoking (because this is an activity that *isn't* happening now!)

3 Speaking and listening

Students work in small groups to answer the questions. Monitor the groups very carefully. Be prepared to help students with vocabulary, especially for clothes. Expect there to be mistakes, as students confuse the two present tenses.

> **Possible problems**
> Short answers – *Are you smoking now?** No, I don't. *Does your teacher smoke?* * Yes, she is.
> Students mix the forms * I'm wear trousers.
> They forget to use the verb **to be** * Maria writing.

● Language review (SB page 8)

Question forms

Read the Language review all together. You can tell students that these are *all* the question words in English. Students might like to translate the question words.

Present Continuous

Read the explanation of the Present Continuous. Ask students in groups of three or four to translate the three sentences in the Translate box.

> **Note**
> Many languages either don't have the forms to express the differences between the two present tenses in English, or use them only occasionally. In many languages, the sentences *He smokes ...* and *He's smoking ...* will be expressed by the same form, so be prepared to explain if this causes your students to worry. Remember that the aims of the Translate section are to check understanding and to make students aware of language systems in L1 as well as English.

▶ **Grammar reference: page 120.**

Ask students to read the Grammar reference at home.

> **Additional idea**
> Play the mime game to practise the Present Continuous. Give an example yourself, first, to show students what they have to do. Mime an action such as doing the

washing-up, playing golf, driving a car. Students have to guess what you're doing, and make a sentence in the Present Continuous:
You're doing the washing-up.

> **Additional material**
> **Workbook Unit 1**
> These exercises could be done in class to give further practice, for homework, or in a later class to revise.
> Question forms – exercises 1–7.
> Present Continuous – exercises 8–11.
>
> **Pronunciation book Unit 1**
> Stress and intonation in question forms – exercise 3.

SKILLS DEVELOPMENT

● Reading and speaking (SB page 9)

This is perhaps the first time with this class that you are doing a fluency-based lesson and as you are no doubt aware, your aims in such lessons are different from accuracy-based lessons. You aim now to have natural language use, with students trying to understand and trying to make themselves understood with all the language they possess. Depending on the type of course your students had before this one, they will be more or less used to the demands of such lessons.

It can be frustrating for students at this level to do fluency work, because their lack of language prevents them from understanding and saying all that they would like. However, if the right topics are found, it can be extremely beneficial and enjoyable for students to realize that they can operate as real language users.

A lot of speaking work in *Headway Pre-Intermediate* comes from activities before and after reading and listening comprehensions. In the pre-reading task to this comprehension, 'Hello, People of the World!', students are talking about animals and people, and what one group can do that the other can't. Let this discussion go on as long as everyone seems interested. You might find that by the time you get to the 'What do you think?' questions, students are tired, having worked hard at the speaking activity and the reading comprehension.

Pre-reading task

1 Students work in pairs (or groups of three or four) to write down the names of as many animals as they can. Maybe some groups will only manage six or seven, but others might come up with thirty! When getting the feedback to this exercise, while students are reading out their lists of animals, you need to take care that the lesson doesn't degenerate into a free-for-all vocabulary session on animals! Teach *some* of the new words to the rest of the class, and put *some* of the words on the board, but you won't be able to deal with *all* of them.

Saying what animals can do that people can't is more difficult, but students should be able to come up with a few ideas, for example:

Fish can swim under the water, because they can get oxygen from water.
Birds can fly thousands of miles and return to the same place.
Cats can see in the dark.
Dogs have a very good sense of smell.
Horses can run fast.
Animals can live in the wild.
Monkeys can climb trees very well.
Insects can walk on walls.

2 Students think of things that people can do that animals can't, for example:

We can live in many different places in the world.
We can draw pictures.
We can communicate very complicated ideas.
We can think about the past and the future.
We can write.
We can laugh.

3 Students look up the words in their dictionaries. You can check their translations in L1.

Possible problems

When they look up *record*, they find only *to save on a tape or disc*.

When they look up *sense*, they find only *reason* or *wisdom*.

When they look up *look after*, they can't find the right definition because it is a multi-word verb, and dictionaries give information about multi-word verbs in different places. Also, it has a subtle meaning, perhaps translated by several different verbs in L1.

Reading

Students read the article. Allow enough time for them to read it at least twice. Some students might want to use their dictionaries once or twice, which is fine, but discourage them from using their dictionaries fifteen or twenty times. That really shouldn't be necessary, and students lose the thread of the article if they spend too much time looking up words.

Note

The words near the top of the article mean *Hello* in different languages.

Salut is French.   صباح الخير *Sabah al khair* is Arabic.
Hola is Spanish.
Ciao is Italian.   你好 *Ni hao* is Chinese.

コんにちは *Konnichi-wa* is Japanese.

Students work in pairs or small groups to answer the comprehension questions.

Answers

1 Paragraph 1 – b.   Paragraph 3 – d.
   Paragraph 2 – a.   Paragraph 4 – c.
2 (No set answer.)
3 With faces, hands, bodies, voices, and writing.

4 Because we can record what happens and read it later. We can read now what someone wrote four hundred years ago.

What do you think?

Discuss these questions as a class. Students might have a lot to say, or they might be tired, having worked hard.

Question 3 will bring out any current news about the environment. Notice that the question (and probably the answer) uses the Present Continuous.

● Vocabulary   (SB page 10)

Using a bilingual dictionary

Bilingual dictionaries are very useful when students are beginning to learn a language, but they need to be used with caution. They vary greatly in amount of detail and accuracy of information. The better ones will separate out different meanings, and give plenty of example sentences. Problems arise especially when students look up a word in the L1 to English section and find perhaps three or four words in English to choose from. They need to look at the information very carefully to know which one is correct in context.

In these exercises, students are asked to look at their own dictionary to see how much information it gives. They then practise using both halves of their dictionary, first English to L1 then L1 to English.

---

1 Students look at the dictionary extract. If they are used to using dictionaries to look words up in their own language, they should be able to do it for a foreign language quite easily. However, the reverse is also the case. If students *aren't* used to using dictionaries in L1, basic skills such as alphabetical order and the standard conventions of dictionary entries (how information is presented; the order of information; symbols) will need to be practised.

2 Students look at their own dictionaries. Ask them to find the entry for *book*. You could conduct the feedback in L1 if you want.

3 Students decide if the words in the box are nouns, verbs, etc.

Answers

bread – *n*	came – *pt*	write – *v*
in – *prep*	quickly – *adv*	hot – *adj*
eat – *v*	on – *prep*	never – *adv*
beautiful – *adj*	went – *pt*	letter – *n*

Students write another example of each word class, and check the abbreviations in their dictionary.

4 Read the introduction to the exercise carefully with your students. Then ask them to use their dictionaries to find the correct definition and translation.

Answers

a. book = reserve
b. fan = supporter (e.g. football fan)
c. sink = doesn't stay on top of water
d. kind = nice, friendly
e. flat = no mountains

f. on strike = not working
g. tap (e.g. in the bathroom)
h. change = small coins
i. mean = not generous
j. ring = phone call
k. branch = local office or shop
l. play (e.g. at the theatre)
m. boot (at the back of a car)

5 You might decide to leave this question for another lesson, or
   you could set the first part for homework and do the second
   part at the beginning of the next lesson.
   Answers
   key   diary   purse   chewing gum   season ticket
   comb   receipt   file   plaster   lipstick   calculator
   pair of scissors   lighter   packet of hankies   wallet

Additional idea
Bring in as many of the everyday objects as you can.
When students have found the word in their dictionaries,
put the object on the floor. Carry on until all (or most) of
the objects are on the floor. Point to an object and ask for
the word to be repeated. Correct any mistakes. Ask a
student to come out to the front and point at an object and
invite a student to repeat.

What follows is a memory game. Remove one object from
the floor. Students must remember what the object was, so
that when you point to the empty space on the floor, they
can still tell you the word. Carry on removing objects until
about a third remain on the floor. After that, it becomes
very difficult to remember exactly what was where!

Additional material

Workbook Unit 1
Exercise 12 is a vocabulary exercise which practises using
dictionaries.

Pronunciation book Unit 1
Exercise 1 is the first of several exercises that introduce
students to the phonemic script, which is very useful if
they want to know how to pronounce a word.

● Listening and speaking   (SB page 11)

T.2a and b

Leaving home

This is the first of several jigsaw activities in *Headway
Pre-Intermediate*. The only drawback of such activities is
that with jigsaw listening (not so much reading), you
ideally need two rooms, as students can't concentrate on
their own tape if they are all together. Hopefully, this
drawback is compensated for by the involvement of the
students. If a jigsaw goes well, they have to speak a lot,
listen a lot, (perhaps) read a lot, and write. So it is a multi-
skills lesson with a built-in information gap – group A
doesn't know what group B knows (and vice versa), and
they have to work together to find the missing information.

Pre-listening task
Students work in groups of perhaps five or six to discuss the
questions. Let this go on as long as everybody seems interested.
You will probably want to have some class feedback, or perhaps
you could discuss question 2 as a class.
The aim of question 3 is to teach or check the vocabulary item *to
keep in touch*, as it appears on the tape.

Jigsaw listening
T.2a and b   Students divide into two groups, with a tape
recorder and the right tape. They will need to listen several
times. You should go between the two groups, making sure that
they are all right, and helping where necessary. Tell them that
they can't answer *all* the questions.

When both groups are ready, bring the class back together, and
ask students to find a partner from the other group. If you have
an odd number of students, you will need a group of three. Be
careful that the class doesn't collapse into chaos at this point!
Students need to find a partner and sit down together *as quickly
as possible*!

Comprehension check
Students will naturally have differing information. By and large,
our sympathies should lie with Jackie more than her father, who
seems to think his daughter is still a little girl.
Answers
1   Jackie says she came to London because she wants to be a
    professional dancer, and the best schools are in London. Her
    father says he doesn't know why she went.
2   Two months ago, says Jackie. Her father doesn't say.
3   They both say she's living in a flat in north London.
4   She says she's living with another girl. He thinks she's
    living with her boyfriend.
5   She says she's doing a course at the National Dance School.
    He thinks she is doing a sort of ballet course.
6   Her father says Tony doesn't have a job. Jackie doesn't say.
7   She says she works with a theatre group, teaching dance to
    children. He thinks she works in a theatre or club.
8   She says it isn't dangerous, it's exciting, and there are a lot
    of things to do.
9   She says she phones home every Sunday, and sends
    postcards when she goes to a museum or art gallery. He says
    she doesn't phone very often.
10 She says she loves them, but she doesn't want to live at
    home for the rest of her life. He thinks that she would like to
    come back home.

What do you think?
Discuss the three questions in groups or as a class. If your class
is motivated, question 3 could extend into a discussion.
–*Do you think 16 is the right age for people to get married?*
–*When would you like to get married?*

Note
In Britain, people can get married at 16 if their parents
agree, otherwise the earliest age is 18. They can vote when
they're 18. They can smoke when they're 16. They can
ride a motorbike when they're 16, and drive a car at 17.

● Everyday English   (SB page 12)

Social English

T.3

1   Students look at the cartoon. 'How do you do' is very formal.

> **Note**
> How do you do does not end in a question mark. This is
> because it is not asking for information. It is always
> answered by How do you do. It is also worth pointing
> out to students that in English How do you do is only
> exchanged once, the first time people ever meet!

Students match a line in A with a line in B. This exercise is
more difficult than it at first appears. Some students will
finish it very quickly, but will probably have made several
mistakes. Look at their work and say how many they have
right and wrong, and ask them to look again.

2   T.3   Listen to the tape to check answers.
   Answers
   Hello, Jane! – Hi, Peter! (Two friends greeting each other
      informally.)
   How are you? – Fine, thanks. (Both formal and informal.)
   See you tomorrow! – Bye! (Both formal and informal.)
   Good night! – Sleep well! (Said as people go to bed.)
   Good morning! – Good morning! (Formal more than
      informal; said, for example, at work.)
   Cheers! – Good health! (When we're drinking.)
   Excuse me! – Yes. Can I help you? (In a shop, for example, to
      get someone's attention.)
   Bless you! – Thanks. (When someone sneezes.)
   Have a good weekend! – Thanks! Same to you! (Said on a
      Friday afternoon or evening.)
   Thank you very much indeed. – Not at all. Don't mention it.
      (Formal rather than informal. Informally, we might say
      That's OK.)
   Make yourself at home – That's very kind. Thank you. (Said
      when a guest comes to your house.)
   Ask students to look at the cartoon and tell you where some
   of the above dialogues are taking place.

Don't forget!

Workbook Unit 1
There are two exercises on writing, exercises 13 and 14.
Students are asked to write an informal letter.

In the Teacher's Book, we sometimes suggest when the
writing activities could be done, but generally we leave it
up to you to decide. The Correcting mistakes exercises, of
which there is one every unit, could well be done in class
as warmers at the beginning of a lesson. You could do the
same yourself by selecting some of your students'
mistakes when you are correcting their written work and
putting them on the board for the class to correct.

It can be productive to use a code when you are correcting
written work, so that you direct students to the nature of
the mistake, and then they have to try to correct it. This is
not always possible – the mistake might be way beyond
what they could be expected to understand. Be selective in
what you ask students to self-correct.
You might like to use the following symbols:

G	Grammar	/	This word isn't necessary.
P	Punctuation	∧	A word is missing.
WO	Word order	T	Tense
WW	Wrong word	Sp	Spelling
Prep	Preposition		

It is a useful, although difficult, skill to teach students to
proof-read their written work before handing it in. Here
are two suggestions.
1   Do the Correcting mistakes exercises in class. Students
   must first identify the nature of the mistake using one of
   the above symbols, then actually correct it.
2   When you collect in written work, you can occasionally
   redistribute it straight away, making sure that a student
   doesn't get his/her own work back. In pairs, and in
   pencil, students try to find and correct mistakes. Do this
   just for ten minutes. Students tend to get very critical,
   and start finding mistakes where there aren't any!

Pronunciation book Unit 1
There is an exercise on word linking – exercise 2.

Word list
Make sure your students complete the Word list for Unit 1
by writing in the translations.

UNIT 2

Introduction to the Unit

The theme of this unit is 'Lifestyles' in various countries. The Presentation section has texts about lifestyles in different European countries, and provides the opportunity to practise the Present Simple and **have/have got**.

The Skills Development section contains readings about how other nationalities find life in Britain, and a listening about 'Life in a Japanese school'.

There are opportunities throughout the unit for students to compare lifestyles in their own country with the lifestyles described. If it is their country's lifestyle being described, they can discuss whether they think what is said is true or not.

Notes on the Language Input

Grammar

It is often a good idea to remind yourself of the grammar in each unit before you prepare your lessons. One way you can do this is to read the appropriate Grammar reference section at the back of the Student's Book.

Present Simple

The Present Simple is revised in its form and uses. It is assumed that students will have a certain familiarity with the Present Simple, although of course mistakes will still be made.

All forms are practised. Particular attention is given to forming questions and short answers using the auxiliary **do/does**. The uses of the Present Simple – present habit and permanent truth – are contrasted with the uses of the Present Continuous (see Unit 1).

Have/have got

The verb **have** for possession is used as part of the practice for the Present Simple. However, it is also contrasted with **have got** for possession in both form and use.

Students at this level are often familiar with **have got** from their beginners' and elementary courses, but they are a little confused about its relation to the verb **to have** both in its form, particularly in questions and negatives, and in its use. In fact they are often interchangeable, but generally speaking **have got** is more informal.

Vocabulary

The vocabulary activity continues the dictionary work from the previous unit and also introduces the idea of word networks as a way of building vocabulary. The lexical area is electrical household goods, chosen because it fits well with the theme of lifestyles, allowing students to talk about what they have in their homes.

The activity widens out as it continues into revision of rooms in a house, and students are asked to produce a similar network diagram for the contents of a room in their house, again involving dictionary work.

Everyday English

This is practice in the recognition and production of numbers in English, an area which often needs revision at this level (and indeed most levels).

Notes on the Unit

PRESENTATION (SB page 13)

Present Simple and *have/have got*

Introduction: Ask students to name (in English!) as many European countries as they can. This should be done *quickly*. You could make it into a little competition. Set a time limit and see who can write down the most in that time.

1 Ask the students (possibly in pairs) to look at the flags in their book, discuss which country they think they belong to and write the name of the country beneath the flag.
  Answers
  1 France   2 Spain   3 Holland   4 Italy
  5 Great Britain
  Check answers with the whole class before the next exercise.

15

2 Tell the students that they are going to read five short texts with some facts about each of the countries. (The information is all from a survey done by a market research organization called Mintel.)

Ask them to work in pairs to read, then discuss which of the five countries they think is being described. This can generate quite a lot of discussion, as some countries are easier to identify than others, so you may have to encourage them to do it by a process of elimination.

If there are any vocabulary problems, deal with them quickly yourself rather than asking students to use dictionaries. You do not want the activity to last too long, because the main aim of the reading here is to provide a context for the grammar.

Before you give the answers, encourage some full-class discussion. Ask questions such as:
– *What did you decide? Why?*
– *How did you decide?*
– *Which facts **most** helped you to decide?*
Answers
a Spain   b Holland   c France
d Great Britain   e Italy

3 The aim here is not only to personalize the activity and have a short discussion about the students' own countries (this can be quite heated if the students do not agree with the information in the text!), but also for you, the teacher, to be noting how well the students are using the Present Simple and **have/have got** before moving on to the grammar work.

● **Grammar questions** (SB page 14)

The Presentation section reaches its main aim at this point. Focus the attention of the whole class on these questions so that your students are clear about the grammatical aims of the lesson.
Answers
– The tense used is the Present Simple (not the Present Continuous) because present habits and permanent/general truths are described.
– **Have** not **have got** is used because of the nature of the texts. They are giving formal and factual information in writing. **Have got** would more likely be used when speaking personally. (You could give and/or ask for one or two examples of **have got** – *I've got a new bag./Maria's got two dictionaries.*, etc.)
They can both be used when speaking informally, but **have** must be used in more formal writing.
– The forms are different – **have** is formed like the Present Simple with the auxiliary **do/does** in questions and negatives; **have got** uses **has/have** as the auxiliary in questions and negatives (see Practice exercise 1).

Students might well come up with the differences of form, but it is unlikely that they will know that **have** is more formal (or more American!) than **have got**.
You could at this point ask students to look back at the texts and find examples of the Present Simple and **have/has**.
They could work in pairs again and focus on one text only, different pairs on different texts, and you could ask them to find examples of any adverbs of frequency as well as the verbs.

PRACTICE (SB page 14)

This section aims to provide controlled oral and written practice of the grammar.

1 Grammar

Focus the students' attention on the examples in the speech bubbles. These are to highlight the differences in form of the questions, short answers, and negatives of **have** and **have got**. Get your students to practise the examples orally.
You could chorus drill them and/or practise them individually, doing the questions and answers around the class. You need to listen carefully, correcting their mistakes and paying attention to the pronunciation, particularly the stress and intonation in the questions and answers:

Do you have a car?   Yes, I do.

Pairwork
Put the students into pairs. Tell them to use the prompts to ask and answer questions.
This practice is personalized but still controlled. It is important that you go round the class to help, monitor, and correct where necessary.
Tell the students to take it in turn first to ask and then to answer the questions. They can choose whether they use **have** or **have got** in the question, but the answer must match.

> **Possible problems**
> Students omit the auxiliary **do/does** and/or **got**:
> * Have you a car?
> * I haven't a computer.
> (Although these forms are possible, they are slightly stylized, and it would be unwise to present students with three forms of **have**.)
>
> They mix the two forms:
> * I don't have got a computer.
> *Have you got a car?*   * Yes, I do.
>
> They are reluctant to use the more natural short answers:
> *Have you got a car?   Yes, I've got a car.* – rather than just *Yes, I have.*
> *Do you have a computer?   No. I don't have a computer* – rather than just *No, I don't.*

A nice way to end the activity and draw the full class together again is to ask one or two members of the class to tell the others about their partner. This also provides practice of the third person after the first and second person practice in the pairwork.
Teacher   *Thomas, tell us about Maria.*
Thomas   *Maria has a camera and a stereo but she doesn't have a computer or a bicycle.* etc.

2 Speaking and listening

This activity is a controlled jigsaw activity and brings together practice of the Present Simple and **have/have got**. It also reminds students of the difference between the uses of the Present Simple and Present Continuous.

Pairwork

Make clear which student is A and which is B. They must only look at their own chart. They each have information about two of the people in the chart. To complete their chart they must question each other about the other people and make notes in the blank boxes in their chart.

1 Ask students to work together to prepare their questions fully. This should preferably be done orally, but some weaker students might feel happier doing it in writing also.
   Answers
   Where does he come from?
   Is he married?
   Does she have any children?
   Has he got any brothers or sisters?
   How many children/sisters/brothers has she got/does she have?
   What does she do?
   What does she do in her free time?
   Where do they go on holiday?
   What's he doing at the moment?
   Check their questions before they start the next part of the activity.

2 While students are asking and answering questions to complete their charts, you should go round the pairs to help and check.
   When the charts are filled ask one or two individuals to tell the whole class about someone in the charts. For example:
   Teacher *Juan, tell us about Chantal.*
   Juan *Well, she comes from Paris; she isn't married. She's got two older brothers and she's a fashion buyer. She likes jogging and going to ... etc.*
   You could also encourage a little bit of discussion at this point by asking the students if the people in the charts are typical of their country in relation to the information in the Presentation texts on page 13.

3 This activity is definitely optional and very short. Students question each other about their own free time and holidays. This is to give some personalized practice of the Present Simple in first and second persons for those students who might benefit from further practice.

3 Writing and listening

T.4

Again, this is a controlled practice activity to bring together all the language points in this unit. It practises the formation of questions with **have/have got**, the Present Simple, and the Present Continuous from the previous unit.
It also picks up on one of the people from the chart, Emma, the schoolgirl, and takes the form of an interview between her and a market research organization.

1 Ask students to read through the interview quickly first to get an idea of the content. There should be no difficulty with vocabulary.
   Then ask them either individually, in pairs, or in small groups

to try and complete the interviewer's questions in the dialogue.

2 T.4 Play the tape and ask the students to listen very carefully to check their answers. There could be some slight variations from the words on the tape, which of course does not matter as long as the English is correct.
   You could photocopy the tapescript on page 119 at the back of this book and give it out if you feel it would be useful (or if the students ask for it).

3 Depending on time available, the students could do this activity in class in pairs or small groups or it could be set for homework.
   Pairs of students could read their dialogues aloud to the others in the class. This would be a good pronunciation exercise.

● Language review   (SB page 15)

Present Simple

Read the Language review on the Present Simple all together. Put students into small groups to translate the sentences.

Present Continuous

Now ask students to re-read the review of the Present Continuous in the previous unit, then translate the next two sentences.
It is important to discuss and highlight the differences and similarities in the use of the two present tenses in English and the present tense (or tenses) in the students' own language. You could use L1 to do this.

Have/have got

Read the review all together. If you want to, you could provide a couple of examples for translation, or use some of the examples in the book for this purpose.

► **Grammar reference: page 121.**

Ask students to read this at home, perhaps before they do some of the Workbook exercises for homework (see below).

Additional material

Workbook Unit 2
These exercises could be done in class to give further practice, for homework, or in a later class to revise.

Present Simple – exercises 1–6.
Present Simple or Continuous exercises 7–9.
Have/have got – exercises 10–12.

Pronunciation book Unit 2
Exercise 1 could be done in a later class, perhaps in the language laboratory.
Sounds /s/,/z/,/ɪz/ – Present Simple third person singular verbs – exercise 1.

SKILLS DEVELOPMENT

● Reading and speaking   (SB page 15)

This is a fluency activity, in the form of a jigsaw reading.
The class divides into three groups and each group reads a
different article about someone from another country who
came to live in Britain.
After the reading, students from the different groups get
together to swap information about the person in their
article. This should result in some natural speaking
practice where the students' main attention is on the
completion of the reading task. The selection of the
articles means that students will need to use (naturally and
without noticing it) some of the grammar taught in this
unit – Present Simple and **have/have got**.
The articles come from a popular weekly magazine. The
three people still live in Britain.

Pre-reading task

1 Ask students to close their eyes for a few minutes and think
   of Britain, then write down the first five things about Britain
   that come into their heads.
   Two examples are given in the Student's Book to help trigger
   ideas and signal that this activity is meant to be fun.
2 You should put the class into the three groups for the jigsaw
   activity at this point.
   Go round the groups as they compare their lists, and draw the
   attention of the whole class to any things that you think are
   interesting or funny. Encourage others in the class to
   comment, thereby generating a short discussion if you can.
   Keep asking them to tell you *why* they thought of the things.

Reading

You need to be very clear when giving instructions for any
jigsaw activity. If necessary give them in L1.

Name the groups A, B, or C and focus each one onto their text
only. Tell them the name and country of origin of the person
they are going to read about and say that they will find out about
the people in the other texts later.
Allow dictionaries to be used while reading, but make it clear
that they should read through quickly first for general
understanding and that this can be lost if they look up too many
words. They need to know the important vocabulary, because
they may be required to help other students with it (see
Comprehension check 2).
Each group has the same three questions to answer after the
reading.
You should also ask them if the person in their article mentions
any things about Britain that they discussed in the Pre-reading
task.

Answers

Group A- Kimiko	Group B – Xavier	Group C – Margaretha
1 She came to Britain because she married an Englishman.	1 He came because of his work. (Probably, but this is not directly stated.)	1 She came first to learn English, then she married an Englishman.
2 She is a translator and a housewife.	2 He is a chef.	2 She's a full-time housewife.
3 She likes: – the greater freedom for women. – the attitude of men to women and the home. She dislikes: – the education system. – no small clothes in the shops.	3 He likes: – British fashion. – shopping, especially the fresh food in supermarkets. – street markets. He dislikes: – British men's attitude to women. – British bathrooms. – the closing times of shops.	3 She likes: – British people because they are friendly. – British men because they are polite and romantic. – British food, especially tea (now!). She dislikes: – British houses (they are not built well). – the litter.

Comprehension check

1 Get the groups to re-form, this time with at least one A, one
   B, and one C in each group. They have to tell each other
   about the person in their article before they go on to read the
   other articles and, as a group, answer more detailed questions
   on all three people.
2 Tell them to read the other two extracts. If they have any
   vocabulary problems they ask the student who has already
   studied that article to help them. This is for speed, and to
   encourage a feeling of co-operation in the group. Dictionary
   work would slow things down at this stage.
3 Tell the group to discuss the true/false questions all together.

Possible problem
If students become very involved in activities they
sometimes start talking in L1.
If this happens just occasionally in a group don't worry,
but if L1 takes over you could remind them to speak in
English as best they can, because it's good practice.
You are not going to be correcting them much in this
activity, as its aim is fluency, not accuracy.

Answers

a. False – Japanese men relax more in Britain and help their
   wives more in the home, so their wives are probably less
   busy.
b. True – He thinks they look good because they don't follow
   fashion so seriously.
c. True

d. False – Xavier thinks that English men don't show consideration for the women; Margaretha thinks that the men are polite and romantic.

e. True

f. False – Kimiko complains because she can't buy small clothes. Xavier complains about the times shops close. Margaretha doesn't give her opinion of the shops.

g. True – Xavier doesn't like British bathrooms, where the shower is part of the bath. Margaretha says that British houses are not built well and have a lot of draughts.

h. True.

You could circulate during this activity, but if the students are working well in their groups, let them get on with the activity and discussion. Don't be tempted to give the answers at this stage.

Draw the class together again to get the feedback on the answers. Ask *why* when they say *false*. Then move on to the last activity.

What do you think?

This activity is to round off the lesson and make the discussion more personal to the students.

They could form groups or pairs again to get some ideas, but it is not expected that it will be a long discussion, as there will probably not be much time.

You could also ask:
– *What five things do you think foreign people think of first about your country?*

Thus bringing the lesson full circle!

Additional Material

Pronunciation book Unit 2

Connected speech – exercise 3 – strong and weak forms of *does, was, has*, etc. This follows on from the reading about Kimiko.

● Vocabulary (SB page 17)

Vocabulary networks

It is hoped that from an activity such as this students will see the advantages of recording vocabulary in related groups. Encourage your students to keep their own special notebook for vocabulary.

Also, as you go through the units of *Headway Pre-Intermediate*, get the students to check the vocabulary list for each unit at the back of the Student's Book.

Begin the lesson by telling your students to look quickly at the box of words. Ask them what the words have in common. Tell them not to worry if they don't know all the words. They should recognize enough to be able to say perhaps:

They're all in a house. or
They're all electric.

Now read through the introduction to the activity with your students.

Check that they understand the words in the diagram.

Ask them to work in pairs to look at the words in the box more carefully, using their dictionaries to check the meaning and also the pronunciation, and then ask them to write the words in the diagram under the correct headings.

The students could practise saying the words to each other as they write.

Answers

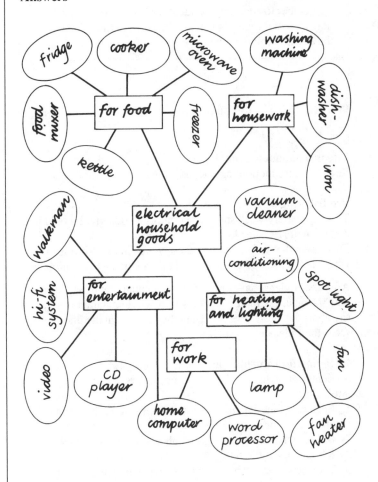

Go through the diagram with the whole class and get the students to practise the pronunciation as you go.

Discussion

You could put the class into small groups to discuss these questions. The idea is that the vocabulary is practised in a personalized way. Also the names of rooms will be revised as students answer the questions.

In the last activity in this section students are asked to make a similar diagram by themselves. You will probably need to spend a little time setting this up. Ask them to suggest a room in their house for the centre of their diagram, then ask what headings could go round this. For example:

The centre word *bedroom* could have the headings *furniture*, *soft furnishings*, *decoration*, *entertainment*, *electrical equipment* around it.

You could set this for homework and your students could describe the room to each other at the beginning of the next lesson.

Additional material

Workbook Unit 2
Exercise 13 is a vocabulary activity which introduces more household items with pictures, and gives further practice in dictionary work.

Additional idea

Remember to encourage students to keep a vocabulary notebook and remind them to add words to this whenever they do a vocabulary exercise such as this one.

● Listening (SB page 17)

T.5

Life in a Japanese school
Read the introduction together as a class.

Pre-listening task

This vocabulary work should be done quite quickly. It could be done in pairs for speed.
Encourage the students to find these words in the Word list for Unit 2 at the back of the book, and to write in the translation.

After the students have studied the vocabulary, and before you play the tape, ask them what they think Graham Grant is going to say about Japanese schools. Then they can listen the first time to see if their ideas were correct.

Listening for information

Students could discuss the questions in pairs.
Answers
1 Because of the Japanese attitude to jobs, Japanese people often have the same job for life.
2 Because they must get a good job as soon as they leave school, or it is too late.
3 They start to work hard at twelve, when they move from primary to junior school.
4 The pupils sit in rows, and before each lesson they bow to the teacher.
5 They go to extra classes; and they do three or four hours' homework every evening.
6 No, they don't.
7 They go to school on Saturday, and in the holidays they go to club activities at school, for example sports clubs, art clubs, English clubs.

At this point it might be a good idea to bring forward the **What do you think?** questions and have a short discussion to compare school life in your students' countries with Japan. (Or, if you have Japanese students, ask them if it is true.)

Asking and answering questions

Clear instructions are needed for this activity. It aims not only to check comprehension but also to practise question formation.

Divide the class into A groups and B groups and focus them on the appropriate box. Make it very clear that the box contains the answers and their job is to write the questions, taking care with the grammar. You will need to help and monitor the groups and check their questions, because students often find it very difficult to form questions from answers.

When the questions are complete each student A finds a student B. First student A asks student B to answer (without looking) the questions that the As have just written, then student B does the same with the B group's questions. Thus every student in the class has practice of both asking and answering questions.

Answers

Group A
1 What is Graham Grant doing at the moment?
2 How long do most Japanese people stay with the same company?
3 How many children are there in each class?
4 Why don't Japanese children ask (the teacher) questions?

Group B
1 How many days a week do Japanese children go to school?
2 How much homework do they do? / How long do they study?
3 Do they enjoy school?
4 What is the interviewer's/presenter's daughter doing at the moment?

What do you think?
1 This personalized discussion could be done earlier (see above).
2 This can be as short or long a discussion as you have time or inclination for:
   – You could just throw it open to the whole class for a few ideas at the end of the lesson.
   – You could put students into groups to get some ideas before having an open discussion.
   – You could ask the students to think about it at home and make notes, using their dictionaries, and have a follow-up discussion in the next lesson.

● Everyday English (SB page 18)

The exercises in this section could be done on different days as warmers before your main lesson or to close the lesson.

Numbers

T.6a and b

Before you do this exercise, remind the class of numbers. You could have them go very quickly round the class from 1–100, or play the following little game: Tell the class you're thinking of a number between 1 and 100. They must ask you questions to find out the number.

Examples

Is it more than 50?

Is it under 30?

Does it begin with a 6?

Are the two numbers the same?

Is it an odd number?

One or two other students could have a turn to think of a number.

1 Read the examples aloud and ask individuals to repeat them. Put the class into pairs to practise saying the next numbers and go round to help and correct them. Pull the whole class together for a final check.

Answers

two hundred and seventy-seven

four hundred and eighty-nine

six hundred and twelve

five thousand, eight hundred and seventy

three thousand, nine hundred and twenty-three

fifteen thousand, eight hundred and four

one hundred and eighteen thousand, three hundred and seven

one hundred and sixty-five million

Possible problem

Students want to add an **s** and say:

* *five thousands* or *sixty millions*   This is wrong.

---

2 Read through the first part with the students and practise saying the numbers. Get them to exaggerate the **-ty** or **-teen** at first when they say them.

T.6a   Ask students to underline the number they hear on the tape.

Answers

a. 16   d. 90

b. 50   e. 13

c. 18

Get them to check their answers with a partner before you ask for the answers from the whole class.

Prices

First ask your students to identify the pictures of English coins on the page.

Then ask them to look at the examples of how prices are written and spoken and practise them by reading them aloud.

1 T.6b   This activity is called a *number dictation*. Students only write down the number they hear in each short conversation.

Play the tape through completely the first time.

Answers

1 62	4 220 (pesetas)	7 £6.50	10 870
2 182	5 £614	8 106	11 435
3 14	6 £87	9 £227	12 £19

To check the answers play the tape again, but pause after each conversation, get the students' suggestions, and establish the correct answer.

2 You should check exchange rates before the lesson because your students might not know them.

Note

In the UK, the average price of a three-course meal for one person in a good restaurant is about £20 a head.

The average price for hamburger and chips is about £2.50.

The average price of a hotel room (bed and breakfast) is about £30–£40 outside of London, £60–£80 in London.

A packet of cigarettes is £2.00 or more (for 20).

---

3 Finally, get students to make a list of some numbers and English prices and dictate them to a partner.

Don't forget!

Workbook Unit 2

There are two exercises on writing – exercises 14 and 15. The linking words **and**, **so**, **but**, **however**, and **although** are practised. Then students are asked to write about their own lifestyle and the lifestyle of someone in their family.

Pronunciation book Unit 2

There is an exercise on stress in nouns with two syllables – exercise 2.

Word list

Make sure your students complete the Word list for Unit 2 by writing in the translations.

Video

Section 1 – Situation: *The Station*

This supplements Units 1 and 2 of the Student's Book. It features David and his Italian friend, Paola, who appeared in *Headway Elementary* video. David goes to the station to meet Paola off the train. Students practise greeting people and the language of stations.

21

UNIT 3

Past Simple – Past Continuous – Time expressions

Introduction to the Unit

The title of this unit is 'Fact and fiction'. In the Presentation sections, students revise and extend their knowledge of two past tenses via newspaper stories. In the Skills Development section, students are invited to read an extract from a James Bond novel. They practise telling a story from pictures, and listen to an interview with the biographer of Ian Fleming, the author of the James Bond books.

Notes on the Language Input

Grammar

It is often a good idea to remind yourself of the grammar in each unit before you prepare your lessons. One way you can do this is to read the appropriate Grammar reference section at the back of the Student's Book.

Past Simple

Students will already have a certain familiarity with the Past Simple, and may be able to use it quite accurately on a basic level.

Possible problems
Many regular verbs will be known, but you can expect problems with the pronunciation of **-ed** at the end, for example:

helped	*/helped /	/helpt/
saved	*/seɪved / instead of	/seɪvd/
watched	*/wɒʃt /	/wɒtʃt/

It is worth doing some work on this problem, but don't expect students to master it easily! It takes a long time to get right. There is an exercise on this in the *Pronunciation* book.

Students will also know some common irregular verbs, such as *came, went, saw, met* and *took*, but there are unfortunately still quite a few for them to learn! Remind students that there is a list of irregular verbs at the back of

---

the Student's Book. You could ask them to learn five new irregular verbs every week. Do a little test on them from time to time.

The use of **did** causes problems. Students forget to use it, for example:
*What time you get up?
*Where you went last night?
*I no see you yesterday.
*You have a good time at the party?

Learners try to form a past tense of **have** with **got**, which is uncommon in English.
*I had got a cold yesterday.
English prefers forms with just **had**.

Past Continuous

The Past Continuous could well be new to students at this level. In the Presentation it is contrasted with the Past Simple, and in this context, the difference between the two tenses is clear. However, the fundamental use of the Past Continuous to describe background events and temporary situations in the past is quite a difficult one to grasp. Learners find it hard to see the difference between sentences such as:

It **rained** yesterday.
It **was raining** when I got up.

I **wore** my best suit to the wedding.
She **was wearing** a beautiful red dress.

The Past Continuous is not dealt with in great depth in this unit. Instead, the Presentation aims to lay a foundation, and students will learn to recognize the tense as they see it in context, and gradually they will begin to produce it.

While is often used with verb forms in the Past Continuous.
While I was having lunch, James arrived.
Learners often confuse **while** and **during**. Exercise 9 in Unit 3 of the Workbook deals with this.

Vocabulary

The Vocabulary section contains the first of several exercises on collocation, that is, words that go together. This unit deals with verbs and nouns that go together, and preposition collocations.

Don't forget to remind students that there is a list of words + preposition at the back of the Student's Book.

Everyday English

The Everyday English section deals with time expressions – saying dates, and phrases with and without prepositions. Both these areas cause problems of form, because there are so many 'bits' to get right.

Notes on the Unit

PRESENTATION (SB page 19)

Past Simple

T.7

1 Introduction: Ask students some questions about last night:
– *What did you do last night?*
– *Did you go out?*
– *Did you watch television?*
– *Who did you talk to?*
– *What did you have to eat?*
– *What time did you go to bed?*
– *Did you sleep well?*
Listen carefully to their replies to see how well they are using the Past Simple. You could ask them *What tense were all my questions?* to see if they know the name of the tense.

Ask students to look at exercise 1. Students write in the base forms of the irregular verbs. They could use the list of irregular verbs at the back of the book. (The base form of the verb is the same as the infinitive without **to**.)
Answers

spend	catch
sink	eat
leave	break
meet	see
hear	can
have	take

You could drill some of the irregular verbs, especially those with a difficult pronunciation.
heard /hɜːd/
caught /kɔːt/
ate /et/

2 Ask students to look at the pictures on page 19. Ask questions:
– *What can you see?*
– *Do the people look OK?*
– *What's this called?* (A whale.)
– *And this?* (A shark.)
– *What happened to their boat?*
– *What's the man doing?* (Catching fish.)
Teach the word *life-raft*. Ask students to read the story.

3 T.7 Read the introduction and the examples very carefully, and play the tape. After the first playing, put students into pairs to compare information. Play the tape again and put students in pairs again. They will need to write down their sentences.

Possible problem
When getting the feedback to this exercise, insist on good pronunciation. This requires a wide voice range to express surprise and strong stress to show contrast.

They weren't from New York.

They were from Miami.

Answers
They didn't meet any sharks. They met some whales.
They didn't have two life-rafts. They had one.
They didn't have tins of fruit. They had biscuits.
They didn't cook the fish. They ate them raw.
They didn't lose the line. It broke.
Bill didn't catch fish in a cup. He caught them with his hands.
One or two ships didn't pass them. About twenty ships passed them.
Bill and Simone didn't jump onto the fishing boat. The captain carried them.

4 Students work in pairs to ask and answer questions. They should write them down. After a while, get the feedback. Insist on correctly formed questions, and make sure the question starts with the voice high.

How   many   days   were   they at sea?

Possible answers
Where did they come from?
Did they survive in good condition?
When did they meet some whales?
What was the name of their yacht?
What did the whales do to their boat?
What food did they have?
Did they have any water?
How did they get fresh water?
How many fish did they catch?
Did they cook them?
How did he catch fish after the line broke?
How many ships passed them? (= a subject question without **did**)
How did they get onto the fishing boat?
Where did the fishing boat take them?

● Grammar questions (SB page 20)

Put students in pairs or threes to answer the grammar questions.
Answers
– The Past Simple, because it is a newspaper report of an incident that happened in the past.
– With **did** + the infinitive (students will probably use the term infinitive instead of base form).
– With **didn't** + the infinitive.

PRACTICE (SB page 20)

1 Grammar

Students write in the Past Simple of the verbs. The first eight are regular. They are all found in the 'Real Life Drama' reading on page 19, so you could ask students to look at the text again, if they want.
When students have the right answers, drill the words for the pronunciation of **-ed**.
Answers

started /ɪd/	passed /t/
jumped /t/	picked /t/
watched /t/	survived /d/
happened /d/	saved /d/

Regular past tenses are formed by adding **-ed**. If the verb ends in **-e**, add **-d**.

carried	married
studied	

If the verb ends in consonant + **y**, change the **-y** to **-ied**.

was/were	went
bought	hit
came	knew
did	made
fell	rang
felt	said
found	sent
flew	swam
gave	threw

2 Speaking and listening

Students work in pairs to talk about what they did last night, last weekend, etc. Monitor the groups carefully. There will no doubt be mistakes of form and pronunciation, but you can't correct them all, so be selective! As you go round the groups, you could write down some mistakes, and after you have conducted the feedback, you could write them on the board for the class to correct.

> **Additional idea**
> This is a variation on a drill to practise the question and the Past Simple. Find pictures of people doing everyday things such as going for a walk, watching TV, playing tennis, fishing, swimming, reading, writing a letter,

playing a piano, etc. You need quite a few. Ask the class to stand up in a circle if you have a small class, or several circles if you have a large class. Give Student A a picture of, say, someone playing tennis. Ask the student *What did you do yesterday?* Student A says *I played tennis.* Student A gives the picture to Student B, and asks *What did you do yesterday?* Student B says *I played tennis*, and hands the card to Student C. B asks C *What did you do yesterday?* etc. You, meanwhile, give another card to Student A and ask *What did you do yesterday?*, etc. All the pictures are passed round in a circle.

● Language review (SB page 20)

Past Simple

Read the Language review all together. Ask students to translate the three sample sentences. Check their translations.

▶ **Grammar reference: page 122.**

Ask students to read the Grammar reference at home.

> **Additional material**
> **Workbook Unit 3**
> Past Simple – exercises 1–6.
>
> **Pronunciation book Unit 3**
> Regular past tense endings – exercise 1.

PRESENTATION (SB page 20)

Past Continuous

> This might be the first time that your students have been formally introduced to the Past Continuous. In the exercises in this unit, there is more emphasis on recognition than production. This is for the reasons mentioned in the introduction to this unit.
> The Presentation consists of three stories, which have had the examples of the Past Continuous taken out. Students must decide which examples of the Past Continuous go with which story, and then where exactly in each story they should go. The idea implicit here is to show students that the main events of a story are expressed by the Past Simple – the stories make perfect sense without the phrases containing the Past Continuous. The Past Continuous phrases give background information and description.

1 Students use their dictionary to check any unknown words in the headlines. They won't find the word *pilotless*! Explain that the suffix **-less** means *without*, as in *useless*.

2 Students read the articles quickly, and match a headline and an article. They put the verbs in the Past Simple in the correct place.

Answers
Miracle escape – Four-year-old Mark Harris
Channel champion – Twelve-year-old Thomas Gregory
Pilotless jet – An American jet

Miracle escape

fell 60 feet	threw him onto some rocks
boys saw Mark	rang the police

Pilotless jet

pilot took off	went wrong
began working	jet flew for more than one
It hit some trees	hour

Channel champion

He swam the 31 miles	He drank hot tomato soup
He felt so cold	he could not see

3 Read the instructions for this exercise and look at the example very carefully. Use L1 if possible, as this is quite a complicated activity.
Students work in pairs or small groups to decide which story the phrases go with, and then where exactly they go in the story.

Answers
. . . fell 60 feet from a bridge into the River Avon when he was running after his dog.
. . . drank soup while he was swimming because . . .
(or While he was swimming, he drank . . .)
. . . in France, where his parents were waiting for him.
. . . a field where a farmer was working.
. . . see anything because the sun was shining in his eyes, and that was . . .
. . . engines went wrong while it was flying over New Mexico.

● Grammar question   (SB page 21)

Ask students to identify the tense. They might not know it.
Answer
– The tense used is the Past Continuous. The Past Continuous is used to give background information and description, and the Past Simple is used to tell the story.

Additional idea
Students have read examples of the Past Continuous, but they haven't repeated any yet. Elicit the following sentences from the class, and write them on the board:
Three boys were fishing.
Mark was running after his dog.
The jet was flying over New Mexico.
A farmer was working in a field.
Thomas drank soup while he was swimming.
The sun was shining in his eyes.
His parents were waiting for him.
Ask students *How is this tense formed?* (**was**/**were** + verb + **-ing**). Point out that **was** and **were** are weak /wəz/ and /wə/. Give models of the sentences yourself, and then drill them around the class.

PRACTICE   (SB page 21)

Before going on to the Practice exercises, you might decide that your students would like some more information about this (new) tense. You could look at the Language review on page 22 and read the Grammar section on page 122. In Unit 3 of the Workbook, exercise 7 is a mechanical drill to practise forming the Past Continuous. Once they have done it, your students might feel more confident about doing the following exercises. Don't be surprised if there are quite a few mistakes with the Past Continuous. You have just introduced students to a new tense, and it will take time for them to see how it operates. Let students have the rules reinforced as they see the correct answers in exercises 1 and 2, and be prepared to re-teach if necessary.

---

1 Grammar

1 Students work in pairs to decide which is the correct verb form.
Answers
a. saw
b. was shopping   lost
c. stopped   was travelling
d. did you cut
e. was cooking
2 Students work in pairs to put the verb in the correct form.
Answers
a. was coming   met
b. didn't want   was raining
c. was listening   rang
d. picked
e. were watching

2 Speaking and listening

Before putting students in pairs, give them a model. Choose a student (a good one), and ask the questions.

Possible problem
Make sure that in answer to the questions in the Past Continuous, another Past Continuous verb form is used.
Examples
What were you doing (at three o'clock this morning)?
I was sleeping. (*Not* I was asleep.)
What were you doing (at eight o'clock this morning)?
I was having breakfast. (*Not* I had breakfast.)

– *Where were you at three o'clock this morning?*
– *What were you doing?*
– *Where were you at eight o'clock this morning?*
– *What were you doing?*
– *Where were you two years ago?*
– *What were you doing?*
– *Where were you in August last year?*
– *What were you doing?*
etc.

Ask another student to ask you the same questions. As he/she does this, write the questions on the board. Drill the questions, paying attention to a high start and weak forms.

Now ask students to work in pairs (or small groups). Point out that in answer to the questions using a Past Continuous, they must use a verb in the Past Continuous.

3 Writing

Students work in groups of four to write a story. Don't underestimate how long activities such as this take if they are to be done thoroughly. Allow 20–30 minutes. You could start by discussing some possible news stories as a class, and ask students to give you some details.

Groups sometimes take a while to get started. They have to decide on a story, decide who's going to write, and decide what the wrong information is, so be prepared to give them a gentle nudge to keep the lesson moving.

● Language review   (SB page 22)

Past Continuous

Read the Language review all together. Ask students in pairs to translate the two sentences.

▶ **Grammar reference: page 122**.

Ask students to read the Grammar section at home.

SKILLS DEVELOPMENT

● Reading and speaking   (SB page 22)

In this activity, students read an extract from a James Bond story. The extract is quite long, but it is very dramatic, and students have the pictures to help them to understand.

Pre-reading task

1 Read the introduction and the titles of the books together. You might need to teach some of the vocabulary items, for example, *diamonds*, *casino*, *golden*.
   Answers
   The hero is James Bond.
   The author is Ian Fleming.

2 Students translate the titles of the films. Some are direct translations, others are different.
   Ask some questions:
   – *Do you like James Bond films?*

– *Which have you seen?*
– *What happens in James Bond films?* (Good against bad/spies/madmen who try to rule the world/fights/women)
– *What sort of person is he?* (Cool, sophisticated, masculine)

3 Students work in pairs or small groups to put the pictures in order. It doesn't matter whether they get the right order or not. When they are ready, ask one or two groups to tell the story as they understand it. Make sure that the story is told using past tenses. When we talk about stories, we often naturally use present tenses, but this is not what you want to practise.

Reading
Students read the story and number the pictures. There will be quite a few words that students don't know, but don't let them over-use dictionaries. The pictures give a lot of help. Ask students to talk about the order of the pictures in pairs, and get the feedback.

Answers

a. – 6	b. – 1	c. – 4	d. – 2	e. – 5	f. – 8
g. – 3	h. – 7				

At this point, you could choose to read the text out loud. Some might say that this is mixing a reading lesson with a listening lesson, but there are several advantages. As you read it out loud, you (the teacher) can add a lot of expression and emotion. Bond is angry. Mary Goodnight is worried. Scaramanga is full of menace. All this aids comprehension. You can also quickly check/teach/demonstrate any items of vocabulary (for example, *thump*, *relief*, *cursed*, *banged shut*, *whispered*), which aren't terribly important, but which might cause students concern if they are not understood.

Comprehension check
Students work in pairs to answer the true/false questions.
Answers
1 False – We know he was excited because his heart was thumping. Perhaps he was in a fight, but he 'breathed in the air with relief', so he didn't feel frightened.
2 False – A noise from behind the curtains woke him.
3 False – He was very angry.
4 False – The window banged shut with a noise like a gunshot.
5 True – He also turned the shower on so no one could hear them.
6 True
7 False – He did know.
8 True
9 False – He wanted to help her get out, but before he could, Scaramanga arrived.

Vocabulary and grammar work
1 Students find the past tense forms of the verbs.
   Answers
   (I) = irregular

had (I)	breathed	woke (I)
took (I)	crept (I)	shone (I)
whispered	put (I)	tried
caught (I)	led (I)	sat (I)
knew (I)	gave (I)	stood (I)

2 Students make a list of the parts of the body in the text.

Answers

heart	chest	eyes	teeth
hair	foot	hands	necks

Additional idea

This is a reading aloud activity, probably best done on another day rather than continuing to exploit the James Bond text in the same lesson.

Appoint a narrator and a character to play James Bond, Mary Goodnight, and Scaramanga. Begin at the third paragraph, when James says 'Mary Goodnight!' The students read their lines, and you correct pronunciation as necessary. The text is quite dramatic, so students should get excited doing it! Then students work in groups of four to do the activity again.

Reading aloud as an activity has long gone out of fashion, but if it is done occasionally, it can be enjoyable and productive.

Speaking

Students should now be ready to retell the story in some detail. Let them first do this in pairs to practise. Monitor them carefully, correcting the most important mistakes. This exercise is mid-way between a fluency- and an accuracy-based activity: you want students to speak at length, but you also want the past tense usage to be correct.

When students are ready, ask one or two of them to tell the story to the rest of the class. You could begin the next class by asking a different student to retell the story. It only takes a few minutes, and you can revise the vocabulary and past tenses.

Additional material

Pronunciation book Unit 3

In the Connected Speech section, there is an exercise on the weak form of prepositions, which follows on thematically from the James Bond extract – exercise 3.

● Vocabulary (SB page 24)

Verbs and nouns that go together

1 Read the introduction all together, and look at the dictionary extracts. The point being made here is that students will probably need to look at the example sentences to find out which words go together.
Ask students to look up *joke* and *draw* in their dictionary to see if the same (or similar) information is given.

2 In pairs, students match a line in A with a line in B. This is harder than it looks.

Possible problems

Be careful with the pronunciation of *wear* /weə/ and *suit* /su:t/.

Students might come up with combinations other than those shown in the answers below. Some of these are

---

possible, for example, *to make a suit*, *to order a taxi*, but by a process of elimination, this is not the desired answer.

Students might want to say 'pay a meal' because they confuse *pay* and *pay for*. You pay for what you actually get, for example, *pay for a book*, *pay for a shirt*.

Answers

wear a suit	post a letter
tell a lie	ride a horse
drive a van	pack a suitcase
take a photograph	pay a bill
do the washing-up	order a meal
make a phone call	watch a film on TV
cash a cheque	take a taxi

3 Students work in pairs to ask and answer questions using the combinations. In answer to some questions, students might want to say *I've never* (driven a van), using the Present Perfect, which is good, but don't go into this in any depth at all! You don't want to start a lesson on the Present Perfect versus the Past Simple.

Words and prepositions that go together

Read the explanation together. Ask students to look up *listen* in their dictionary to see if it gives similar information.
Students work together to put the right preposition into each gap. You could direct them to the list of dependent prepositions at the back of the book to correct the exercise.

Answers

a. for	e. for	i. to
b. at	f. in	j. with
c. for	g. to	k. of
d. for	h. to	l. at

● Listening and writing (SB page 24)

T.8

An interview with a biographer

Pre-listening task

Read the introduction as a class. Students use their dictionary to check the meaning of any of the professions they don't know.

In pairs, students discuss which jobs they think Ian Fleming had. This exercise is mainly to get students to think about what the creator of James Bond might have been like. They have no real way of knowing which jobs he did.

Listening

Ask students to read the two questions.

Note

Eton is a famous and very expensive private school in England.

T.8   Students listen and try to answer the two questions.

Answers

1 Ian Fleming was a soldier, journalist, stockbroker, and a member of Naval Intelligence. He was perhaps a member of MI5, but we don't know for sure.
2 His family were rich, and James Bond seems to be rich. He travelled a lot. He was a spy. He was good-looking, dressed well, and liked women. He drank and smoked.

Comprehension check

Play the tape again, then ask students in pairs to answer the questions.

Answers

1 28 May, 1908.
2 His brothers liked Eton, but he hated it. He also hated the army, and the suggestion is that his brothers liked it.
3 To Geneva.
4 He didn't pass the exams.
5 No. He was working as a stockbroker.
6 North Africa, Portugal (Lisbon), and America.
7 An expensive way of life. He dressed well and had a lot of girlfriends.
8 No. He smoked and drank too much, and had a bad heart.
9 He got married, he had a son, and he started writing about James Bond.
10 In 1964. He was 56.
11 Ian Fleming was nine when his father died.
   He smoked sixty cigarettes a day.
   He wrote fourteen books about James Bond.
   Over forty million James Bond books were sold while he was alive.

> **Additional idea**
> Choose four or five lines from the tapescript and use them as a dictation. The paragraph beginning *Well – they all went to Eton* has some past tenses, positive and negative. You could ask one student to do his/her dictation on the board. You correct this one, and the other students can correct theirs from the board.

Writing

Students write a short biography for homework. This may seem to be asking a lot of such low-level students. The aim is process writing, or writing for fluency. It can be very interesting to give students a writing task and see how they get on on their own. They will use dictionaries and perhaps grammar reference books to produce something that they find interesting. As you correct it, you might choose not to correct every single mistake, or you might choose to correct only one or two mistakes.

> **Additional idea**
> When you read what students have written, don't necessarily correct all mistakes. Make a note of those mistakes which you think your class could work out, and put them on the board at the beginning of the next lesson. The class as a whole works to correct them. You then give back the homework, and students see if they made any of the mistakes on the board.

● Everyday English   (SB page 25)

Time expressions

T.9

Introduction: Ask students what today's date is, and practise saying it in the two ways.
July the eighth – the eighth of July

> **Possible problems**
> Students forget to say the definite article.
> **I came here on fifth August.*
> Students might not know all the ordinal numbers, especially *first*, *second*, *third*, and *twenty-first*, *twenty-second*, etc. You might want to practise these first.
> The pronunciation of some ordinal numbers is difficult because of consonant clusters.
> *fifth   sixth   twelfth*

1 Read the introduction as a class. In pairs, students practise saying the dates and years. Before they listen to the tape, let the students concentrate on getting the *form* of the dates and years right. When students are ready, get the feedback.

   T.9   Listen to the tape. Stop the tape after each date, and drill it around the class. Concentrate now on correct form *and* pronunciation. It is very important that dates are said with strong and weak stresses.

   •   ●   •   ●   ●   •   ●
   the fourth of June   June the fourth

2 Practise the dates in open and closed pairs. (Open pairwork is when two students talk to each other and the rest of the class listens.)

> **Note**
> Note the different questions and answers.
> *When is your birthday?   March the eighth.*
> *What is your date of birth?   March the eighth, 1960.*

3 Look at the chart together.

4 Do question 4. It might be interesting to answer the first question as a class, partly so that you can check students' answers, and partly because people are usually very interested to hear what time of day other people were born!

   Students answer the final two questions in pairs.

> **Additional material**
>
> **Workbook Unit 3**
> Past time expressions – exercise 6.
>
> **Pronunciation book Unit 3**
> Saying dates – exercise 2.

Stop and Check   (WB page 20)

There is a Stop and Check revision section in the Workbook after every three units. Revision is very important, especially at lower levels.

Suggest to students that they buy a supplementary grammar book. Recommend one with exercises and key. At the end of the Stop and Check, they should decide for themselves which areas of the language they need to do more work on, and refer to the relevant parts of the grammar book. If their problem is remembering vocabulary, suggest they buy a special vocabulary notebook, and start recording vocabulary items and reviewing them regularly.

Here is one suggestion for using the Stop and Check sections.
1 Students do the Stop and Check for homework.
2 In the next lesson, they go over the Stop and Check in groups of four or five, trying to agree on the right answers. Allow enough time for this. It can be very productive for students themselves to try to persuade their peers of the right answer. Many previous lessons are recalled.
3 Go over the Stop and Check as a class, reminding students of language items covered.
4 Ask students which areas they themselves feel they need to revise, and suggest ways in which this might be done.

UNIT 4

Expressions of quantity – Articles – Requests and offers

Introduction to the Unit

> **Note**
> Prior to starting this unit you could ask students, as part of their homework, to think about their favourite recipe/dish, and find out what the ingredients are in English.

The title of this unit is 'Going shopping'. The expressions of quantity in the Presentation section are brought together in dialogues where two friends discuss the ingredients of recipes for a dinner party. Also, in a separate Presentation section, there is some work on the use of articles in English, which involves the use in class of the Grammar reference section at the back of the Student's Book. The Skills Development section has a reading about one of Britain's most famous stores – Marks & Spencer, and the listening consists of five radio adverts from a commercial radio station.

Notes on the Language Input

Grammar

Remember that it is often a good idea to remind yourself of the grammar in each unit before you prepare your lessons. One way you can do this is to read the appropriate Grammar reference section at the back of the Student's Book.

Expressions of quantity

It is assumed that students will have some knowledge of expressions of quantity, but that the intricacies of this area (particularly in relation to countable and uncountable nouns) will mean that mistakes will still be common. We feel that it is worthwhile bringing some of the expressions together to study and practise them.
The point is also made that the rules about the use of **something/anything**, etc. are the same as for **some** and **any**. These are also practised.

Articles

It is expected that students will not have actually studied articles in English to any great extent. However, they will probably be aware that the use of articles varies between languages. Those students whose L1 has no articles, such as Japanese and Arabic, find their use particularly difficult. It would be a good idea to compare for yourself article use in English with the language(s) of your students to help in your lesson preparation. This way you might be able to anticipate problems or questions that might emerge.
In the Presentation section students are encouraged to find examples of articles in a very short text and then work out the rules using the Grammar reference section on page 123.

Vocabulary

The lexical areas of food and cooking are chosen to fit the theme of the unit and the activity involves the use of bilingual dictionaries and personalized speaking, where students tell each other how to make a favourite recipe. (There could be the opportunity here for a class party!)

Everyday English

Requests and offers also are chosen to fit the theme of shopping. These are practised in a variety of everyday shopping situations.

> **Note**
> This Everyday English section has its own Grammar reference section on page 124.

Notes on the Unit

PRESENTATION (SB page 26)

Expressions of quantity

> T.10

Introduction: Ask which students like cooking. Have a very brief discussion about favourite meals/recipes. (Later, students are asked to describe their favourite dish in more detail.)

1 Ask them to look quickly at the ingredients for Ben and Sam's Shepherd's Pie. Do they think they would like it? You may want to save time here by quickly dealing with any vocabulary problems yourself (perhaps by a quick translation), rather than having a longer session with dictionaries.

> **Note**
> lbs (pounds, /paʊnz/ not to be confused with £s!) and ozs (ounces, /aʊnsɪz/) are imperial measures still widely used in Britain, often alongside metric measures.
> 16 ozs = 1 lb
> 2.2 lbs = 1 kilogram
> 1.76 pints (/paɪnts/) = 1 litre

2 This exercise focuses on **much** and **many** only and aims to highlight the difference between countable and uncountable nouns in English, with just these two expressions of quantity, before going on to study more expressions.

Before you ask the students to work in closed pairs, practise the sample questions and answers in open pairs across the class. Encourage good pronunciation of the questions, particularly the intonation:

How much   beef   do we   need?

Put students into pairs to ask and answer about the other ingredients. Go round the class and monitor them carefully, correcting any mistakes and checking their understanding of when to use each.

Answers

How many carrots		Two.
How many mushrooms		50 grams.
How much flour		25 grams.
How much stock		300 millilitres.
How many potatoes	do we need?	700 grams.
How much butter		25 grams.
How much milk		60 millilitres.
How much cheese		50 grams.
How much salt and pepper		Just a little.

● **Grammar question**   (SB page 26)

Ask the students to tell you the answer and perhaps write it on the blackboard.

Answer

– We use **many** with countable nouns (things you can count one, two, three, etc. of) and **much** with uncountable nouns (things you can't count).

Encourage the students to give you more examples of countables and uncountables. You could build a short list on the blackboard:

Sample list

Countables		Uncountables		
bananas	books	sugar	beer	
stamps	apples etc.	money	music etc.	

3   T.10   Before you do this exercise ask the students if they can tell you any other expressions of quantity.

Play the tape and ask students to read and listen at the same time and see if any of the expressions they thought of occur.

● **Grammar questions**   (SB page 26)

Ask students to work in pairs to answer the questions. The idea is that they use the examples in the dialogue to work out the grammar rules for themselves.

Answers

– countable: onions, potatoes, mushrooms, carrots, Shepherd's Pie.
– uncountable: minced beef, milk, butter, cheese, salt, pepper, flour, shopping.
– **The first two sentences:**
 The plural verb, in this case **are**, is used with countable plurals, but a singular verb, in this case **is**, is always used with uncountables.
 The next three sentences:
 any is used with countable and uncountable nouns in questions and negatives.
 The last two sentences:
 a lot of can be used with both countable and uncountable nouns.
– **a few** is used with countable nouns; **a little** with uncountable nouns.
 many is used in questions and negatives with countable nouns; **much** is used in questions and negatives with uncountable nouns.

● **Language review**   (SB page 27)

Expressions of quantity

Ask students to check the rules they worked out when they answered the Grammar questions by reading the Language review section. Then read it through with the whole class.

> **Note**
> You could ask your students to translate one or two sentences at this point. However, it might be preferable to move now to the practice exercises. Some sentences for translation come at the end of this section.

PRACTICE   (SB page 27)

1 Grammar

Encourage your students to do this quite quickly. They should be able to. Ask them to do 1 on their own as quickly as possible, then check with a partner. Do the same for 2, then go through all together. Point out that in 2 **a lot of** could be used in all the sentences, and check that students understand that it can only be replaced by **many** and **much** in questions and negatives.

Answers

1 a. any   d. some
   b. any   e. any
   c. some

2 a. much/a lot of   d. a lot of
   b. many/a lot of   e. many/a lot of
   c. a lot of

2 Speaking and writing

1 Put students into pairs to look in their dictionaries (or ask each other) for any unknown words in the dessert recipe. However if you want to move more quickly check them yourself.

> **Note**
> Always remember to encourage your students to add new words to their vocabulary notebooks, and/or find them in the Word list for the unit at the back of the book and write in the translations.

Get them to look carefully at the picture of the fridge and cupboard and use the prompts to form their questions.

Possible answers

Are there any cooking apples?	No, there aren't.
Have they got any raisins?	Yes, they have, but only a few.
Are there any sultanas?	Yes, there are. There are a lot.
Is there any milk?	Yes, there's a little.
Is there any soft brown sugar?	Yes, there is.
Have they got any flour?	Yes, they have.
Is there any butter?	No, there isn't.
Have they got any eggs?	Yes, they have.

Go round the individual pairs and check and correct their questions and answers. Ask them not to write them down at this stage but to concentrate on speaking. They can write in the next exercise.

2 Now ask them to look back at the dialogue on page 26 and use it as a model to write a similar dialogue about the Apple Cake.
(This could be set as homework if you run out of time.)

Sample dialogue

Ben   Have we got everything for the dessert?
Sam   Well, let's see. There aren't any cooking apples, but there are a few raisins and a lot of sultanas.
Ben   Is there any milk?
Sam   A little. But we don't need much, and there's a lot of sugar and flour.
Ben   Have we got any eggs and butter?
Sam   Well, we've got some eggs but we haven't got any butter.
Ben   OK! Let's go shopping.

You could simply ask students to look at and correct each other's dialogues. Alternatively, let the class *hear* examples of each other's work. Ask a few pairs to act out their dialogue. Each dialogue should be a little different. The students can listen to see if they can identify any mistakes.

3 Grammar

> **Note**
> You might want to set this exercise for homework at this point and move on to exercise 4.

Ask your students to look at the chart. Point out that **somebody** and **someone** mean exactly the same. Read through the explanation and examples together.
The exercise should not take them very long to do. They could do it individually then check their answers with a partner.

Answers

a. anyone/anybody	e. somewhere
b. someone/somebody	f. anywhere
c. something	g. something; someone/
d. anything	somebody; somewhere

4 Speaking and listening

The idea here is to have a short personalized speaking activity about students' favourite dishes at the end of the lesson after all the grammar work.
Students could have been asked to prepare this a little before the lesson (see note at the beginning of this unit).
It should be *fun* (and mouthwatering!) as they tell each other about the dishes. Listen to see if they are starting to use the expressions of quantity correctly (if at all!) but don't be too quick to correct – you'll spoil the fun!

> **Note**
> On the right, there are two recipes from the unit.
> Photocopy them and give them to your students if they are interested. They could make them with some of their own dishes for a class party later on!

● Language review   (SB page 28)

Expressions of quantity

Translate the sentences together and compare the languages.

▶ **Grammar reference: page 123.**

Ask students to read this at home, perhaps before they do some of the Workbook exercises for homework (see below).

> **Additional material**
>
> **Workbook Unit 4**
> These exercises could be done for homework, or in a later class to revise.
> Countable and uncountable nouns – exercises 1 and 2.
> Expressions of quantity – exercises 3 – 6.
>
> **Pronunciation book Unit 4**
> Exercise 2 could be done in a later class and/or as a fun activity at the end of the week/term, etc.
> Word focus – containers, weights and measures e.g. *a bottle of wine*.

Shepherd's Pie

Shepherd's Pie is a very popular English dish. It originated in the north of England, but is now eaten all over the country.

1 Slice the onions, carrots, and mushrooms.
2 Fry them in a pan with the minced beef for about 8 – 10 minutes, stirring all the time.
3 Add the flour and stir for one more minute.
4 Add the beef stock and some salt and pepper and stir again until the mixture becomes thicker.
5 Transfer to a casserole dish and put into the oven at 190°C (Gas mark 5) for 25 minutes.
6 Meanwhile, cook the peeled potatoes in boiling salted water for 20 minutes.
7 Then drain and mash together with the butter and milk.
8 Put the potato on top of the mince mixture, grate the cheese and put it on top.
9 Return the dish to the oven at 200°C (Gas Mark 6) for 15 minutes.

Serve hot with a green vegetable.

Apple Cake

1 Peel and chop the apples.
2 Mix together the apples, raisins, sultanas, milk, and sugar.
3 Mix together the flour and butter (softened) in another bowl.
4 Add the fruit mixture and the egg and mix very well.
5 Put into a buttered 20-centimetre square cake tin. Put a little white sugar on the top.
6 Cook in the oven at 170°C (Gas Mark 3) for 1 hour 45 minutes.

Serve hot or cold with fresh cream.

Note
At this point it might be a good idea to do the first activity in the Skills Development section (the reading text on Marks & Spencer, page 29) *before* you do the next grammar presentation. Your students might like the variety.

PRESENTATION (SB page 28)

Articles

Note
This is the only presentation in *Headway Pre-Intermediate* where we suggest that the Grammar reference section plays an active part in the presentation. Usually we suggest the reading of the section as revision after the lesson, or perhaps prior to the lesson if the language area is a difficult one.

Ask your students to look at the picture of the shopkeeper and read the text about him quite quickly at this stage. The vocabulary is simple and should cause no problems.

Ask the students to read it again more carefully and underline all the definite and indefinite articles. They may need a quick reminder that this means *a* and *the*!

Answer
My uncle is <u>a</u> shopkeeper. He has <u>a</u> shop in <u>a</u> small village by <u>the</u> River Thames near Oxford. <u>The</u> shop sells almost everything from bread to newspapers. It is also <u>the</u> post office. <u>The</u> children always stop to spend <u>a</u> few pence on sweets and ice-cream on their way to and from school. My uncle doesn't often leave <u>the</u> village. He doesn't have <u>a</u> car so once <u>a</u> month he goes by bus to Oxford and has lunch at <u>the</u> Grand Hotel. He is one of <u>the</u> happiest men I know.

Before they turn to the Grammar reference section you could ask them a few general questions about articles:
Sample questions
– *Can you give any rules about the use of articles in English with examples from the text?*
– *Can you find some examples of nouns in the text where there is no article? Do you know why?*
– *Do you know of any differences between the use of articles in English and in your own language?*

▶ **Grammar reference: page 123.**

Now ask the students to turn to the Grammar section and find examples of the rules in the text on page 28. Point out to the students that after each rule listed, there is a letter (A, B, C, etc.) which they can use to identify the rule easily when they find examples. This should also facilitate the feedback session.

Answers (The words are in the order they appear in the text.)

a shopkeeper	**C**
a shop	**A**
a small village	**A**
the River Thames	**F**
Oxford	**J**
The shop	**B**
bread	**I** (uncountable noun)
newspapers	**I** (countable plural noun)
the post office	**G**
The children	**B** or **G** (we understand it means the children of the village, B, and there is only one group of these, G.)
a few pence	**D**
sweets	**I** (countable plural noun)
ice-cream	**I** (uncountable noun)
to and from school	**K**
the village	**B**
a car	**A**
once a month	**D**
by bus	**K**
has lunch	**J**
the Grand Hotel	**F**
one of the happiest men	**H**

Ask students to check their answers with a partner first, then conduct a feedback session with the whole class.

PRACTICE (SB page 28)

Grammar

Put students into pairs to do these two exercises. They can refer to the lists of rules.

1 Ask them to identify the mistake and discuss why it is wrong.
 Answers
 a. He's <u>a</u> milkman, so he has breakfast at 4 a.m. (C)
 b. I want <u>the</u> government to do something about the problem of unemployment. (G)
 c. Cities are usually exciting – in London, for example, you can have tea at the Ritz and then go to the theatre in <u>the</u> evening. (G – there is only one evening in a day.)
 d. I must go to <u>the</u> bank and see my bank manager. I want to borrow one hundred pounds. (B)

2 **Answers**
 a. I have two children, <u>a</u> girl and <u>a</u> boy. <u>The</u> girl is six and <u>the</u> boy is four. (A and B)
 b. She goes to work (K) in <u>the</u> City (B) by train (K) every day. Her office is in Baker Street (J).
 c. I never read newspapers (I) during the week, but I buy *The Observer* (F) every Sunday and I read it in bed (K).
 d. When you go to France (J), you must take <u>a</u> boat (A) on <u>the</u> Seine (F) when you are in Paris (J).

Pull the class together to go through the exercises. Ask them *why* they have reached their decisions, and in this way you will revise the rules.

● Language review (SB page 28)

Articles

These sentences for translation have been chosen because they should lead to discussion about the differences in the use of articles between languages. Ask students to do them in small groups.

Additional material
Workbook Unit 4
These exercises could be done as homework or in a later class to revise.
Articles – exercises 7–9 (Exercise 8 would be suitable as a quick warmer at the start of almost any lesson.)
Vocabulary
Spelling of plural nouns – exercise 10 (This would also be a good warmer.)

SKILLS DEVELOPMENT

● Reading and speaking (SB page 29)

Ask your students if they have heard of Marks & Spencer. Do they have any in their country? What can you buy there?

Pre-reading task
Get students to work in pairs. They should be able to make a guess at some of the connections, but if you have a less imaginative class you may have to push them a little.

Possible ideas – the correct answer is underlined.
– *Princess Diana* – probably <u>a customer</u> (Check they know this word.)
– *£10 million* – perhaps this is how much Princess Diana spent last week; or perhaps the <u>profit made by M&S every day/week/year</u>
– *a Polish immigrant* – <u>the man who started the shops</u>
– *shoelaces* – perhaps M&S sells a lot of these; or <u>the first shop sold them</u>
– *Spain* – <u>there are shops in Spain</u>
– *Paris and Newcastle* – there are shops in Paris and Newcastle; <u>the same/different things sell in Paris and Newcastle</u> (Newcastle is a city in the north-east of England.)
– *jumpers* – they have very beautiful jumpers; they sell more jumpers than anything else; <u>jumpers are one of the best-selling things</u>
– *chiropodists* – they look after the tired feet of customers; <u>they look after the feet of the staff</u>.

Note
In England, chiropodists only look after minor disorders of the feet.

Get the students to read the article quite quickly and then discuss the list again with their partner to see if their guesses were right. Go through the list with the whole class. You could ask a few more comprehension questions as you go (see below), but take care not to ask the questions from the Comprehension check exercise.

> **Possible additional questions (and answers)**
> 1 – *Who else likes Marks & Spencer?*
>   Tourists, housewives, millionaires, the Prime Minister, Dustin Hoffman.
> 2 – *Can you see a picture of a stall on the page? What is the difference between a shop and a stall?*
>   A stall is a small, open shop, usually outside.
> 3 – *Why did the notice say 'Don't ask how much.'?*
>   Because everything cost one penny.
> 4 – *Why are the staff happy?*
>   Because they have good conditions of work. Doctors, dentists, hairdressers, and even chiropodists look after them. They get cheap (subsidized) lunches.

Comprehension check
This activity is designed to give some more practice of expressions of quantity as well as to check comprehension. Students could continue working in pairs and be encouraged to help each other. They often find it more difficult to make the questions than to give the answers, so go round and help.

Answers
1 How much profit did Marks & Spencer make last year?
2 When did it start?
3 Where did Michael Marks/the man who started it come from?
4 Did he have many/a lot of things to sell at first?
5 How many stores are there in the world?
6 Why is Marks & Spencer so successful?
7 Does it only sell clothes?
8 How much does lunch cost for the staff?/How much do the staff pay for lunch?

Vocabulary work
The examples from the text should be found quite quickly. The aim here is to revise these lexical areas when the students give their three further examples.

Clothes	Food	Professions
shoelaces	bread	housewives
bras	Chicken Kiev	prime minister
dressing gowns	fresh chickens	fashion designer
jumpers	sandwiches	chiropodists
knickers	vegetables	dentists
pyjamas		doctors
shirts		hairdressers
socks		
suits		
underwear		

Ask students to compare and share their additional three examples. Take care that this useful revision does not develop into an extensive and over-long vocabulary exercise.

> **Additional material**
> **Workbook Unit 4**
> **Vocabulary**
> This could be given as homework to revise and extend the clothes vocabulary from the lesson.
> Clothes – exercise 11.

Speaking
1 This should be a short activity. Ask several students to give a one- or two-line summary under one of the headings. The aim is to follow all the language work with some fluency work, so don't correct too heavily.
2 The aim here is to give some brief personalized free-speaking practice to round off the lesson. Most countries have famous and popular stores.
  If you feel your students will have little to say, you could do a little research into the backgrounds of these stores (if this is possible) and use the information to further the discussion. Don't worry if you only get a few sentences – at least it's something!

● Vocabulary   (SB page 30)

> **Note**
> Don't forget to encourage your students to keep adding words to their own vocabulary notebooks and/or find the words in the list at the back of the book and write in the translation.
> Also you could, by this stage of your course, have regular short vocabulary tests/competitions. Ask students to study the word lists for the first four units. Test via pictures, definitions, and translation. This could be done in teams and students could sometimes devise their own tests for each other to increase motivation.

Food and cooking
1 This activity aims to revise and extend the lexical area of food and also to practise further the use of a bilingual dictionary.
  Ask students first to write in the names for all the items of food they know, and only then go to their dictionaries to look up the unknown words. They could check their answers with a partner before you have a full-class feedback session.
  Answers
  peas   cauliflower   orange
  banana   strawberries   mushrooms   carrot
  leg of lamb   potato   cucumber
  celery   roast beef   cabbage
  saucepan   frying pan
  lettuce   tomato   grapes   garlic
  plum   onion   apple   chicken
  melon   pear   peach
  Brussels sprouts   beans
  raspberries   lemon   cherries   pineapple
  bowl   wok   casserole dish

2 The aim in this activity is to put the vocabulary in a wider context – in this case by seeing which verbs can be used with the food in the pictures. You could ask students to work in small groups, and put a time limit on it of 10–15 minutes.

> **Note**
> Take great care not to let this activity run away with itself and go on too long. Just one or two examples from the pictures and other food should be sufficient. Too many new words would be non-productive. Leave time to move on to exercise 3, where students give their favourite recipes.

Some common combinations (not a definitive list)

bake potato (baked potato is a potato cooked in its 'jacket' or skin); apple (baked apple is a popular English dessert. The core is removed from the apple and brown sugar and cinnamon are inserted before baking.)
Other: bread, cakes, biscuits

boil carrots, potatoes, cauliflower, cabbage, sprouts, peas, beans, chicken
Other: water, milk

chop onions, mushrooms, garlic, carrots, celery
Other: meat, herbs

cut most things except perhaps peas! (Often used with preposition **into** – *cut into small/two/four pieces*, etc.)

fry/grill onions, mushrooms, tomatoes, chicken, steak
Other: eggs (fry only), bacon, hamburgers

peel onions, potatoes, apples, pears, oranges, bananas.

roast potatoes, beef, lamb, chicken
Other: pork

slice onions, cucumber, mushrooms, melon, orange, banana
Other: bread, cake

squeeze orange, lemon

Go round and monitor the groups and then pull the whole class together for some feedback.

3 Use the pictures to check students understand the equipment.

> **Note**
> Before this stage in the unit, students should have already thought (as part of their homework) about their favourite recipe, its ingredients, and how it is made (see introductory note to this unit).

You could ask them just to tell each other about the dishes rather than write it down first. Let them do this, still in their small groups. Try to listen out for one or two dishes that sound particularly interesting and ask those students to tell their recipes to the whole class.

● Listening and speaking (SB page 31)

Five radio advertisements

| T.11 |

> **Note**
> These are actual advertisements taken from London radio stations. However, the nature of the advertisements means that they should be largely comprehensible to students at this level. The aim here is fluency, i.e. to develop the listening skill for itself. The tasks are designed to do this. It would not be appropriate to analyse the tapescripts for language work.

Pre-listening task

1 This should be a very brief discussion to set the scene. You could begin by telling the students about your favourite advert and ask if they know it. This might encourage their ideas. Do this quite quickly with the whole class.

2 Read through the definitions together. Point out that *break* and *fair* are nouns here.

3 Put the class into small groups and set a maximum time limit of five minutes.

Possible ideas

a soft drink	the taste, the price. You can drink and drive.
a musical	which theatre, the stars in it, the wonderful music, the newspaper reviews
a cross-Channel ferry	which ports, the speed, the comfort, the price, the facilities
a frozen potato dish	the taste, the speed, the price, better than chips
a motor fair	the place, the dates, the beautiful new cars

Ask students from different groups to give their suggestions and the others can compare.

Listening for information

| T.11 | Play the tape and pause briefly after each advertisement for students to write down which advert they think it is. At the end ask them first to check their order with a partner, then conduct a full-class feedback.

Answers

1 A new kind of frozen potato dish
2 A cross-Channel ferry
3 A musical at the theatre
4 A motor fair
5 A soft drink

Ask the students to tell you if they heard any of their ideas to sell the products. Did they hear any other ideas?

Comprehension check

The students could stay in their groups to do this. Get them to go through the questions quite quickly at first and tell them not to worry if they cannot answer them all.

Play the tape again for them to check their answers and complete any questions they were unable to answer. Get a final feedback from the whole class and establish the correct answers.

Answers
1 (Ross) Oven Crunchies
2 P & O European Ferries
3 *Anything Goes*
4 Sunday the 29th
5 Coca-Cola
6 You can bake, fry, or grill them.
7 £10.50
8 Prince Edward Theatre or your local ticket agent
9 Television, video, three telephones, a bar, solar deck, and a swimming pool
10 A free meal for your child

Group work

Probably the students will stay in the same groups to do this. Go round and help and encourage them. If they need it, give them extra ideas. This activity does not need to be very long.

> **Additional idea**
> It would be nice to record the finished advertisements and play them to the whole class for them to judge whose was the best. Each group could choose one student to make the recording and they could help her/him practise reading it aloud. This would be good pronunciation practice.

● Everyday English (SB page 32)

Polite requests and offers

T.12

1 You could ask students to do the matching in pairs. Ask them to think about where the conversations are taking place at the same time.
Answers
1 – b. (a post office)
2 – e. (a fast food restaurant)
3 – a. (a department store)
4 – c. (a chemist's)
5 – g. (a railway station)
6 – h. (a baker's)
7 – d. (an airport)
8 – f. (a supermarket)

2 T.12 Play the tape for students to check their answers. Then get a full-class feedback on where each dialogue is taking place.
Give students a few minutes to practise the dialogues in their pairs. Go round and help with their pronunciation. You could ask one or two pairs to act some out in front of the class.

3 Now we move to some language study. Students can stay in their pairs to do this or do it on their own.
Answers
The different structures for polite requests in A are:
Can I have/take (1 and 7)
Can you tell me (5)
We'd/I'd like (2 and 6)

Could you tell me (3)
Could I have (8)
Have you got (with polite intonation!) (4)

The three offers in B are:
I'll check (c)
I'll give you a label (d)
I'll show you (g)

▶ **Grammar reference: page 124.**

Read through the Grammar reference with the whole class. This is the first short reference to modal verbs. It is enough for the moment.

4 Either ask pairs to choose two or three places to write similar dialogues for, or allocate the places, so that all are covered. You could make the activity more challenging and interesting by getting the pairs to act out their dialogue and asking the other students to guess where it is taking place.

> **Additional material**
> **Pronunciation book Unit 4**
> Intonation and sentence stress – exercise 3 – polite/impolite requests and offers – Students have to discriminate.

> **Don't forget!**
> **Workbook Unit 4**
> There are two exercises on writing – exercises 12 and 13. There is practice at filling in forms.
>
> **Pronunciation book Unit 4**
> Sound symbols – Long and short vowel sounds are practised in exercise 1.
>
> **Word list**
> Make sure your students complete the Word list for Unit 4 by writing in the translations.
>
> **Video**
> Section 3 – Situation: *Car Hire*
> This section supplements Unit 4 of the Student's Book. It is a short situation in which Paola hires a car.

UNIT 5

Verb patterns (1) – Going to – Will – Spelling

Introduction to the Unit

The title of this unit is 'Plans and ambitions'. In the Presentation sections, various verb patterns are introduced and practised via three people talking about their ambitions, and **going to** is contrasted with **will**. There are two reading texts, one a quiz to find out how ambitious you are, and the other a newspaper article about two people's experiences of computer dating. In the listening activity, eight learners of English talk about how they organize their vocabulary learning.

Notes on the Language Input

Grammar

Verb patterns

Students might well have come across several of the verb patterns in this unit, either formally or informally, but they will probably not have seen them presented under the heading *verb patterns*. It is worth explaining what a pattern is, i.e. something that repeats itself.

> **Possible problems**
> Mistakes of form are common with verb patterns.
> *I'm going work as a designer.
> *She hopes finding a job soon.
> *He want have a restaurant.
>
> Two possible patterns with **like** are also presented, and these cause problems of form and use. With the two forms being similar, they are easily mixed up, but learners also find the conceptual difference of 'general versus specific preference' difficult to grasp.
> **Common mistakes of form**
> *I like play football.
> *I'd like having a drink.
> **Common mistakes of use**
> *I'm thirsty. I like a Coke.
> *Do you like to come to the cinema tonight?

In this unit, we suggest that for a general preference, **like + -ing** is used. Students might come across **like** + the infinitive to express this use.
I like to relax at the weekend.

The verb patterns presented in this unit are such high-frequency items (with the exception of **hope**), that once you have presented them, they will automatically be revised and practised in many classroom activities. If mistakes occur in subsequent lessons, remind students of the rules.

Going to and will

Going to is contrasted with **will** in this unit, but only one use of each verb form. Both items are traditionally taught in a first year book, so the forms will not be new. **Will** to express a (spontaneous) offer was practised in the Everyday English section of Unit 4. In this unit it is seen in a very similar use, to express a future intention or decision made at the moment of speaking. This is in contrast with **going to**, which expresses a pre-planned intention. Students might well perceive this conceptual difference quite easily, but it is another matter to apply the rule thereafter. Selecting appropriate future forms causes many problems for a long time.

Common mistakes
'Have you booked a holiday yet?'
*'Yes. We'll go to Spain.'

*What will you do tonight?
*What do you do tonight?
*What you do tonight?

'The phone's ringing.'
*'OK. I answer it.'

As was noted in the teaching notes for Unit 4, students often use the base form of the verb to express a spontaneous offer or intention, rather than **will**.
*I open the door for you.

Making offers and expressing intentions are common occurrences in the day-to-day interactions of classrooms, whether students are acting in roles or just being themselves. If (and when!) you hear mistakes with this use of **will**, it is worth reminding learners of the rule. They might learn it all the better for seeing the item in a real context. For example, if a student offers to help you collect in some books and says 'I collect the books for you', take the opportunity to point out to the class how **will** should be used here.

This unit deals with the modal use of **will**. **Will** as an auxiliary verb to show future time is dealt with in Unit 9.

Vocabulary

There are two parts to the Vocabulary section. The first part consists of several students of English describing what they do to learn vocabulary. The idea is to suggest to your class various approaches that they could adopt themselves.

The second part picks up on one of the approaches mentioned, and does some work on word families, and shifting stress in word families. In the Workbook, another suggestion is exemplified with an exercise on putting words into sense groups.

Everyday English

Spelling is practised both productively and receptively.

Notes on the Unit

PRESENTATION (SB page 33)

Verb patterns

Introduction: Teach the word *pattern*, either by translating it or demonstrating it, for example, by pointing to a plain shirt and a patterned shirt. Explain that the grammar practised in this unit is verb patterns, which means verbs followed by the infinitive or **-ing**.

If your students are too young to have a job, ask questions such as the following:
– *What do you want to do when you leave school?*
– *Would you like to go to university/college?*
– *What would you like to study?*
– *Are you going to travel?*

If your students are already employed, ask questions such as the following:
– *What would you like to do after this course?*
– *Do you want to stay in your present job for a long time?*
– *Would you like to change jobs?*
Listen carefully to their answers to see if they use any of the target language of this unit.

1   Look at the photos and read the introduction as a class. Students read the three texts, and decide who is sure about what they want to do, and who isn't.
   Answer
   Angela and Steve are sure; Pippa isn't.

   Check any unknown vocabulary, for example *caring profession* (jobs where you work with people, for example, teaching, nursing, social work), *paediatrician, chef*. Careful with the pronunciation of the last two items – /piːdɪətrɪʃn/ and /ʃef/. Check also *a year off* (a year not working).

Ask questions:
– *What does Angela want to do?* (She wants to be a doctor.)
– *Why?* (She likes working with people.)
– *What does Steve want to do?* (He wants to be a chef.)
– *Why?* (He loves cooking.)
– *What does Pippa want to do?* (She probably wants to work for a tour company.)
– *Why?* (She enjoys travelling.)

2   Students work in pairs to complete the chart. They can either write notes (*doctor*) or sentences (*She wants to be a doctor*).
   Answers

Angela	wants to be a doctor; would like to be a paediatrician	likes working with people; loves children	going to medical school
Steve	wants to be a chef	loves cooking	going to work in a restaurant in Paris
Pippa	would like to work for a tour company	enjoys travelling	going to have a year off

● Grammar questions (SB page 33)

– Students underline the verb forms that express plans and ambitions. Make sure that the verb forms that express general preferences (*like working; love cooking; enjoys travelling*) are not included.
   Answers
   Angela
      wants (to be)
      'm going (to medical school)
      'm going (to work)
      would like (to specialize)
   Steve
      wants (to be)
      's going (to work)
      hopes (to learn)
      'd like (to have)
   Pippa
      would (probably) like (to work)
      want (to do)
      'm going (to have)
      'm going (round the world)
      hope (to find)

– Students work in pairs to underline the correct verb form.
   Answers
   to be   to work   to find   to have
– This question is quite difficult. Answer it as a class. Try to get from students the idea that **like working** is a general, all-time preference. It applies to the past, present, and future. **Would like to be** refers to the future. If you feel it would help your

class to do so, translate these two sentences. Alternatively, you could put the following two sentences on the board, and ask students to tell you the difference between them.

I like Coke.
I'd like a Coke.

Additional idea

So far, students have read the target structures, perhaps written them, and perhaps spoken examples of them, but not to any great extent.

Elicit the following sentences and write them on the board:

She wants to be a doctor.
He wants to be a chef.

She's going to medical school.
She's going to work very hard.
He's going to work in a restaurant.
She's going to have a year off.

She likes working with people.
He loves cooking.
She enjoys travelling.

He'd like to have his own restaurant.
She'd like to be a paediatrician.
She'd like to work for a tour company.

She hopes to find work.

Drill the sentences around the class, correcting as necessary. Ask students to practise saying the sentences in pairs.

PRACTICE   (SB page 34)

If you feel your students would benefit from looking at the Language review and translating the sample sentences before doing these Practice exercises, do so.

1 Speaking

Read the introduction as a class. Ask one or two students to read out the example sentences and correct carefully. Students work in pairs to think up sentences. Tell students that it isn't necessary to think of a sentence for every structure.

Allow enough time for this. When most groups have finished, get the feedback.

Possible answers
a. They're going to go skiing in Switzerland.
   They want to stay in a hotel.
   They hope to have good weather.
b. She wants to live in the country.
   She's going to look for a new job.
   She'd like to find a little cottage.
c. She wants to buy a car.
   She's going to borrow some money from the bank.
   She'd like to have a VW.
d. He wants to work in a hotel.
   He's going to work hard.
   He hopes to have his own hotel one day.

e. She wants to be a professional player.
   She'd like to play all over the world.
   She hopes to win Wimbledon.
f. She's going to work as a teacher.
   She'd like to get a job in Argentina.
   She wants to learn Spanish.
g. They're going to get married.
   They'd like to find somewhere to live.
   They want to have three children.

2 Grammar

Students work in pairs to complete the sentences.
Answers
a. Would you like to see
b. I'd like
c. I like
d. I like swimming and playing
e. she would like to go
f. Do you like learning

3 Speaking and listening

Before students work in pairs, make sure they can ask the questions correctly. Drill them around the class.
Possible answers
Which countries would you like to go to?
When do you want to get married?
How many children do you want to have?
What are you going to do after this course?
Would you like to have your own business?

Students work in pairs to ask and answer questions. You could finish this activity by asking one or two pairs to say their questions and answers again while the rest of the class listens.

● Language review   (SB page 34)

Verb patterns

Read the Language review as a class. Ask students to find the reference to the list of verb patterns at the back of the book.

Like doing/ would like to do

Read the Language review as a class. Ask students to translate the three sample sentences.

▶ **Grammar reference: page 124.**

Students read the Grammar reference for homework.

Additional material

Workbook Unit 5
Verb patterns – exercises 1–3.
Would like (to do) and like (doing) – exercises 4–6.

Before moving on to the next presentation of **will** and **going to**, you and your class might prefer to do some skills work. You could do the reading activity on page 36 of the Student's Book, a questionnaire to find out how ambitious you are.

PRESENTATION

Will and *going to*

T.13

If you think your students already have an idea about the difference between **will** and **going to**, do the Presentation exercises as they are in the Student's Book. If you think that they would make a lot of mistakes (which is discouraging), do the following introduction first.

Introduction: Write the following sentences on the board.

Ann   *I'm going to buy some sugar. It's on my shopping list.*
Bill   *Can you buy some tea?*
Chris   *OK. I'll buy some in the supermarket.*

Underline the words as shown, and ask students the following questions.

– *When did Ann decide to buy some sugar? Before she spoke or while she was speaking?*
– *When did Chris decide to buy the tea? Before he spoke or while he was speaking?*

Ask students if they can tell you the difference between the two forms. Explain that *going to* is used to express an intention that is thought about before the moment of speaking, and *will* expresses a spontaneous intention.

1   Read the introduction as a class. Students work in pairs to put a form of **going (to)** or **will** into each gap.
    Answers
    I'm going to Bristol.
    my parents are going to retire
    I'll give you a lift
    I'll get a taxi home.
    I'll pick you up

2   T.13   Students listen to the tape and check their answers.

● Grammar questions

Answer the Grammar questions as a class. Make sure students are concentrating hard at this point.
Answers
– Before he spoke to Jenny.
– While she was speaking to him.
– **Going to** expresses an intention that is thought about before the moment of speaking. **Will** is used to express a spontaneous intention.

PRACTICE

1   Speaking and listening

1   Read the introduction to the exercise as a class. Drill the two sample sentences (*I'll make some sandwiches*; *I'll buy some bread*). Make sure that students pronounce the **'ll**.

Do the next part quite briskly, so that suggestions are coming from students all the time. The suggestions must be spontaneous! Try to get an idea from most of the class. If there are any mistakes with **'ll**, correct them.

2   Read the introduction as a class. Model the four sample sentences yourself, and exaggerate the stressed **I'm**. If you think it's necessary, ask the class why **going to** is now used, and not **will**.
    You need to remember the suggestions your students made. Repeat them, using **will**, and invite the student who made that suggestion to say it again using **going to**. Again, try to do this briskly, otherwise the exercise will pall.

2   Grammar

Students work in pairs to decide which is the correct verb form.
Answers
a. I'll carry . . .
b. I'm going skiing.
c. I'll give . . .
d. We're going to see . . .
e. I won't tell . . .
f. you and John are going to get . . .
g. I'm going shopping . . . I'll post . . .
h. are you going . . . we will go . . .

3   Speaking and listening

Before students work in pairs, establish the questions:
– *What are you doing tonight/next weekend?* (Or) *What are you going to do tonight/next weekend?*
– *Where are you going on holiday?*
Students work in pairs to ask and answer questions.

● Language review   (SB page 36)

Going to and *will*

Read the Language review as a class. Ask students to translate the sample sentences.

▶ **Grammar reference: page 124.**

Students read the Grammar reference for homework.

Additional material

Workbook Unit 5
Will and *going to* – exercises 7–9.
Pronunciation book Unit 5
Intonation and sentence stress – exercise 3. This exercise picks up on the theme of plans and future intentions.

SKILLS DEVELOPMENT

● Reading and speaking   (SB page 36)

It is best to do the questionnaire as a class, rather than students reading silently, so that you can sort out any problems of vocabulary as you go through it. However, let students use their dictionaries if they prefer.

1 Ask a student to read a question out loud. Students tick the choice that is nearest to their own ambition. As often happens in such questionnaires, there isn't the exact option you would choose, and if students are reluctant to choose one, say it's just a game.

> **Note**
> A *white lie* is a lie told for good reasons. For example, if someone is wearing some clothes which you think are awful, and you are asked for your opinion, you might say they are nice.
> *'Every man for himself'* is a saying which means everybody must fight for what he or she wants, and nobody else is important.

Students look at the answers, add up their scores and read the interpretations.

2 Ask the class if they agree with the interpretations. Encourage discussion at this point.

3 Students choose a question. This is a 'milling' activity, where students stand up and talk to everybody in the class. If you have a large class, it isn't essential that *every* student is asked, because it might take too long.
When students are sitting down again, allow them a minute to think about how to report back, then get the feedback.

> **Additional idea**
> After the questionnaire, you might want to encourage a discussion, either short or long, on your students' professional aspirations.
> Alternatively, find pictures of some of the professions mentioned in question 3 of the questionnaire, and add some professions that are particular to your country.
> Ask students in groups to put in rank order who *should* earn most (according to merit and usefulness to society) and who *in fact* earns most.

● Vocabulary and listening   (SB page 37)

How to learn vocabulary

T.14

> Before this lesson, try to find some of the following items, which are mentioned on the tape: an address book, a notebook, some stickers which peel off easily, quite a lot of graded readers, a picture dictionary.

Introduction: Have a discussion about what your students do to learn vocabulary. Perhaps they do very little; some might have some interesting approaches. Ask what sort of dictionary they have, and how often they use it.

> **Additional idea**
> Memory is obviously very important in the learning of vocabulary. Research suggests that one of the best ways of remembering words is via association. A learner meets a word he/she wants to remember and associates it with something else, probably in L1. *What* the association is doesn't matter at all.
>
> Example
> I want to remember the Italian word for ice, which is *ghiaccio*. I think of *ghee*, which is a kind of Indian butter used in cooking, and I think of someone sneezing, and I get to *ghiaccio*.
>
> It might seem rather long-winded, but it would appear to work! Tell your students about it. You could put ten pictures on the board and the English word next to them. Encourage students to think of some way of associating the words with something else. Let them do this in silence, as it is a personal activity. Then test them on the words over the next few lessons.

1 T.14   Students listen and take notes. Before you check as a class, put students in pairs to compare notes. Let them listen again if they want.
Answers
1 (Swiss German) She has an address book, and she writes in the word, a translation, and a sentence.
2 (Italian) He has a notebook, and has special pages for certain things.
3 (French) She sticks bits of paper all over the house.
4 (Turkish) He writes the words on bits of paper, and moves them from one pocket to another when he has learned them.
5 (Brazilian) She reads stories in easy English.
6 (Hungarian) She has a picture dictionary.
7 (Japanese) He records the new words onto a tape.
8 (Spanish) She finds different parts of speech. She also marks her dictionary when she looks up a word.
Discuss these different approaches to vocabulary learning as a class. Try to get your students' reactions to each one. Show them the address book, the notebook, etc., that you brought in. You might like to encourage your class to read simplified readers, either now or next lesson.

2 Students work in groups to discuss the dictionaries they have.

3 Students work alone to decide which approach they are going to try. Once you have started to encourage students to do *something* to learn vocabulary, ask them again regularly. It doesn't really matter *what* approach students adopt, as long as they do *something*.

Word families

1 Read the introduction, and look at the dictionary extract, as a class. Ask different students to repeat some of the different parts of speech (*photograph*, *photography*, etc.), and drill them around the class, paying careful attention to word stress. Ask students to practise them in groups for just thirty seconds.

Students check in their dictionaries to see how word stress is shown. Different dictionaries adopt different methods. If there *are* several methods, put them on the board so that the whole class can see.

2　Read the introduction to question 2 as a class. Students work in pairs to complete the charts with the other parts of speech.

Answers

am'bition	am'bitious	
'happiness	'happy	
'power	'powerful	
'science	scien'tific	
tech'nology	techno'logical	
'health	'healthy	
'person	'personal	
'fashion	'fashionable	
im'provement	im'prove	
a'rrival	a'rrive	
'government	'govern	
de'cision	de'cide	
e'lection	e'lect	
organi'zation	'organize	
com'plaint	com'plain	
imagi'nation	i'magine	
invi'tation	in'vite	
des'cription	des'cribe	
em'ployment	em'ploy	
suc'cess	suc'ceed	suc'cessful
at'traction	at'tract	at'tractive
speci'ality	'specialize	'special
natio'nality	'nationalize	'national

When most of the class have finished, get the feedback. Ask one or two students to read out the words, and pay attention to correct word stress.

3　Do this question as a class.

Answer

The words are both nouns and verbs, with no change.

Additional material

Workbook Unit 5

Word groups – exercise 10. This exercise practises the kind of vocabulary building described by the second student on the tape.

● Reading and speaking　(SB page 38)

The right person for you

Pre-reading task

Read the introduction as a class. Encourage discussion with the three questions. To use a dating agency, you often have to fill in a detailed questionnaire about the kind of things you like doing, and the kind of person you would like to meet. People are sometimes matched by computer. With some agencies, you also make a short video.

Vocabulary

Students match a line in A with a line in B.

Note

They are unlikely to find *high-flier* and *high-powered* in their dictionaries, but you can explain by saying a *high-flier* is someone who flies high (that is, someone who does well), and *high-powered* means having a lot of power. Point out that *fed up* is colloquial, and quite strong. *I'm fed up with the weather* is acceptable, but *I'm fed up with you* isn't.

Answers

If you are desperate for something, you want it very, very much, and will do anything to get it.

If you are seeking something, you are looking for it.

A high-flier is someone who is ambitious.

A high-powered job is one that is important and well paid.

A documentary is a TV programme that gives factual information about something.

If you get on well with someone, you have a good relationship.

A degree is the qualification you get from university.

If you are fed up with something, you are unhappy or bored with it.

A considerate person is someone who is kind, and pays attention to other people's feelings.

Check that students know the word *lonely* before they read.

Jigsaw reading

1　Read the introduction as a class. Students read the headline and the introduction, and answer the two questions.

Answers

People over thirty with good jobs but no partner.

Because they want to find a partner, but have no time to look.

2　Students divide into two groups. They read about one of the people, and answer the comprehension check questions. Allow enough time for this. If one or two students finish quickly, look at their answers to the questions and tell them how many they have right and wrong, but don't say which ones. They should then read the article again.

When students are ready, they find a partner from the other group and compare answers.

Answers

John Frantz

1　He's a sales manager.

2　Yes, it is. He earns more than £65,000 a year.

3　Yes, he does, a big one.

4　He wants to stay in his house in Washington DC.

5　Someone who is intelligent and who has their own opinions. He likes British women because they have an air of independence.

6　Women who are more interested in how much money he has.

7　He says they aren't so important to him, so maybe yes and maybe no.

8　A secretary called Sandy.

9　We don't know exactly, but it sounds all right.

10　He's going sightseeing with Sandy, and he's going to see some other women while he's in England.

Nicolette Morganti

1 She's a personal assistant with a TV news agency.
2 Yes, it is.
3 Yes, she does.
4 She'd like to live in London for six months of the year and in the United States for the other six months.
5 A caring, well-educated, non-smoking animal lover with a professional job and a sense of adventure.
6 She's fed up with British men who are materialistic, have no imagination, and are boring.
7 Yes, she does.
8 She met one or two men after she put an advertisement in a magazine, and she has met five American men.
9 We don't know, but the meetings probably weren't successful. She says she's looking for someone very special.
10 She is going to stay with English Rose until she finds a partner.

What do you think?

1 Answer question 1 as a class.
   Answer
   In some ways they would get on, in some ways they wouldn't. The main reason they would get on is that he likes English women and she likes American men. She doesn't like men who are materialistic, and he doesn't like women who only want his money. She likes men with a sense of adventure, and he likes exotic holidays. He likes women who are intelligent and who have their own opinions, and Nicolette seems to be like this.
   However, she would like to live in both London and the States, but he wants to live where he is now. She would like to have children; for him, children aren't so important.
2 Answer question 2 as a class.
3 Question 3 could be done in different ways, either quickly if you don't have time, or as a discussion. People often find the subject of arranged marriages interesting. If you want to have a discussion, you could put students into two groups. Group A must think of reasons in favour of arranged marriages, and Group B reasons against. When students have some ideas, get the feedback.
   You could extend the discussion by doing the same for marriages which *aren't* arranged by parents. What are the advantages and disadvantages of marriages arranged by the couple themselves?

● **Everyday English**   (**SB page 39**)

Spelling

T.15

This exercise could well be done as a warmer.

1 Read the introduction as a class. Ask different students to practise saying the letters in the columns. Then pick letters from different columns. You could write letters on the board which the students have to say.

Note
Learners of English often find the following letters hard to remember, so practise these especially.
a, e, i
j, g
h, k, v, w
r

2 Read this as a class.

3 T.15   Students listen to Henry and write down the names of his relatives.
   Answers

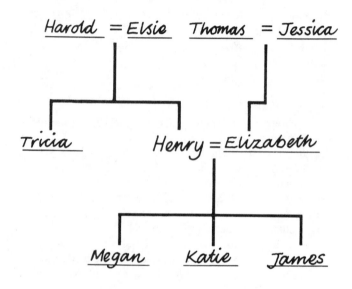

4 Students work in pairs to dictate names and addresses to each other.

Don't forget!

Workbook Unit 5
There are two exercises on writing – exercises 11 and 12. Students are asked to write a postcard.

Pronunciation book Unit 5
Exercise 1 is a sounds exercise on /w/.
Exercise 2 is a word focus exercise on words that students confuse because of their pronunciation.

Word list
Make sure your students complete the Word list for Unit 5 by writing in the translations.

Progress test
There is a Progress test for Units 1–5 on page 147 of the Teacher's Book.

UNIT 6

What ... like? – Comparatives and superlatives – Directions

Introduction to the Unit

The theme of the unit is describing people and places. This provides a useful context to practise the grammar for this unit, **What ... like?**, and comparatives and superlatives. The Skills Development section contains a reading text with some interesting facts about the world's richest man, and the listening exercise compares living in Madrid with living in London.

Notes on the Language Input

Grammar

Remember, if you are unsure about the form and uses of any of the grammar, check the Grammar section in the Student's Book, page 125, before you start work on the Presentation sections of the unit.

What ... like?

This question, which asks for a description, causes difficulties for students for several reasons:

1 – the use of **like** as a preposition, when students only have experience of it as a verb, as in *I like dancing*.
2 – the fact that the answer to this question does *not* contain *like* with the adjective. Students often make the following mistake:
   What's John like?   *He's like nice.
3 – It seems to many students a strange construction to ask for a description. In many languages the question word **how** is used to do this. In English *How is John?* is an inquiry about his health, *not* about his character and/or looks, and the answer is *He's very well*.

What ... like? is introduced first in the unit to provide a staged approach to the practice of comparatives and superlatives in the second Presentation. It is a useful question in the practising of these.

Comparatives and superlatives

It is assumed that students will have a certain familiarity with these, although of course mistakes will still be made. The exercises bring together all aspects of comparatives and superlatives:

– the use of **-er/-est** with short adjectives, **-ier/-iest** with adjectives that end in **y**, and **more/most** with longer adjectives.
– irregular adjectives such as *good, better, best; bad, worse, worst*.
– **as ... as** to describe similarity.

Students experience little difficulty with the concept of these structures but experience more difficulty in producing and pronouncing the forms because of all the different 'bits' involved. One of the most common problems is that they give equal stress to every word and syllable, so that utterances sound very unnatural.

Common mistakes

*She's more big than me.
*He's the most rich man in the world.
*She's tallest in the class.
*It's more expensive that I thought.
*He is as rich than the Queen.

There are a lot of controlled activities which aim to practise the form, and a pronunciation drill to practise natural connected speech.

Vocabulary

Adjectives are practised in the Vocabulary section, where students are asked to explore the use of synonyms and antonyms. The activities extend their vocabulary and also show how the prefixes **un-, in-, im-** are used to form opposite adjectives, e.g. *happy/unhappy, patient/impatient*. It is important that students should start to study some of the grammar of vocabulary, such as prefixes.

Everyday English

This section practises getting and giving directions with prepositions of place, e.g. *behind, in front of*, and prepositions of movement e.g. *along, across*. A picture map is used to do this. The final activity is personalized, and the students give each other directions to get to their homes from school.

Notes on the Unit

PRESENTATION (SB page 40)

What ... like?

T.16a

Read through the introduction to Tina Stanley with your students.

> **Note**
> The first stage of the lesson focuses only on the adjectives and giving descriptions before moving to the introduction of the question **What ... like?**. This is so that when the question is introduced students will understand from the start that the answer to this question is a description and does not contain **like**.

1   T.16a   Ask your students to listen carefully and write down the adjectives Tina uses to describe the cities she visited.

It is not expected that the students will have much difficulty understanding the tape. The language is quite simple. They should be familiar with most of the adjectives, although possibly *crowded*, *polluted*, and *noisy* will need some explanation (you could give a quick translation), and they will certainly need some pronunciation practice: /ˈkraʊdɪd/, /pəlˈuːtɪd/, /ˈnɔɪzɪ/.

Answers
New York   exciting, busy, dirty, cold
Tokyo   busy, crowded, clean (streets), polluted (in the centre)
Rome   beautiful, not too hot, noisy, expensive, interesting

● Grammar questions (SB page 40)

Before you ask the students to answer the Grammar questions, give your students the opportunity to tell you if they heard the question **What ... like?** Ask:

– *Did anyone hear the question the friend asked about all the cities?*

Now read through the questions all together. The aim is to make clear the difference between the verb **to like** and **like** the preposition.

Answers
– No, the friend isn't asking if Tina likes the cities.
– Yes, she is asking Tina to describe the places.

Reinforce the concept by explaining to the class that *What's X like?* means the same as *Tell me about X.*

You could photocopy the tapescript and give it to your students to read it and see the questions in context. You could ask them to underline the questions.

PRACTICE (SB page 40)

1 Grammar

1   The aim of the exercise is very controlled oral practice. You could chorus drill the question to practise the contraction **What's**, and the intonation.

Put students into pairs. Go round, helping and correcting. You may need to point out that **have/have got** can also be used in the answers.

Ask your students to do this exercise without looking at the tapescript if possible.

Sample Answers

What's New York like?	It's very exciting, but it's very busy and the streets are dirty. It's sometimes very cold in winter.
What's Tokyo like?	It's busy too, and very crowded. The centre is sometimes polluted, but the streets are clean.
What's Rome like?	It's beautiful, it's got/has beautiful old buildings. It's very interesting but it's noisy and expensive.

2   Ask students to do this on their own and compare their answers with a partner when they finish. They should be able to do it quite quickly. Drill the questions around the class.

Answers
a. What's the weather like?
b. What are the people like?
c. What's the food like?
d. What are the buildings like?
e. What are the shops like?

2 Speaking and listening

Focus students on the examples in the book and the fact that this time the practice is in the past – **What was/were ... like?**

Put students into small groups to do the activity. If you think they may find it difficult to come up with ideas you could brainstorm the topic with them first and add to the examples in the book.

Further ideas
What was the journey like? ... the entertainment ...? the night life ...? the swimming pool ...? the countryside ...? your hotel room ...?
What were the people like? ... the other guests ...? the roads ...?
Go round and help and correct while they ask and answer the questions. The activity will probably not last very long.

● Language review (SB page 41)

They could read this through together in their small groups and discuss the translations. These are designed to reinforce the message of the difference between verb and preposition.

Ask the class how they ask for descriptions in their language(s) and point out that *How is your sister?* in English is asking about her health.

▶ **Grammar reference: page 125.**

Ask students to read this at home, perhaps before they do some of the Workbook exercises for homework (see below).

Additional material

Workbook Unit 6
These exercises could be done in class to give further practice, for homework, or in a later class to revise.
What . . . like? – exercises 1–2.

Pronunciation book Unit 6
Exercise 3 could be done as further practice, perhaps as a warmer to another lesson, or in the language laboratory. Connected speech – Varieties of **like**.

PRESENTATION (SB page 41)

Comparatives and superlatives

T.16b

Note
It is assumed that your students will already have some familiarity with comparatives and superlatives, and so different aspects of them are brought together in this listening text.
Only if your class is very weak should you give them a photocopy of the text to read as they listen, although you could give them a copy at the end of the lesson.

---

1   T.16b   Ask your students to listen very carefully, and then ask them to tell you any of the structures they can remember that Tina uses to compare the cities.
At this point just go through the examples orally, getting them from different members of the class. There is the opportunity to write the answers and practise the pronunciation in later exercises (3 and 4).
Answers
London is **more** exciting **than** Tokyo (for a musician).
New York is **the most** exciting.
London is (**much**) **older than** New York.
London isn't **as** old **as** Rome.
Rome is **the oldest** city (she visited).
London doesn't have **as many** old buildings **as** Rome.
London has **more** old buildings **than** New York and Tokyo.
New York has **more** parks **than** Tokyo.
London has **the most** parks.

2   Read through the examples of how comparatives and superlatives are formed and then ask your students to work in pairs to do the exercise. It should not take long because they simply have to insert the correct number 1, 2, or 3, except for *far, good/bad* where they need to write out the words in full.

Answers

beautiful (3)	cold (1)	old (1)
ugly (2)	hot (1 and	near (1)
big (1 and	doubles the	far, farther/
doubles the	consonant –	further, farthest/
consonant –	hotter)	furthest
bigger)	crowded (3)	noisy (2)
small (1)	exciting (3)	quiet (1)
busy (2)	friendly (2)	polluted (3)
cheap (1)	heavy (2)	wet (1 and
expensive (3)	interesting (3)	doubles the
clean (1)	boring (3)	consonant –
dirty (2)	modern (3)	wetter)
		dry (2)
		good, better, best
		bad, worse, worst

Go through the table with the whole class together.

● Grammar question

Students should be able to work out the rules from the table quite easily.
Answers
– You use **-er/-est** with short adjectives.

Note
At this point you could also ask your students if they can work out the rule about the doubling of the consonant: where there is *one* vowel and *one* consonant, the consonant doubles.

– You use **ier/iest** when the adjective ends in **y**.
– You use **more/most** when the adjective has two syllables or more.

3   Ask students to do this written consolidation exercise on their own and then check their answers with a partner. Afterwards, you can play the tape again for a final check.
Answers
a. Tokyo's exciting, but, for a musician, London is *more* exciting *than* Tokyo and, of course, New York is *the most* exciting of all.
b. London is, of course, much older *than* New York, but it isn't *as* old *as* Rome. Rome is *the* oldest city I visited.
c. London doesn't have *as* many old buildings *as* Rome, but it has *more than* both New York and Tokyo.
d. New York has *more* parks than Tokyo, but London has *the most* parks.

4   T.16c   This is a short pronunciation exercise. The aim is to practise the links between words in connected speech and weak forms, which students often find difficult because they are trying to remember all the different 'bits' of these structures.
Play the first sentence on the tape (or model it yourself) and highlight the weak forms, *than* /ðən/ and *as* /əz/, and the word links:

London is older than New York but it isn't as old as Rome. /lʌndən ɪz əʊldə ðən nju: jɔːk bʌt ɪt ɪznt əz əʊld əz rəʊm/

Ask students to work in pairs on the next set of sentences. They could mark in the word links and say them to each other. If your students have a knowledge of the phonemic script you could transcribe the sentences (see below) and give them out to help them practise.

I'm not as tall as you. /aɪm nɒt əz tɔːl əz juː/
But I'm taller than Ann. /bʌt aɪm tɔːlə ðən æn/
It's not as cold today as it was yesterday. /ɪts nɒt əz kəʊld tədeɪ əz ɪt wɒz jestədeɪ/
But it's colder than it was last week. /bʌt ɪts kəʊldə ðən ɪt wɒz lɑːst wiːk/
This book is more interesting than I thought. /ðɪs bʊk ɪz mɔː(r) ɪntrəstɪŋ ðən aɪ θɔːt/
But it isn't as interesting as the one I read last week. /bʌt ɪt ɪznt əz ɪntrəstɪŋ əz ðə wʌn aɪ red lɑːst wiːk/

Play the sentences on the tape one by one (or model them yourself) and get the whole class to chorus them, then ask individual students to repeat them.

PRACTICE   (SB page 42)

The exercises bring together the grammar from both the Presentations – **What ... like?** and comparatives and superlatives.
You could set some of these exercises for homework.

1 Grammar

Go round and monitor the pairs as they correct the sentences.
Answers
a. He's older than he looks.
b. Ann's as tall as her mother.
c. 'What is Paris like?'
   'It's beautiful, especially in spring.'
d. Concorde is the fastest passenger plane in the world.
e. Trains in Tokyo are more crowded than in London.
f. Oxford is one of the oldest universities in Europe.
g. He isn't as intelligent as his sister/He isn't more intelligent than his sister.
h. This is harder than I expected.
i. Who is the richest man in the world?
j. Everything is cheaper in my country.
Conduct a feedback with the whole class.

2 Speaking

Allocate different conversations to different pairs, or let the pairs choose one for themselves, but make sure that there is variety in the class.
Some sample answers are given here so that you can give additional prompts to reluctant students. Make it clear to the students that not every line of the conversation needs to contain examples of the structures – the idea is to broaden the context of use.

Possible answers
The car: It's bigger, more comfortable, and it has more space for luggage. It was more expensive than my old car but it's much better. I love driving it.
The house: It's bigger – it has a much more beautiful garden. It has more bedrooms. It's nearer to the town centre but further from the countryside. My family are very happy there.
New girl/boyfriend: She's/He's taller, prettier/more attractive and very funny, much funnier than Julia/John. I enjoyed the party.
Go round and help with ideas and ask them to go back through their dialogues to get them right and aim for good pronunciation. At the end, ask one or two pairs to act out their conversation to the rest of the class.

3 Speaking and writing

Ask students to do this in pairs or individually and then to compare their sentences with a partner's.
You could ask the students to focus on *one* of the cities and compare it with the others. Tell them to write sentences using all of the structures and remind them that the box of adjectives on page 41 will help, and that they do not have to make sentences just using the facts about the cities – if they know the cities they can give their own opinions.
Sample answers (using London)
Facts
It's older than Tokyo and New York but not as old as Rome.
The population is bigger than Rome but smaller than New York and Tokyo – Tokyo has the biggest population.
It has the biggest area of all the cities.
In winter it's colder than Rome but warmer than New York and Tokyo.
It isn't as wet as Rome. Tokyo is the wettest city.
Of all the cities, London is the furthest from the sea.

Ask your students if any of the facts surprise them.

4 Speaking and listening

This activity should follow naturally from the one before. The aim is to give an opportunity for freer speaking practice by personalizing the topic.
Put the students into small groups to compare their towns or different parts of their country. Go round the groups and take an interest in their ideas, but don't be as quick to correct in this activity. Encourage the flow of ideas and general use of language, not just sentences containing the structures.

● Language review   (SB page 43)

Ask students to translate in pairs or groups. It should be quite straightforward.

▶ **Grammar reference: page 125.**

▶ **Grammar reference: page 125.**

Ask students to study the Grammar section at home.

Additional material

Workbook Unit 6
Comparatives and superlatives – exercises 3–8.

SKILLS DEVELOPMENT

● Reading and speaking (SB page 44)

Tell students to look at the picture of the Sultan of Brunei. Ask a couple of very general questions:
– *Have you heard of him?*
– *How old do you think he is?*

Pre-reading task

1 Direct these questions at the whole class. The aim is to try and stimulate your students' interest in the topic before they read.
See if your class as a group can reach a consensus about where Brunei is. Many people seem to think it is in the Middle East, but it is in fact in East Asia. Don't tell your students where it is at this point because they have to check if they were right when they read the article.

2 You could put students into pairs for this dictionary work. Ask them to put the words in their vocabulary notebooks with the translation. Make sure they find the part of speech that is indicated when they look up the words.
You do not want this vocabulary work to go on too long because the impetus to read the text will be lost.
Tell them that all the words appear in the text.

Reading for information

Ask them to read through quite quickly the first time (tell them that there will be the opportunity to read it more carefully later), and then check with a partner if they were right about where Brunei is, and if they agree about the most extravagant way the Sultan spends his money.
Is it:
– *the party for his daughter?*
– *the huge new palace?*
– *the second new palace?*
– *his many hotels?*
– *his fleet of private planes and airbus?*
– *his big house in London?*

Comprehension check

Let the students remain in their pairs and ask them to read the text again more carefully as they do this exercise.

Answers

1 Four hotels are mentioned.
  – *Claridges* Hotel in London because that is where the Sultan had a party for his daughter, which cost £100,000.
  – The *Dorchester* in London, the *Beverley Hills* Hotel in Los Angeles and the *Hyatt* Hotel in Singapore because he owns them.

2 His first new palace has 1,788 rooms.
This palace also has 257 toilets and a dining room where 4,000 people can sit.
A servant changes 200 light bulbs a day.
Brunei earns $229,000 an hour from its oil and gas.
The population of Brunei is 230,000.
The Sultan married his cousin, Princess Saleha, when he was 19.

3 Brunei is rich because it has oil and gas, which it sells to Japan, and only a small population to share the money.

4

5 He's very shy and looks very young.

6 The first wife, Princess Saleha, was sweet and pretty when she was sixteen, but she became more and more reserved when she was older.
His second wife, Mariam Bell is more outgoing. She is a mixture of Bruneian, Japanese, and English.

7 The five mistakes:
  – He does not own Claridges hotel.
  – He did not build a multi-storey car park for his guests' cars.
  – He does not have the biggest garden in London, the Queen does.
  – He did not divorce his first wife.
  – His first wife does not now live in Japan. Both wives live in the new palace.

Correct version

The Sultan of Brunei spends his great wealth in many ways. For example, he gave a party for his daughter in Claridges Hotel in London. The party cost £100,000.
He built a new palace but his friends said that it looked like a multi-storey car park so he built another one. He has a few houses in London and one of them has the biggest garden in the city, except for Buckingham Palace.
He did not divorce his first wife when he married an air hostess, he has two wives. They both live in the new palace.
Brunei is a rich country because it has a lot of oil and gas and can sell it to Japan.

Discussion

This should be a brief personalized free speaking activity to round off the lesson and change the pace after all the comprehension questions. Conduct it either in small groups or with the whole class together if you are running out of time.
It would be a good idea if you asked your students to think about these questions at home in preparation for the lesson. It would facilitate the discussion at this stage.

Note

The richest person in Great Britain is, of course, the Queen. She is the wealthiest woman in the world. It is estimated that she owns land, property, and other assets worth £6.7 billion. Her yearly income is about £86,158,000 but her expenditure on property, land, and staff is about £22,000,000.

● **Vocabulary** (SB page 45)

Synonyms

T.17

Check that your students know what synonyms are: *words that are the same or similar in meaning*. You could make the point by asking them to give you some examples in their own language, and also by reading through the introduction to the exercise with them.

1 Put students into pairs to complete the conversations. They may need to use their dictionaries to check the meaning of some of the words.
   Answers
   a. wealthy   e. generous
   b. modern   f. messy
   c. handsome   g. annoyed
   d. marvellous   h. fed up

2 T.17 Ask your students to listen to the tape to check their answers.
   Now play the dialogues through one at a time and after each ask the pairs of students to repeat the dialogues, and try to imitate the stress and intonation.

Antonyms

Remind students what antonyms are: *words that are opposite in meaning*. You could do this in the same way suggested for synonyms above.

1 Let your students stay in the same pairs. You need to focus them again onto the adjectives in the previous exercise to do this exercise.
   You could do the first one with them to demonstrate more clearly what is meant.
   Answers

awful	wonderful, marvellous
interested	bored, fed up
mean	kind, generous
old	new, modern
poor	rich, wealthy
pleased	angry, annoyed
tidy	untidy, messy
ugly	good-looking, handsome

2 Read through the introduction with your students. Draw particular attention to the response containing **not very** + the antonym. Then ask them to work together in their pairs to construct B's more polite answers.
   Sample answers
   a. Well he's certainly not very generous.
   b. Yes, it isn't very cheap there, is it?

c. Well it's certainly not very tidy.
d. Yes, he doesn't look very happy, does he?
e. Well, she's certainly not very clever.
f. Yes, they weren't very good, were they?
g. Yes, she wasn't very polite, was she?

Bring the whole class together to conduct the feedback. Allocate pairs of students across the class to be A or B and get them to act out the little dialogues. Encourage good stress and intonation. The main stress in both sentences is on the adjective.
Example

● • ● • ● • ● • ● • ●

A *John's so mean.*   B *Well, he's certainly not very generous.*

3 This final activity aims to point out how sometimes opposites can be created with the use of prefixes. It should only take a very few minutes to do. Students could do it quickly on their own and then check their answers with a partner. They should use their dictionaries to check those they are unsure of. Expect them not to know those underlined.
   Answers

impossible	uninterested	unhappy	inexpensive
unfriendly	unemployed	impatient	uncomfortable
impolite	unimportant	inconvenient	incorrect

Additional material

Pronunciation book Unit 6
Stress in three-syllabled words – exercise 2. This exercise recycles vocabulary from this unit.

● **Listening** (SB page 46)

T.18

The aim of this activity is primarily to develop your students' listening abilities. They have to listen at length and pick out the main information as required by the selected tasks. The comparing of the cities provides a natural context for practising the language input in this unit, but the main aim is general fluency. You hope that they are beginning to use comparatives and superlatives spontaneously, but let them draw on all their language resources. Avoid overcorrecting.

Pre-listening task
Look at the picture of a café, and read the introduction as a class. Ask students what they know about Madrid. Put them into pairs to consider and discuss the true or false statements.

Listening

T.18 Play the tape and ask your students to listen and check whether their true/false decisions were right or not. Go through the statements with the whole class. Encourage your students to offer a bit more information about each one.
Answers
1 False   (They start work later than in London. Kate starts at ten o'clock.)
2 True   (About seven or eight)

50

3 True   (They close for about three hours, until five o'clock.)
4 False (Only in the summer because it is so hot and the work hours change. Everyone works from eight thirty to three.)
5 False (They eat all day.)
6 False (They have their main meal at lunchtime.)
7 False (Madrid is smaller.)
8 False (There are problems because there are a lot of accidents.)
9 True   (It is also cheap but people still like to use their cars.)

Comprehension check

Play the tape again and ask students to make notes on their own. Tell them that they should be very brief. At the end ask them to get into small groups to compare their notes.

Answers

> **Note**
> Students are not expected to write down all the information but most of it will probably emerge when they compare notes in their groups.

The time of day that things happen
– start work about ten, earlier in summer, about eight thirty; lunch from two to five, three in summer; bed at one or two in the morning.
Food
– eat all day – snacks in the morning, omelette and a beer; main meal lunchtime; *tapas* in the evening.
People
– easier to get to know; spend more time outdoors, in the streets.
Where people live
– in flats; in the city centre.
Cost of living
– cheaper than London.
Shops
– open until late.
Safety
– safer on the streets.

Driving
– terrible drivers, lots of accidents.
Public transport
– good, cheap, ten tickets for about two pounds.
Weather
– very hot in summer; better than London.

What do you think?

The aim of this is to provide some personalized free speaking. Ask students to stay in their groups to compare their town(s) with Madrid. Go round and listen and show interest but don't be too quick to correct mistakes.
At the end, listen to some of the comments as a class.

> **Additional material**
>
> **Workbook Unit 6**
> Exercise 11 does some work on relative clauses and provides a model text, which leads to students writing a description of their home town.

● Everyday English   (SB page 47)

Directions

> T.19

The aim is to direct students in stages towards being able to understand and give directions. Students could work in pairs from the start of the lesson.
Ask them to look at the picture.
1 Ask them to point out the things on the picture to their partner. Go round the pairs to check and then go through with the whole class together.
2 Tell them to read the descriptions of the things which are not named and to insert the name in the correct place. The aim of this is to teach/revise prepositions of place.
Answers

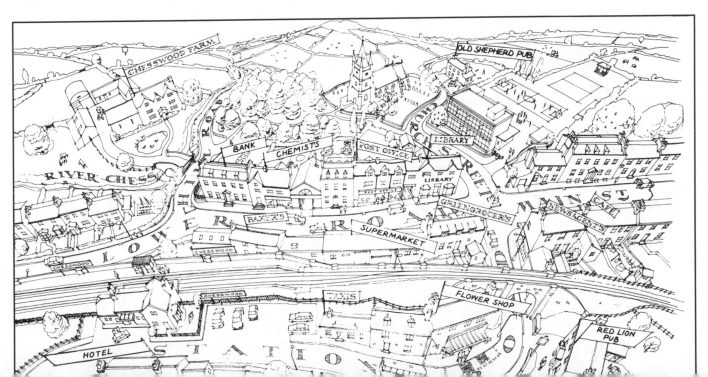

3 This activity is very controlled. Before you ask the students to do it in pairs, go through the introductory example with the whole class, and then do one or two further examples yourself with individual students across the class, to check their understanding of the prepositions.
Go round helping and correcting.

4 This is designed to teach/revise prepositions of movement. Ask students to do it on their own and then compare with a partner.

Answers

You go *down* the path, *past* the pond, *over* the bridge, and *through* the gate. Then you go *across/over* the road and take the path *through* the wood. When you come *out of* the wood you walk *along/up* the path and *into* the church. It takes five minutes.

Go through the text with the whole class.

5 ☐ T.19 ☐ Play the tape and ask your students to take notes and then compare their notes with a partner. Play the tape again for them to check and probably complete their notes. The aim of the final part is that students practise getting and giving directions in a personalized fashion. After they take the notes ask them to relate the directions back to their partner:
'Now, you come out of the school and go across the road to the bus stop, is that right?'
'Then you catch the number 23.' etc.
'No, that's wrong. You turn left and . . .'

Don't forget!

Workbook Unit 6
There is a vocabulary exercise on putting similar nouns into pairs – exercise 9, a writing exercise to practise correcting mistakes – exercise 10, and an exercise on relative clauses – exercise 11.

Pronunciation book Unit 6
The sounds practised in exercise 1 are /n/, /y/, /ŋ/, /ŋg/, and /ndʒ/.
The stress in three-syllable nouns is practised in exercise 2.

Word list
Make sure your students complete the Word list for Unit 6 by writing in the translations.

Video
Section 4 – Report: *Purple Violin*
This video section supplements Units 5 and 6 of the Student's Book. It is a short documentary about a musician in Oxford who busks with an electric violin.

Stop and Check (WB page 36)

It is time to revise the work so far!
A suggestion for approaching the Stop and Check sections in the Workbook is at the end of Unit 3 of this Teacher's Book.

UNIT 7

Present Perfect Simple (1) – Short answers

Introduction to the Unit

The title of this unit is 'Fame'. This topic was chosen because it lends itself to talking about people's experiences, which is one of the uses of the Present Perfect. Students are introduced to the Present Perfect via texts about an actress and a writer. In the Skills Development section, they read about the actor Paul Newman, and listen to an interview with a singer in a rock band. There is a roleplay, where students pretend to be members of a group of musicians.

Notes on the Language Input

Grammar

Present Perfect

This is the first unit in *Headway Pre-Intermediate* where the Present Perfect is dealt with. Two of its uses, to express experience and to express unfinished past, are introduced and practised. The 'evident now' use is dealt with in Unit 14, along with the Present Perfect Continuous.

The Present Perfect causes problems for learners of English because it expresses an aspect which is not present in many other languages. Its use is dictated not by 'time when' but by 'how the speaker sees the event', which is what the term aspect means.

The Present Perfect means 'completed some time before now, but with some present relevance', and so joins past and present in a way that many other languages do not feel the need to. They can express the same ideas, but by using either a past tense or a present tense. In English, we can say *I have seen the Queen* but not *I have seen the Queen yesterday*. In many other European languages, the same form of **have** + the present participle can be used for both these sentences to express both indefinite (Present Perfect) and definite (Past Simple) time.

In the use of the Present Perfect to express an experience some time before now, students' mistakes are usually of the above kind.

Common mistakes
*I have watched TV last night.
*When have you been to Russia?
*Did you ever try Chinese food?

For the Present Perfect to express unfinished past, many languages (very logically) use a present tense. However, English 'sees' not only the present situation but the situation going back into the past, and uses the Present Perfect.

Common mistakes
*I live here for five years.
*She is a teacher for ten years.
*How long do you know Paul?

Students are usually introduced to the Present Perfect very gently in their first year course, so they will not be unfamiliar with the form. This unit aims to lay a foundation in the aspects expressed by this tense, but your class will not have mastered it by the end of the unit! It takes a long time to be assimilated.

Vocabulary

The first vocabulary exercise introduces students to homophones. These are very common in English, especially with one-syllable words, as English spelling is not phonetic.

The second vocabulary exercise practises adverbs of different kinds: focusing adverbs (*even, only, too, especially*), comment adverbs (*of course, fortunately*), adverbs of degree (*nearly*) and adverbs of frequency (*always*). Adverbs of manner are dealt with in Unit 12.

Everyday English

This section practises short answers. There are exercises on short answers throughout the Workbook whenever a new tense or verb form is introduced, and this section aims to bring the area together, and to give some oral practice.

Notes on the Unit

PRESENTATION (SB page 48)

Present Perfect

> **Note**
> We usually suggest that students look at the Grammar section at the back of the Student's Book for homework *after* the presentation in class. However, with certain difficult items, it is worth asking students to spend five or ten minutes looking at the information in the Grammar section *before* you have the Presentation in class, so that they can begin to understand and think about the area. The Present Perfect is a case in point, so set this for homework (see Student's Book page 126).

In this first Presentation section, the use of the Present Perfect to express an experience some time in one's life is introduced.

> **Additional idea**
> If you feel you would like to remind your students of the form and basic use of the Present Perfect before you begin this Presentation section, you could do the following mini-revision lesson.
> Ask a student (who you know has travelled) *Which countries have you been to?* If the student is puzzled by the verb form, prompt with *In your life.*
> Write the names of the countries on the board. Say to the class *X has been to A, B, C, and D. Do we know when X went to A?* Ask X a question with *When …?* to elicit the question in the Past Simple *When did X go to A?*
> The class now asks X the questions, and X replies with the dates.
> Put two sentences on the board.
> *X **has been** to A, B, C, and D.*
> *X **went** to A in (1989).*
> Ask the class if they know the names of these two tenses. The Past Simple should be known, but probably not the Present Perfect. Explain (in the students' language, if possible) that the Past Simple is used to talk about definite time, and the Present Perfect is used to talk about indefinite time, to talk about an action which happened some time before now.
> Ask some other students *Which countries have you been to?*, and encourage the class to ask *When did you go there?*

Introduction: Have a short conversation about films. Ask questions such as the following:
– *Who are your favourite film actors and actresses?*
– *What films were they in?*
– *What sort of films do you like?*
– *When did you last go to the cinema?*

1 Read the text about the actress, Andrea de Silva, as a class.

● Grammar questions (SB pages 48 and 49)

– Students work in pairs to underline the examples of the Past Simple and the time expressions. The aim is to consolidate what is known (i.e. the Past Simple) before moving on to the new (i.e. the Present Perfect), and to reinforce the idea that the Past Simple is used to refer to definite time.

Answers
started   at the age of fourteen
spoke   last week
said
went   a year ago
made
won   in 1987

– Answer the second question as a class.

Answer
The Present Perfect is formed with the auxiliary verb **have** + the past participle.

– Students work in twos or threes to answer the third Grammar question. They might be able to infer the answers, or they might have no idea. If students can manage something such as *Charlie Chaplin is dead*, they are doing well!

Answers
She has made over twenty-five films – Present Perfect, because she is still alive, and can make more in the future.
Charlie Chaplin made over fifty films – Past Simple, because he is dead and can make no more.
She has travelled to many parts of the world – Present Perfect, because this is up to now in her life. She can travel some more.
She went to Argentina last year – Past Simple, because the definite time is given.
She has won three Oscars – Present Perfect, because this is up to now in her life. She can win some more.
She won her first Oscar in 1987 – Past Simple, because the definite time is given.

> **Additional idea**
> Students have read example sentences containing the Present Perfect, but they have not practised saying any yet. Elicit sentences about Andrea, and put them in two columns on the board, with the sentences containing the Past Simple on one side and the examples containing the Present Perfect on the other.
>
> | *Past Simple* | *Present Perfect* |
> | --- | --- |
> | She started acting at the age of 14. | She has made over 25 films. |
> | I spoke to her last week. | She has travelled to many parts of the world. |
> | I went there a year ago. | She has won three Oscars. |
>
> Drill the sentences containing the Present Perfect around the room, paying attention to the contracted **has**.

2 Students work in pairs or small groups to put the verbs in the correct tense. Encourage them to look back at the text about Andrea de Silva if they want help, as the texts are parallel.

Answers

> Barbara Lively, the writer, is married with two children. She <u>has written</u> over 40 books. She <u>started</u> writing after the death of her first husband. She <u>has lived</u> in many parts of the world, including Japan and India.
> She spent her childhood in Egypt, but <u>came</u> to England in 1966.
> She <u>has written</u> both prose and poetry, but is best known for her romantic novels. She <u>has won</u> many awards, including the Booker Prize, which she <u>won</u> in 1988 for the novel *Dark Times to Come*.

Additional idea

For more controlled practice of the Present Perfect, you could again elicit sentences about Barbara Lively that contain examples of the Present Perfect, and drill them around the room.

3 Do questions a. and b. as a class to establish the two question forms, one in the Present Perfect and one in the Past Simple, and drill them to establish a model.

Answers
a. How many films has she made?
b. When did she start acting?
c. When did she go to Argentina?
d. How many Oscars has she won?
e. When did she win her first Oscar?

When you get the feedback, drill the questions around the room, making sure students start with the voice high.

Students work in pairs to ask and answer similar questions about Barbara Lively. They should write their questions down. When you get the feedback, ask one person from a pair to ask another person from another pair. Their questions and answers will be similar.

Sample questions
How many children has she got/does she have?
How many books has she written?
When did she start writing?
Where has she lived?
Where did she spend her childhood/where did she grow up?
When did she come to England?
What sort of books has she written?
Has she won any awards?
When did she win the Booker Prize?
Which book did she win it for?

Rule

In some units, we give a rule in a box before students move on to the Practice section. This is in part to preview the Language review, so that students have a rule 'to hang on to' before they embark on further practice. This will not ensure that all mistakes are eliminated, but it is hoped that it might provide a base to refer back to.

Read the rule as a class. Translate it into L1 if you can.

PRACTICE   (SB page 49)

1 Grammar

Students write in the past tense forms and past participles. All the verbs occur either in the Presentation prior to this exercise, or in the Practice exercises which follow. Encourage them to look at the list of irregular verbs at the back of the Student's Book either to help them do the exercise, or to check their answers from.

Answers

be	was/were	been
try	tried	tried
act	acted	acted
read	read	read
have	had	had
win	won	won
break	broke	broken
work	worked	worked
write	wrote	written
meet	met	met
make	made	made
sell	sold	sold

2 Speaking and listening

This is a mingle activity, where students must ask the same question to everyone in the class. Photocopy page 56 of the Teacher's Book, and cut it up into sentences. (If you paste them onto card, you can use them again.)

1 Every student must have a sentence. Read the example in the Student's Book, showing that they have to turn their sentence into a question beginning *Have you ever ...?* If you aren't careful, students go round the class saying 'Find someone who has been to Russia.'
Before you ask the class to stand up, check that everyone's question is correct. There is little point in students asking the same wrong question fifteen or twenty times.
Students stand up and ask everyone, making a note of the answers.

2 When they have finished and have sat down, allow them a minute to decide what they are going to say when they report back to the class. Ask all the students to report back.

3 This question could go on a long time if you want it to. Work as a class, so that everyone can hear the questions and the answers. People are usually fascinated to hear about other people's experiences! Don't hesitate to come in yourself and ask questions.
Be prudent in your correction. Don't stop too often to correct, but glaring mistakes in the use of the Past Simple and Present Perfect are worth correcting.

3 Grammar

Students work in pairs or small groups to make sentences and questions. They should write their answers down.
When they have finished, ask various students for their answers. You should correct carefully, and you could drill some of the sentences around the room.

Answers
a. He's climbed mountains all over the world.

Find someone who has been to Russia.

Find someone who has been to Portugal.

Find someone who has written poetry.

Find someone who has been to the United States.

Find someone who has been water-skiing.

Find someone who has cooked a meal for more than twenty people.

Find someone who has tried Indian food.

Find someone who has flown in a helicopter.

Find someone who has been horse-riding.

Find someone who has acted on the stage.

Find someone who has won a competition.

Find someone who has been sailing.

Find someone who has read a book by Charles Dickens.

Find someone who has broken an arm or a leg.

Find someone who has been wind-surfing.

Find someone who has had a camping holiday.

Find someone who has been to university.

Find someone who has broken something expensive.

Find someone who has been to Scotland.

Find someone who has worked in a factory.

He's climbed Everest without oxygen.
He's written several books.
Has he ever had an accident?
b. He's directed many films.
   He's never won an Oscar.
   Has he ever written a script?
c. They've sold over five million records.
   They've been on tour all over the world.
   They've had ten number one records.
   Have they ever been in a film?

Additional material

Workbook Unit 7

Exercises 1–5 practise the form of the Present Perfect.

Note

Your students might be tired of doing accuracy work at this point. It might be a good idea to do something from the Skills Development section, for example the reading about Paul Newman, and do the second Presentation (of Present Perfect to express unfinished past) in a later lesson.

PRESENTATION   (SB page 50)

Present Perfect

1   T.20   Students read and listen to the dialogues. You could ask the students to practise the dialogues in pairs.

Grammar questions

– Ask students in pairs to identify the three different tenses used in the questions.
   Answers
   Present Simple
   Where do you live, Ann?
   What do you do, Ann?
   Past Simple
   Why did you move?
   What did you do before that?
   Present Perfect
   How long have you lived there?
   How long have you worked there?

– If you think your students will be able to discuss in pairs *why* the different tenses are used, ask them to do so. If you feel they would prefer more guidance, answer this question as a class.
   Answers
– The Present Simple is used to ask questions about things that are true for a long time or all time.
– The Past Simple is used to ask about a definite time in the past.
– The Present Perfect is used to ask about an action which began in the past and continues to the present.

– Students answer the third Grammar question in pairs.
   Answers
   She has lived near Brighton for three years.
   She has worked in a bank for eight years.
   She moved because she needed somewhere bigger to live.
   She worked for a travel agent before she joined the bank.

2   Students work in pairs to complete the two dialogues between Tony and Ann.
   Answers
   Do you have a car, Ann?
   Yes, I do.
   How long *have you had* it?
   For a year.
   How much *did you* pay for it?
   About two thousand pounds.

   Do you know a man called Lionel Beecroft?
   Yes, *I do.*
   How long *have you known him*?
   For years and years.
   Where *did you meet him*?
   I met him while I was working for the travel agent.

   Read the Rule box as a class. The aim of this is to preview the Language review, and to give students a rule 'to hang on to'.

Additional ideas

1   Students have read some examples of the Present Perfect, and spoken them to each other, but you haven't drilled any yet.
Elicit the following questions and answers, and drill them round the class:
– *How long have you lived there?*
– *How long have you worked there?*
– *I've had a car for a year.*
– *I've known Lionel for years and years.*

2   This is a little situation for highlighting the uses of the Present Perfect. You could do it as a revision exercise following the Presentation.
Write the following on the board:

For sale
1989 Ford Cortina. Red. 1 owner. No accidents. 20,000 miles. £5,000.

Explain to the class that this is an advertisement for a second-hand car. In pairs, they must think of the question for each piece of information. For example:
How old is it?

Allow time for students to think of the questions. As you go round the groups, help students with the necessary verbs.
to have an owner
to have an accident
to do 20,000 miles

Notice that three items of information require the Present Perfect in the question:
How many owners has it had?
Has it ever had an accident? or *How many accidents has it had?*

How many miles has it done?

It can be useful for students to perceive the use of the
Present Perfect in such a definable context. The Present
Perfect is needed because the car isn't 'dead'! It is still
going!

Answers

How old is the car?/When was it made?
What sort of car is it? What make is it?
What colour is it?
How many owners has it had?
Has it ever had an accident?
How many miles has it done?
How much is it?

PRACTICE   (SB page 51)

1 Grammar

Students work in pairs to decide which is the correct verb form.
You could do the first one or two as a class to act as an example.

Answers

a. Have you ever seen
b. I saw
c. have liked
d. was
e. bought
f. have you known
g. have known
h. did you get
i. have been   got

2 *For* or *since*?

Read the explanation and look at the diagram as a class. Students
work in pairs to decide whether **for** or **since** is needed.

Answers

a. for
b. for
c. since
d. since
e. since
f. for
g. since
h. for
i. since
j. for

3 Speaking and listening

Before students begin this activity in pairs, give them an idea of
what you want. Choose one or two students, and ask them the
sample questions. You should know enough about them to ask
questions that relate to their lives, their homes and their
possessions. Try especially to ask some questions in the Past
Simple, i.e. having established a fact using the Present Perfect,
you then ask several more questions in the Past Simple to get
further information.

Students can now work in pairs to ask and answer questions.
After a while, get some feedback.

● Language review   (SB page 51)

Present Perfect

Read the explanation of the Present Perfect as a class. Ask
students in pairs to translate the sample sentences. It is important
that you translate for concept, not form. For example, in the last

sentence in the Translate box, the Present Perfect is used in
English, but in many languages this use is expressed by a present
tense. The aim is to make students consciously aware of
differences between their language and English.

▶ **Grammar reference: page 126.**

Students reread the Grammar reference for homework.

Additional material

Workbook Unit 7
Students are asked to discriminate between the Present
Perfect, the Present Simple, and the Past Simple in
exercises 7–9.
Exercise 6 practises *for* and *since*.

Pronunciation book Unit 7
Exercise 3 on connected speech practises the
pronunciation of 's' in the auxiliary verb *has*.

SKILLS DEVELOPMENT

● Reading   (SB page 52)

Pre-reading task

1 Read the introduction as a class, and discuss the pictures. The
pictures show Paul Newman – as a racing driver, with Joanne
Woodward; as a cowboy; and a bottle of Newman's Own
Salad Dressing.
2 Students work in groups to add to the charts. If they are slow
to start you could prompt with another couple of suggestions,
for example, *He's got blue eyes; He races cars; How many
children has he got? How many times has he been married?*
3 Get the feedback to the group work.

Reading

Students read the article, and try to find the answers to their
questions. If students want to look up one or two words in their
dictionaries, that's fine, but don't encourage them to do this too
often. It's better that they read for pleasure and overall
comprehension, rather than stopping at every unknown word.
Just say *Don't worry if there are words you don't know. We'll
look at them later.*

Comprehension check

Answer questions 1 and 2 as a class. Encourage discussion at
this point.

Students work in pairs or small groups to answer questions 3 and
4. When you get the feedback to question 4, make sure students
start the question with the voice high. **Wh-** questions in English
start high and fall.

Answers

3 a.–5   b.–3   c.–4   d.–1   e.–6
   f.–2   g.–7

4 a. When was he born?
   b. When did he start working in the theatre?
   c. When/where did he meet his first wife?
   d. When did he get married for the first time?
   e. How many children did they have?

f. How old was he when he made his first film?

g. What was his role/who did he play?

h. Did he enjoy making the film?

i. What did he and Graziano talk about?

Possible questions (paragraphs 4–7)

Where did he meet Joanne Woodward?

Did they make films together?

When did he get married for the second time?

What are some of the films he has made?

How many films has he made?

Has he won an Oscar?

How many children has he got from his second marriage?

When did he come second in the Le Mans race?

What did his son die of?

What does the Scott Newman Foundation do?

What are some of the causes Paul has supported?

What does he do with the money from his Newman's Own food products?

Vocabulary

Students work together in pairs to answer the questions. They can use their dictionaries if they want.

Answers

1 a movie; a picture. *Movie* is American English.

2　a. waste　　　f. overdose

　　b. career　　　g. abuse

　　c. slave　　　h. conscience

　　d. break　　　i. charity

　　e. stardom　　j. keep (trying)

Additional ideas

Ask students to take it in turns to read the text out loud, paragraph by paragraph, to the rest of the class. As a language classroom activity, reading aloud has been much maligned for many years, and of course, reading aloud is a very different skill from reading silently; nevertheless, it can be fruitful to do it occasionally. You can check any other vocabulary, and you can check the pronunciation of the student speaking. If a pronunciation problem arises, you can make it a class problem.

You could choose one of the paragraphs and use it as a dictation. This might be a good way to start the next lesson, as it would serve as revision. Paragraph 6 has several examples of the Present Perfect.

Writing

Do exercise 12 (Relative clauses (2)) in the Workbook before asking students to write their biography. When marking such work, be selective in your correction. Try to give praise for effort, and avoid the demotivating effect of a homework handed back full of corrections in red.

● Vocabulary　(SB page 53)

Homophones

Of course, it is not important that your students learn the linguistic term *homophone*, but it is an important fact about

English lexis that there are many words with the same pronunciation but different spellings and different meanings, and it is worth drawing your students' attention to this. They need to be aware of homophones especially when they are listening. When they are reading, they can see the different spellings. Read the introduction to the exercise as a class.

1　Students find a word in the text about Paul Newman with the same pronunciation but a different spelling. Do the first one together as an example. Stress that the two pronunciations are *exactly* the same. Check the meaning of the pairs of words.

Answers

waist/waste	knew/new
roll/role	our/hour
too/two	sun/son
brake/break	

2　This exercise is more difficult, as students have to think of the new words themselves. Encourage them to close their eyes and say the word out loud, then try to think of another spelling. Check the meaning of the pairs of words.

Answers

there/their	ate/eight
red/read	sea/see
been/bean	check/cheque
sail/sale	fair/fare
by/buy/bye	week/weak
I/eye	right/write

3　Students write the words on the correct line according to the vowel sound.

Answers

a. son	f. their; fare
b. waste; break; sale; eight	g. buy/bye; eye; write
c. two; new	h. hour
d. bean; see; weak	i. role
e. read; cheque	

Adverbs

1　Read the introduction as a class. Ask students to find three adverbs that end in **-ly** in the text about Paul Newman (there are four).

Answers

seriously　immediately　endlessly　passionately

2　Read the introduction as a class. Ask students to work in pairs to fill the gaps.

Answers

a. Fortunately	g. exactly
b. still	h. at least
c. especially	i. always/only
d. nearly	j. Of course
e. even	k. At last
f. too	l. only

● Listening and speaking　(SB page 54)

T.21

Interview with a musician

Introduction: Talk to students about the kind of music they like.

Ask questions:

– *What sort of music do you like?*

– *Who are your favourite singers?*

– *What bands/groups do you like?*

Additional idea

Ask the following question:
– *If you met your favourite singer or band, what questions would you ask them?*

You could prompt with questions such as *How long have you been together? What are you doing at the moment? When are you going to make another record?*

Pre-listening task

1 Students work in groups to think of the names of as many musical instruments as they can. Some groups might come up with fifteen or twenty, others just a few. Put the names of some of the instruments on the board, especially if students ask for them, but avoid having a long list of words which students won't remember.

2 Read the definitions as a class.

Listening

T.21   Read the introduction, and check that students understand the words in the chart, and what they have to do while they are listening. Play the tape.

Ask students to work in pairs to compare their answers. Avoid asking questions such as *How much did you understand?* or *Do you want to hear that again?* Students often have a natural antipathy to the tape recorder, and feel that if they have not understood everything, they have understood nothing. Putting them in pairs to pool information can be constructive and morale-boosting.

Answers

Instruments he plays		Bands he has played with		Places he has visited	
guitar	✓	Roxy Music	✓	France	✓
saxophone	✗	U2	✗	Japan	✗
trumpet	✗	The Smiths	✓	America	✓
drums	✓	The Pretenders	✓	Eastern Europe	✗
keyboards	✓	Simply Red	✗	Germany	✓
violin	✗	Madness	✓	Italy	✓
piano	✓	Queen	✗	South America	✗
		Ace	✓		

Ask individual students to tell you the bands he has played with, and the countries he has been to. This is to give further controlled practice of the Present Perfect. You could also ask about the bands he *hasn't* played with, and the countries he *hasn't* been to, to get practice of the negative.

Answers

He has played with Roxy Music.
He has played/given concerts with The Smiths.
He has played/made records with The Pretenders.
He has played/made records with Madness.
He has played with Ace.

He has been to France.
He has been to America.
He has been to Germany.
He has been to Italy.

Comprehension check

Play the tape again. Ask students to work in pairs to answer the comprehension questions.

Answers

1 Only one – a musician.
2 No. He taught himself to play.
3 Yes. He was playing in pubs and clubs.
4 It was his first hit record.
5 Yes. He always wanted to go there.
6 People know his name, and his records are often played on the radio, so they buy his albums.
7 He's toured the States twice, he's made his own album, he's done a tour of Germany, and he's had a number one record.
8 A
He started playing the drums when he was five years old.
He left school when he was sixteen years old.
He had his first hit record in 1974.

B
He has played with Mike and the Mechanics since 1985.
He has made about twenty records.

Language work

1 Answer question 1 as a class.
   Answers
   – The verb forms in box A are in the Past Simple, because they refer to definite time.
   – The verb forms in box B are in the Present Perfect, because they refer to the past up to the present, and probably into the future.
2 Do the first question together as an example, then ask students to do b–f in pairs. Be very careful in establishing the correct answers to this exercise, as it is all about the target language of the unit, i.e. Present Perfect versus Past Simple, and Present Perfect versus Present Simple.
   Answers
   a. Paul has been
   b. He started playing
   c. He has played with
   d. He has never been
   e. He had a hit
   f. He has been interested

Roleplay

This activity could last a short while or nearly an hour, depending on how you organize it (and whether you and your class are interested). If you allow the musicians and journalists about fifteen minutes to prepare, then have the interviews and record them, then listen to the taped interviews for feedback, you should easily fill an hour, depending on the size of your class. You could ask students to prepare their roles for homework; you could save some of the taped interviews for the next class. The success of a roleplay often depends on the effort put in during preparation.

When the students are preparing, the journalists will probably be ready before the groups of musicians. If this happens, tell the journalists that they too are a group of musicians and should prepare information. When the time comes for their interview, you can ask the questions yourself.

For the actual roleplay, you need to decide if you want all the interviews to go on at the same time or one by one. The advantage of the latter is that students are often interested in each other, and want to hear what the 'groups' have to say. Expect some funny answers!

Recording students from time to time can also be useful. You need a good microphone and a long lead! Ideally, you need a cassette recorder with batteries to be able to get round the groups easily.

● Everyday English   (SB page 55)

Short answers

This is a short Everyday English, as the rest of the unit is quite long. Short answers have been practised throughout the Workbook. The aim here is to practise them orally.

1 Read the introduction as a class.
2 Students work alone to think of questions.
3 Students work in pairs to ask and answer questions. Learners often find short answers difficult. Although it is a purely mechanical process to know which auxiliary to use and whether it should be positive or negative, these decisions have to be made so quickly in the natural course of conversation that learners complain they don't have time to think.
   Try to be aware of short answers in your teaching generally, and remind students of them whenever appropriate. The use of short answers, reply questions, and question tags is often quoted as the sign of a successful speaker of English, as they are employed to 'lubricate' conversation.

Don't forget!

Workbook Unit 7
There is a vocabulary exercise on words that go together – exercise 10.
There are two exercises on writing, including a second activity on relative clauses – exercises 11 and 12.

Pronunciation book Unit 7
There is an exercise on consonant sound symbols – exercise 1.
There is an exercise on the sounds /ð/ and /θ/ – exercise 2.

Word list
Make sure your students complete the Word list for Unit 7 by writing in the translations.

Video
Section 5 – Situation: *The Hotel*
This video section supplements Unit 7 of the Student's Book. It is a short situation in which Paola has to make a complaint at the hotel where she is staying in Cornwall. Students practise making complaints and ordering from the room service menu.

UNIT 8

Have to – Should – Invitations

Introduction to the Unit

The themes of this unit, 'Pros and cons', are obligation and advice. In the Presentation sections, students talk about the duties, advantages, and disadvantages of different professions, and offer advice to troubled teenagers. In the Skills Development section, students read about two very successful young people, who talk about their job and how they achieved success, and listen to three people from different parts of the world, giving advice about holidays in their countries.

Notes on the Language Input

Grammar

Have to

This might be the first time that your class has been introduced to **have to** to express obligation. **Must** is often taught in first-year courses to express the obligation of the speaker. This can cause students problems, as they don't realize that **must** with second and third persons sounds too authoritarian. **Should** would be more appropriate. They also use **must** to refer to a general obligation, when **have to** sounds more natural.

Common mistakes
*You've got hiccups. You must have a glass of water.
*My parents must work six days a week.

In *Headway Pre-Intermediate*, we do not introduce **must** to express obligation. This is because the difference between **must** to express the obligation of the speaker, and **have to** to express obligation in general, is too subtle for the level. However, **must** is used to express strong advice or recommendation, for example, *You must see that new film – it's marvellous!*

Students often find the verb **have** a problem, because it has so many guises. In Unit 2, it was seen as a full verb with two forms, one with **got** and one with **do/does**. In Unit 7, it was seen as an auxiliary verb in the Present Perfect. In this unit, it is seen operating with another verb in the infinitive, and only the **do/does** forms are introduced and practised.

Have got to can also express an obligation.
I've got to go now. Goodbye.
Have got to expresses an obligation now, or at a specific time. It cannot be used to refer to a habitual obligation.
*I've got to travel a lot in my job.
To avoid problems of meaning and confusions of form, we do not introduce **have got to** in this unit.

Should

There is an introduction to modal auxiliary verbs on page 127 of the Grammar section. Ask students to read this before you begin the presentation of **should**.
Should presents few problems of meaning, but learners often want to put an infinitive with **to**.

Common mistake
*You should to do your homework.

Vocabulary

Two areas of collocation are dealt with, compound nouns and **make** or **do** + noun.

Everyday English

Inviting, accepting and refusing invitations are practised. This is partly to revise **have to** and other verb patterns such as **would like to**, **would love to**, and **going to**.

Notes on the Unit

PRESENTATION   (SB page 56)

Have to

T.22a and b

Introduction: Ask your class the following questions:
– *What job would you like to do? Why?*
– *What job would you hate to do? Why?*
– *Would you like to work in a hotel?*
– *Would you like to have a restaurant?*

1 T.22a Read the introduction as a class. Students listen to the interview between Kathy and a friend, and fill in the chart. Ask students to compare notes with a partner before you get feedback. You might want to, or need to, point out that many examples of *you* in the interview refer to people in general, for example, *If you run a restaurant, you have to work very long hours.*

Answers
Advantages of having a restaurant:
You don't have to get up so early in the morning.
You don't have to do the same thing every day. Every day is different.
You are your own boss. You don't have to work for someone else.
You don't have to wear a uniform.
Disadvantages of having a restaurant:
You have to work very long hours.
You have to work in the evenings and at weekends.

2 T.22b Listen to the pronunciation of **have to**. There are pauses to allow your class to repeat. Drill the words and sentences around the class.

3 Play the interview again, and ask students to tell you to stop the tape when they hear an example of **have to** or **don't have to**. Again, drill these sentences around the class. Students practise the same sentences in pairs.

● Grammar questions (SB page 56)

Answer the two Grammar questions as a class.
Answers
– In the first sentence, **have** means *own* or *possess*.
  In the second sentence, **have** expresses an obligation. (It is unlikely that students will use the word *obligation* in L2, but they might use a similar word, or use L1.)
– When **have** means *own*, it is pronounced /hæv/.
  When **have** expresses *obligation*, it is pronounced /hæf/ because it is followed by 'to'.

PRACTICE (SB page 56)

1 Grammar

Ask students to read the instructions and the chart. Ask for suggestions from the class. Drill some of the sentences around the class.
Sample answers
Politicians have to make speeches, but they don't have to wear a uniform.
Postmen and women have to wear a uniform, and they have to get up early, but they don't have to do any work at home.
Teachers have to do some work at home, but they don't have to make speeches.
Nurses have to work in shifts, and they have to wear a uniform.
Air hostesses have to work in shifts, but they don't have to do any work at home.
Factory workers have to work in shifts, but they don't have to wear a uniform.

Note
Your students may not know what a *shift* is. Discourage them from looking up the word in their dictionaries. See if they can work out the meaning, by telling them who works in shifts and who doesn't.

2 Listening and speaking

1 To set this activity up, check that your students know the names of the jobs illustrated. Then choose one of the jobs from the pictures on page 57 yourself, and invite students to ask you questions to find out which it is. Make sure the questions are in the second person singular (*you*), not third person plural (*they*). Correct any mistakes carefully at this stage, as you will not be able to monitor when students are working together. Students then work in pairs or small groups. Let them have several goes each.
The following jobs are illustrated:
shopkeeper, hotel receptionist, fisherman, taxi-driver, painter (artist), engineer, watch repairer, businessman, dancer, soldier, painter and decorator, coalminer, nurse, vet, housewife, dentist, mechanic, chef, farmer

2 Ask students to discuss as a class the jobs they would like to do, and those they wouldn't like to do. This second question should prompt examples of **have to**. Notice that students are expected to use the third person plural here, not second person singular.

3 Grammar

Read the introduction as a class. Drill *She had to wear a uniform* around the class, paying attention to the lingering on the /t/ sound. Ask students to recall the other reasons Kathy didn't like her job as a shop assistant.
Answers
She had to get up early in the morning.
She had to do the same thing every day.
She had to work for someone else.

Additional material
Workbook Unit 8
Have to/had to/don't have to/didn't have to – exercises 1–5.

Note
You might decide that your class would like some freer work at this stage. You could do the Discussion on page 62 (see notes on page 65 of the Teacher's Book), and then come back to the presentation of **should**.

PRESENTATION (SB page 58)

Should

Read the introduction as a class. Ask students to match a heading with a letter and a reply. Pre-teach or check that students know the words *dye* and *punishment*.

> **Note**
> In the introduction to the problem page, there is an idiom. *'To get a problem off your chest'* means to tell someone about your problem, and so feel better.

Answers
Never been kissed – I'm 16 ... – People of your age ...
Food for thought – I live on a farm ... – I think you're being ...
To dye, or not to dye? – My parents went away ... – I think you should dye ...

You could ask various students to read out the letters and replies, and ask the class if they agree with the advice.

● Grammar questions (SB page 58)

Answer the Grammar questions as a class.
Answers
– **Should** is used to ask for and give a suggestion.
– *She has to cook for herself* expresses an obligation.

PRACTICE (SB page 59)

1 Speaking and writing

1 Students work in pairs or small groups. Ask them to read the letters, and then compare ideas about what advice to give.
Sample answers
Not fair
Sharon should help more in the house. She's 14, and old enough to help her parents. She could get a Saturday job or a newspaper round. (In Britain, children can earn some money by delivering newspapers in the morning or evening.)
Weighty problem
Peter should talk to his parents about his diet, and he should visit his doctor for advice about diet and exercise. He should try not to eat between meals.
Bullies at school
Jeremy should talk to his teacher and his parents. He shouldn't give them money. The bullies should be punished.
Roses are red
It doesn't matter *how* Andrew gets in touch, but if he doesn't talk to the girl, how is she to know how he feels about her? He should give her a ring and invite her to a dance or the cinema.
Problems with lessons
Suzie should talk to her teachers and her parents. She should ask her friends for help, and do homework together. She should borrow a friend's notes, and try reading her books again.
My friends steal
Simon is right not to steal. This is a serious problem, and it's difficult to say what he should do, because he doesn't want to get his friends into trouble. He should try to make new friends, and forget about those that steal.
2 Students work in pairs to write a letter in reply. This can take

quite a while to do well, so you need to decide how long you want the activity to last.
Ask the pairs to read out their letter, and ask the rest of the class if they think it is good advice.

2 Speaking and listening

Students work in groups to think of advice to give someone coming to their country for six months. You could set this task for homework, so that when they start to talk about it, the students have some ideas prepared.

● Language review (SB page 59)

Expressing obligation

Read the explanation as a class. Students translate the sample sentences.

▶ **Grammar reference: pages 126 and 127.**

Ask students to re-read the introduction to modal auxiliary verbs, and the sections on **have to** and **should**.

> **Additional material**
> **Workbook Unit 8**
> *Should* and *have to* – exercises 6–8.

SKILLS DEVELOPMENT

● Reading (SB page 60)

Introduction: Ask the students to look at the pictures on pages 60 and 61. Ask the following questions:
– *How old is the boy?*
– *What's he doing?*
– *Does he still go to school?*

– *He writes computer programs – do you think this is easy?*

– *How old is the girl?*
– *What's she doing?*
– *Does she still go to school?*
– *Do you think it's easy to work as a model?*

Reading and vocabulary
1 Read the introduction as a class. Ask students to read the text about David Bolton quite quickly, and to check no more than four words that they don't know.

> **Note**
> The word *troubleshooter* might not be in students' dictionaries. A troubleshooter is a person whose job is to solve big problems in a company.

2 Students compare and teach each other their words.

Reading for information
Students read the text more carefully and answer the questions.

Comprehension check

Students work in pairs or small groups to answer the questions.

Answers

1 He is only 15, but he has already learned an adult's profession, and he has earned a lot of money. He has a reputation as one of the country's top troubleshooters in the computer world.
2 His parents bought him a computer when he was nine, and he learned to program it.
3 It seems that it was easy to learn to program his first computer, but after that he had to work hard to save up for a bigger computer. He also went to night school, and did a correspondence course.
4 He has to send a monthly report to a computer seller, Eltec. He also helps companies by suggesting which computers they should buy, and he writes programs for them.
5 He is obviously very clever at programming computers, and companies pay a lot of money to get the right hardware and software. He can work more quickly than many other older professionals.
6 He says you should be ambitious, you should believe in yourself, and you should tell yourself that you're the best.
7 a. How much has David put in the bank?
   b. What sort of computer did his parents buy him? *or* What was his first computer?
   c. Why did he have to save for a long time?
   d. How does he help companies?
   e. What has he bought with his money?

Arranging a jumbled text

> **Additional idea**
> If your class is quite strong, and they find the reading about David Bolton easy, ask them to cover up page 61. Write the seven paragraph summaries which appear at the top of page 61 on the board in random order, and ask students to identify which paragraphs they go with in the text about David.

Read the seven paragraph summaries as a class, and ask students to read the jumbled paragraphs about Kimora Lee Perkins and put them in order. They should work with a partner to do this.

Answers

1 – e.	3 – c.	5 – d.	7 – f.
2 – a.	4 – g.	6 – b.	

Comprehension check

1 Students work in pairs to answer the first six Comprehension check questions.

Answers

1 She is a top model working in Paris at the age of fourteen.
2 She felt different from other girls because she was so tall, so her mother took her to a modelling school because she would be with other tall girls.
3 We don't know if it was easy to learn – perhaps it was and perhaps it wasn't. She had to learn how to walk and pose. Also, she was still going to school, so she needed to work hard and have a lot of energy.
4 She spends eight to ten hours a day modelling clothes in various parts of the world.

5 She has remarkable looks, being part Korean and part black American. Chanel chose her because she has the look of the 90s.
6 She says you should go to a good modelling school, you have to work hard, and give your whole life to modelling.

2 Students work alone or in pairs to write some questions about Kimora. They then ask them to the other students in the class.

Sample questions

Where does she come from?
Does she speak French?
How tall is she?
Who does she work for?
What nationality are her mother and father?
Why did she feel different from other children?
Why did her mother take her to a modelling school?
Did she like it?
Is it an easy job?
Does she earn a lot of money?
Why did Chanel choose her?
How many hours a day does she work?
Does she have to travel a lot?
Does she still have to do school work?

● Discussion (SB page 62)

Ask students to look at the cartoons and tell you which one they find funnier. They then work in groups to discuss the questions. Some students might be happy to talk about their relationship with their parents, whilst others will prefer to remain silent. The discussion could last for ten minutes or an hour – it depends entirely on how interested your students are!

● Vocabulary (SB page 62)

Nouns that go together

1 Read the introduction as a class. Drill the compounds *post office*, *headache*, and *horse-race* to make the point about the stress being on the first word. You will probably need to exaggerate the stress pattern yourself as students' natural inclination is to give both words equal stress.
Students work in pairs to match a line in A with a line in B. Tell students that English people have to check whether compounds are spelt as one word, two words, or hyphenated, and dictionaries often disagree.

Answers

alarm clock	hair-drier (can also be
car park	spelt *hairdryer*)
traffic lights	fire engine
toothpaste	sunset
cigarette lighter	screwdriver
tin opener	word processor
tape recorder (or tape-recorder)	earring (or ear-ring)
earthquake	dustbin
departure lounge	signpost
pocket money (or pocket-money)	bookcase
timetable	noticeboard
raincoat	rush-hour (or rush hour)
	safety belt (or safety-belt)

Check that students understand the compound nouns, and ask three or four students to read out the list, making sure that the stress is on the first word.

2 On their own or in pairs, students think of sentences to test the compound nouns. Give some more examples if necessary.
It wakes you up in the morning.
It's where you leave your car.
They have red, orange, and green lights.
You put this on your toothbrush.

3 Students look again at the texts on pages 60–61 to find the noun + noun combinations. Be prepared to step in and stop students seeing compound nouns everywhere! *Teenage tycoon, part-time work, South London* and *software* are not examples of compound nouns.
Answers

computer consultant	credit card
electronics expert	modelling school
night school	school lessons
business programs	daytime
correspondence course	fashion house
computer seller	

Make or *do*?

Read the introduction as a class.

1 Students work in pairs to put **make** or **do** before the nouns.
Answers

make a phone-call	do my homework
make a mess	make my bed
do the washing-up	do someone a favour
do the ironing	do the shopping
make a cup of tea	make a mistake
do your best	make a noise

2 Students work in pairs to write conversations to practise some of the **make/do** + noun combinations. These will probably sound very contrived!

● Listening   (SB page 63)

Holidays in January

T.23

Pre-listening task
Students discuss the two questions in groups. Let this go on as long as they are interested.

> **Note**
> Many British people go abroad in summer, especially to Europe. Spain is the most popular destination. People also take holidays in Britain, either in the countryside or on the coast, especially the south coast.

Listening and note-taking

T.23   Read the instructions as a class. Pre-teach the following words:

valuable	*mint*
inflation	*cruise*
lime (fruit)	*waterproof shoes*
cool	*melt*

Students listen and take notes. Stop the tape after each section for students to compare notes with a partner.

Answers

1 *Weather and clothes*
It's hot all day and night. You only need light clothes and a swimming costume.
Things to do
Go to the beach, surfing and windsurfing. Go to piano bars, listen to music. Go up the Sugar Loaf Mountain at sunset.
Food and drink
Restaurants are cheap. The speciality is beans and meat, called *feijoada*. Fish and seafood are very good. There is a drink called *caipirinha*, which is made of rum and lime.

2 *Weather and clothes*
It's mild, and doesn't often rain. Take a light coat and a jumper.
Things to do
Go round museums and mosques. Visit the Pyramids. Go on a Nile cruise.
Food and drink
The local food is koftas, kebabs, and falafel. Mint tea is refreshing.

3 *Weather and clothes*
Very cold, lots of snow, but in the mountains it can be warm. Bring warm clothes and waterproof shoes.
Things to do
Go skiing and walking. Visit the towns. Go for a boat trip on the lake.
Food and drink
Fondue is cheese melted in a pot, and you eat it on bread.

Comprehension check
Answer question 1 as a class, then ask students to discuss questions 2–5 in pairs. Question 6 might lead to a class discussion.

Answers

1 The first speaker talks about Brazil. It is very hot there in January. She suggests going up the Sugar Loaf Mountain, which is in Rio de Janeiro.
The second speaker talks about Egypt. He suggests visiting the Pyramids and going on a Nile cruise.
The third speaker talks about Switzerland, where there are mountains and lakes. It is famous for its winter sports.

2 The first and third speakers talk about sports. They mention swimming, surfing, windsurfing (Brazil), skiing, and walking (Switzerland).

3 The first and second talk about money. The Brazilian woman says there is high inflation in Brazil, so it's best to take dollars and change money daily.
The Egyptian man suggests bringing travellers' cheques and changing money in Egypt.

4 The holiday in Egypt sounds the most cultural, with visits to museums, mosques, and the Pyramids.
5 Brazil – sea food, people on the beach, music in a bar
Egypt – Islamic art, pyramids, riding horses
Switzerland – a fondue pot, people having lunch, people skiing, and mountains.

Language work/speaking
1 Students work in pairs to form the questions.
   Answers
   a. What is the weather like in January?
   b. What clothes should I take?
   c. What sort of things can I do?
   d. Should I take cash or travellers' cheques?
   e. What food do you recommend?
   f. Are there any special places I should go to?

2 If you have a monolingual class, you could ask one student to talk about a place he/she has visited that the others don't know. It needn't have been in January! Alternatively, *you* could talk about a place you know, or you could invite in a guest speaker. Inviting someone into your class can be very motivating and interesting.

Additional material

Workbook Unit 8
Exercise 9 is a vocabulary activity which practises words associated with winter. It could follow on from this listening.

● **Everyday English**   (SB page 64)

Invitations

T.24

Introduction: Ask students the following questions:
– *Where do you like to go in the evening and at the weekend?*
– *What do you like doing?*
– *What do you do with your friends?*

1 T.24 Listen to the three dialogues. Students decide which follows which pattern.
   Answers
   1 – b.   2 – c.   3 – a.
2 This will work best if you photocopy the tapescript, or put it on an overhead transparency. Let students practise the dialogues first by reading, then by following the patterns on page 64 of the Student's Book.
3 Read the lists of functional phrases. You could practise them in open pairs by asking student A to invite student B to do one of the things in the box in exercise 4. Student B either refuses or accepts. Put a list of excuses on the board, for example:
   I have to do my homework.
   I have to help my mother/father.
   I'm going shopping.
   I'm already going out.
4 Students practise similar dialogues in pairs.

Don't forget!

Workbook Unit 8
These are two exercises on writing, including a second activity on formal letters – exercises 10 and 11.

Pronunciation book Unit 8
Exercise 1 practises the sounds – /ʃ/,/s/, and /tʃ/; exercise 2 contrasts the sounds /uː/ and /ʊ/.
There is an exercise on intonation and sentence stress – questions with *or* – exercise 3.

Word list
Make sure your students complete the Word list for Unit 8 by writing in the translations.

Video
Section 6 – Report: *Wales*
This video section supplements Unit 8 of the Student's Book. It is a short documentary about the Welsh-speaking areas of Wales and the threats to the survival of the Welsh language.

UNIT 9

Will – First Conditional – Time clauses – Travelling

Introduction to the Unit

The theme of this unit is 'Life in the 21st century'. In the Presentation section, students read about an incredible building being planned in Japan, and they study the future form **will** and its use in various clauses. In the Skills Development section, there is a listening activity on the need to protect the environment, and a reading text about the effect of cars on our lives. The topic of travel is dealt with in the Vocabulary and Everyday English sections.

Notes on the Language Input

Grammar

Will

The use of **will** to express an offer was dealt with in Unit 4, and the use of **will** to express a future intention or decision made at the moment of speaking was presented in Unit 5. In this unit we see **will** as an auxiliary of the future, where it merely signals future time. This use is also called the neutral future.
The distinction is very fine, and not always discernible.
The house will cost fifty thousand pounds is an example of the neutral future.
I'll phone you when I arrive is an example of a decision.
I'll see you tomorrow can have elements of both meanings.
We don't suggest you explore this area with your students!

First Conditional

Tense usage in any sentence containing the word **if** causes learners of English a lot of problems. In this unit, the First Conditional is presented, and in Unit 13 the Second Conditional is introduced. The problems seem to be that there are two clauses to get right, and whereas **will** is used in the result clause, it is *not* used in the condition clause, even though it might refer to future time. In many languages, a future form is used in both clauses.
Common mistakes
*If it will rain, we'll stay at home.
*If it rains, we stay at home.

Time clauses

Speakers of Germanic languages confuse *when* and *if*, as they are translated by the same word. Tense usage in time clauses presents the same problem as in the First Conditional, i.e. a future verb form is not used in the time clause, even though it might refer to future time.
Common mistakes
*When it rains, we'll stay at home.
*When I will arrive, I'll phone you.
*As soon as I arrive, I phone you.

Vocabulary

Two lexical areas of travelling by rail and travelling by air are explored.

Everyday English

Students practise dialogues at an airline check-in desk and in a railway ticket office.

Notes on the Unit

PRESENTATION   (SB page 65)

Will, the First Conditional, time clauses

Introduction: Ask students the following questions:
– *What's the population of (the city you're in)?*
– *What will the population be at the end of this century?*
– *Where will people live?*
– *What problems will the city have?*

Ask students to look at the picture on page 65, and explain that this is a plan of a building that Japanese architects want to build. Ask the following questions:
– *What do you think of it?*
– *Would you like to live in it?*
– *How much will it cost?*
– *How much is that in (your currency)?*

1 Ask students to read the text about Japan, then read it through as a class, checking any vocabulary that you think students might not know, for example, *height*, *robot*, *containing*, *bay*, *according to*, *put out* (a fire).

2 Do this question first as a class activity, so you can establish a good model. Drill the questions around the class, correcting as necessary. Have open pair question and answer practice.

Answers
How much will it cost? – Two thousand million pounds.
How high will it be? – Two kilometres high.
How many floors will it have? – Five hundred.
How many people will live in it? – Over three hundred thousand.
How long will it take to get from the top to the bottom? – Fifteen minutes.
What will the population of Tokyo be at the end of the century? – Over fifteen million.

3 Answer this question as a class. Students should have more to say this time, as they know more about the building.

4 Ask students to find the two intentions with **going to** and the two hopes. Students may find these difficult questions as they are of quite a linguistically analytical nature, so be prepared to help a lot.

Answers
We're going to start doing tests …
We're going to have green floors …
I hope people will like living on the 500th floor.
I hope we'll get the money we need …

● Grammar questions   (SB page 66)

Answer the Grammar questions as a class. If you feel students would benefit from answering them in their own language, do so. They are quite complex. You might want to translate words such as *intention*.

Answers
– They express future facts.
– The first sentence with **When** expresses something that is sure to happen. The second sentence with **If** expresses a possibility.
– They will start to build Aeropolis as soon as they get the money they need.
Ask students the following question:
– *What's the difference between* **when** *and* **as soon as**?
Explain that *as soon as* has the idea of *immediately*.

PRACTICE   (SB page 66)

1 Speaking

T.25

1 Read the introduction as a class. Do the sentences about Jenny all together, and drill the sentences around the class. Pay careful attention to contractions and sentence stress.

●● ● ● ●● ● ● ●● ● ●
If I don't go out so much, I'll do more work.
Answers
If I do more work, I'll pass my exams.

If I pass my exams, I'll go to university.
If I go to university, I'll study medicine.
If I study medicine, I'll become a doctor.
If I become a doctor, I'll earn a good salary.

Ask students for suggestions to continue the sentences.

Students work in pairs to do the same with the sentences about Mark.
Answers
If I stop smoking, I'll have more money.
If I have more money, I'll save some every week.
If I save some every week, I'll be rich when I'm thirty.
If I'm rich when I'm thirty, I'll have my own business.
If I have my own business, I'll make a lot of money.
If I make a lot of money, I'll retire when I'm forty.

2 T.25   Students listen to the sentences and repeat them. There is a pause after each clause in the sentences about Jenny, and a pause after the whole sentence in those about Mark.

3 In pairs, students ask and answer questions about Jenny and Mark. The aim is to practise questions in the third person singular.
Sample questions
What will she study if she goes to university?
How much will she earn if she becomes a doctor?
What will Mark do with his money if he stops smoking?
What will he do with his money if he's rich when he's thirty?
If he makes a lot of money, when will he retire?

2 Speaking and listening

Read the introduction as a class. Do the first three or four questions and answers as a class, so students see what they have to do, then put them in pairs.
Questions and sample answers
What will you do if you don't like the food?
I'll buy some from a shop.

What will you do if it rains?
I'll wait for it to stop./I'll go to a movie.

What will you do if you don't learn to ski?
I'm sure I'll learn to ski./I'll go for walks in the snow.

What will you do if you hurt yourself?
I'll go to the doctor.

What will you do if you lose your money?
I'll phone you and ask for some.

What will you do if you don't understand the language?
I'll buy a dictionary.

What will you do if you don't know anyone?
I'm sure I'll make friends.

What will you do if there's nowhere to go in the evening?
I'll read.

3 Grammar

1 Do the first two as a class, then ask students to do the rest in pairs.

Answers

a. When d. when g. when
b. If   e. if   h. If
c. If   f. If

2 Read the introduction as a class. Ask students to work in small groups.

Answers

Paul Bye, darling. Have a good trip.

Mary Thanks. I'll ring you when/as soon as I arrive at the hotel.

Paul That's lovely, but remember I'm going out.

Mary Well, if you're out when I ring, I'll leave a message on the answer phone so you know I've arrived safely.

Paul Great. What time do you expect you'll be there?

Mary If the plane arrives on time, I'll be at the hotel at about 10.00. That's 8.00 your time.

Paul All right. And remember. Give me a ring when/as soon as you know the time of your flight back, and I'll pick you up.

Mary Thanks, darling. Bye!

● Language review (SB page 67)

Will, First Conditional, and time clauses

Read the explanations together. Ask students to translate the sample sentences.

▶ **Grammar reference: pages 127 and 128.**

Ask students to read the Grammar reference at home.

Additional material

Workbook Unit 9

The form of *will*, and *will* versus the Present Simple – exercises 1–4.
First Conditional and time clauses – exercises 5–9.

Pronunciation book Unit 9

Connected speech – word counting and sentence stress patterns in first conditional sentences – exercise 2.

SKILLS DEVELOPMENT

● Listening (SB page 68)

T.26

How 'green' are you?

Additional idea

The obvious way to introduce this activity and exploit it subsequently is to incorporate current environmental issues, both local to you and global. Have a discussion about what is happening in the world, both the good news and the bad.

Your class might want to write to one of the many environmental pressure groups to get an information pack.

Here are the addresses of two of them.

Greenpeace   Friends of the Earth
Canonbury Villas   26–28 Underwood Street
London N1 2PN   London N1 7JQ

Pre-listening task

1 Students work in groups to think of things we should and shouldn't do to look after the planet.

Sample answers

We should use less energy – petrol, electricity, gas.
We should use public transport.
We should use renewable energy such as solar power and wind power.
We should recycle our waste.
We should look after the countryside and the animals.
We shouldn't pollute the atmosphere or the land or the sea.
We shouldn't consume so much.
We shouldn't cut down the tropical rain forests.
We shouldn't use so many chemicals on the land or in our food.

2 Have a discussion about current environmental issues.

Listening for information

Read the introduction as a class. Look at the pictures in the Student's Book, and check that students know words such as *aerosol*, *bottle bank*, *recycled paper*, *packaging*, *save energy*, *candles*, *washing powder*, *washing-up liquid*.

T.26 Play the tape, and ask students to put a tick next to the things in the pictures that John Baines talks about.
Students compare what they ticked in pairs.

Answers

He talks about the following:
bicycles
walking, using cars less
saving bottles
washing-up liquid and washing powder

Comprehension check

Ask students to read the questions while you play the tape again. They compare answers in pairs.

Answers

1 Using public transport; using unleaded petrol; saving cans and paper; looking after animals; becoming a vegetarian.

2 *More* – uses his bike; walks; uses public transport; saves things to be recycled
Less – uses his car less, doesn't throw as many things away

3 **Sample answers**

a. . . . he wants to use less petrol.
b. . . . driving ten per cent fewer miles every year.
c. . . . it's cheaper, and it keeps the air cleaner.
d. . . . he takes them to places in the village where they are collected for recycling.
e. . . . animals are part of the environment and we should look after them. Also they eat food that people could eat.
f. . . . the environment, our life will not be as comfortable.

What do you think?

Discuss the two questions as a class. You could decide to do some kind of project work resulting from your discussions.

● Reading and speaking (SB page 68)

Pre-reading task
1 Students work in three groups to discuss the advantages and disadvantages of one of the forms of transport.

Sample answers

Advantages	Disadvantages
Cars You can feel free in a car to go where you want. You can travel when you want.	There are often traffic jams. Cars pollute the air. Cars need petrol, which is expensive. Driving is stressful.
Trains They are fast. You can relax. There are no traffic jams.	They are expensive. You can't travel when you want. They are sometimes cancelled.
Bicycles They are cheap. You can keep fit. You can go where you want. It's easier to park a bike than a car.	They are slow. Cycling uphill isn't much fun! You breathe car fumes. You get wet if it rains.

2 Discuss this question as a class. You might like to bring in some current magazine advertisements for cars.

Sample answer
Car advertisements traditionally show the power and speed of the car. They illustrate the freedom you have 'on the open road'. They suggest that if you buy this car, you will feel good, and perhaps superior to other people. They are often trying to appeal to men rather than women, and perhaps have a certain aggression about them. They try to create the impression that ownership of the product will give the buyer the image he/she wants.

Reading and gap-filling
Look at the picture on page 69. Ask questions such as the following:
– *Where is this motorway?* (In Britain. They're driving on the left. In fact it is the M25, which is the orbital road around London.)
– *What time of day is it?* (The rush hour. It could be morning or evening.)
– *Why aren't the cars moving?* (Because there are so many cars, or perhaps there has been an accident.)

Check that students understand the words in the box. *Stuck* is the past participle of the verb *stick*; *race* in this context refers to a group of people. Ask students to read the article and fill each gap with one of the words in the box.

Answers

a. crashes	d. too	g. choice	j. race
b. way	e. stuck	h. timetable	
c. century	f. huge	i. person	

Comprehension check
Students work in pairs to answer the questions.

Answers
1. a. False   e. False
   b. False   f. True
   c. True   g. True
   d. True   h. False
2. (No set answer)
3. Because there are more and more people, and more and more cars.
4. Because this would take more cars off the road.

What do you think?
Discuss these two questions as a class. This activity could go on for a long time!

Speaking
In this section, we give two ideas for extended speaking practice. You could ask your students which one they would like to do in the next lesson, so that you have time to prepare. It is probably best not to try to have the two activities going on at the same time, as this would double the amount of work for you.

Suggestion 1
As with all roleplays and project work, the more preparation that goes in at the initial stages, the better the outcome. The five roles in the first suggestion need fleshing out. The obvious way to do this is to personalize them to your local situation. Is there at the moment a debate about the traffic situation in your town or city? What are the various options being considered? Who are the interested parties? If at all possible, make these parties the roles, and adapt or reject those on page 69 of *Headway Pre-Intermediate*. Make the situation of the roleplay *your* situation. If you can do this, then here are some possible guidelines.

1 In one lesson, have a discussion about the traffic problem in your town, and the possible solutions. Discuss how different people view the situation. Try to draw up four or five or six different interested parties, perhaps politicians, developers, residents, shopkeepers, cyclists, etc. Allocate roles to your students so they can prepare at home.
2 In the next lesson, put the roles together, i.e. all the shopkeepers together, all the developers together, etc. This is to help them share their ideas. Monitor them to see how long they need.
3 Do the roleplays. You need to decide if you want all the groups talking at the same time, or if you want them one by one so everyone can hear. There are pros and cons to both approaches. Do you want to record them, so you can examine them later?
4 Have a feedback session, where you ask students if they enjoyed the activity, what they think they learned from it, if everyone participated, how good they thought their listening and speaking was, etc.
5 Give some feedback yourself on their performance.

Suggestion 2
This activity too would work best if it was related to your particular town or city. Is there an underground system? A tramway? How do people actually get around? These factors will dictate the kinds of questions that should go into the survey. Here are some possible guidelines.

1 In one lesson, have a discussion about the traffic situation in your town, the problems of certain roads, where to park, the advantages and disadvantages of various forms of public transport. Ask students for homework to start thinking about questions to ask in a survey.

2 In the next lesson, share the ideas, and try to organize them logically. Someone needs to write the survey! It will probably have to be you, unless you have access to word processors.

3 Your students need to arrange a time and a place to meet with other classes. Maybe other teachers would oblige, and let you go into their class for fifteen minutes. The survey would be more fun to do orally, with your students actually *asking* the questions and writing down the answers, rather than just giving out a piece of paper and hoping to get it back completed.

4 Your students collate the information, and present it, with their conclusions, as a poster or series of posters.

> **Additional material**
> There is a writing exercise in the Workbook on linking words to express advantages and disadvantages which picks up on the theme of travel – exercise 12.

● Vocabulary (SB page 70)

1 Travelling by rail

Read the introduction as a class. Students use their dictionaries to put the words in the diagram.
Answers

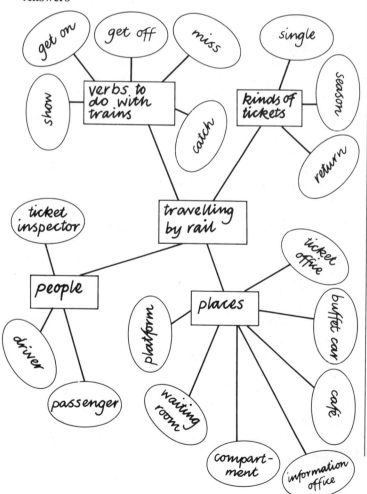

2 Travelling by air

1 The instruction to this exercise suggests that students work in pairs, but you might decide to set it for homework. Students will then come up with their own groups and words. However you do it, ask students to compare their diagrams and teach each other any new words.

2 Read the introduction as a class. Students use their dictionaries to put the sentences in order. There is, of course, no absolute answer to this question, as different people do different things, and not all airports are the same! Be prepared for your students to argue about the order!
Possible order
7 You go to the departure lounge.
2 You get a trolley.
1 You arrive at the airport.
11 You go to your gate.
3 You go to the check-in desk.
8 You go to the duty-free shop.
5 You get a boarding card.
12 You board the plane.
4 You check in your luggage.
9 You look at the departure board to see if your flight is boarding yet.
10 The board tells you which gate to go to.
6 You go through passport control.

3 You might decide to set this for homework, as it could take quite a while for students first to think what happens when you fly in to an airport, and then to use their dictionaries to find the English for it.
Possible answers
The plane lands.
You unfasten your seat-belt.
You get your hand luggage from the overhead compartment.
You wait for the doors to open.
You go into the arrival hall.
You go through passport control.
You wait for your luggage to arrive.
You collect your luggage.
You go through customs.
You leave the airport.

● Everyday English (SB page 70)

Travelling

T.27

1 T.27a Students listen to the lines of dialogue and say if they are taking place at an airline check-in desk (A) or at a railway ticket office (R).
Answers
1 A   2 A   3 R   4 R   5 A

2 T.27b Students listen to the dialogue at the check-in desk, and with a partner try to remember it. You could help with this by putting prompts on the board such as the following:
A Hello. Can I . . . passport and . . ., please?
B Here . . .
A . . . Do you have . . .?
B Yes.
A . . . hand . . .?   etc.

3 | T.27c | Students listen to the dialogue at the railway ticket
office. Play it through once and ask some check questions
such as:
– *Where does the traveller want to go?*
– *How many trains are there to Edinburgh?*
– *What time do they leave?*
– *What sort of ticket does she buy?*
Play it through again, and stop after the questions. Elicit the
questions and drill them.

4 and 5   Students do the roleplays.

Don't forget!

Workbook Unit 9
There is a vocabulary exercise 'Odd man out' – exercise
10.
There is a writing exercise – exercise 11.

Pronunciation book Unit 9
There is an exercise on the sounds /i:/ and /ɪ/ – exercise 1.
There is an intonation and sentence stress exercise on
showing interest and surprise – exercise 1.

Word list
Make sure your students complete the Word list for Unit 9
by writing in the translations.

Stop and Check   (WB page 50)

It's time to revise the work so far!
A suggestion for approaching the *Stop and Check* section in the
Workbook is at the end of Unit 3 of this Teacher's Book.

UNIT 10

Used to – Question forms (2) – Question tags

Introduction to the Unit

The title of this unit is 'The way we were'. The topics for the texts go from recent history (the sixties) to the less recent (the twenties and the suffragette movement). These provide appropriate contexts for the grammar to be introduced and practised. The introduction of **used to** has the subsidiary aim of allowing revision of the Past Simple and comparing and contrasting similarities and differences in their uses. Question forms are also practised again with subject/object questions and question tags.

Notes on the Language Input

Grammar

Remember, if you want to check your own understanding of the form and uses of any of the grammar, look at the Grammar section in the Student's Book, page 128, before you start work on the Presentation section of this unit.

Used to

It is assumed that **used to** will be a new structure for your students. The aim of the Presentation is to introduce it and compare it with the Past Simple.
Used to + infinitive exists only in the past, and expresses past habits or states that do not happen now. The Past Simple can express the same idea but needs a clear context and/or an adverbial expression of frequency to convey the idea of habit. Compare the following sentences:
When I was a child, we went to Scotland for our holidays.
When I was a child, we used to go to Scotland for our holidays.
The first sentence needs the addition of *often* or *every year* to convey habit, otherwise it could mean once only, because the Past Simple is also used to talk about an event that happened only once in the past. **Used to** cannot do this.

Students may find it strange that this structure only exists to express past habit, not present habit and sometimes they try to use it in the present.

Common mistake
*He uses to get up at seven o'clock.
The pronunciation of **used to** /ju:stʊ/ compared with the verb *to use* /ju:z/ can also cause students problems and needs to be highlighted.

Another problem is that the pronunciation of **used to** is the same in positive and negative sentences. This means that students forget to drop the **d** in the negative when writing the structure:
I used to /ju:stʊ/ *smoke.*
I didn't use to /ju:stʊ/ *smoke.*
Common mistake
*I didn't used to smoke.

> **Note**
> Even among native English speakers and grammarians there is some difference of opinion on whether to drop the 'd' or not in written English.

Question forms

Subject questions cause particular problems in the Present Simple and Past Simple tenses because students tend to want to include the auxiliaries **do/did**.
Common mistakes
*Who did see the film?
*What did happen?
*Who does like dancing?
It is not expected that your students will have studied this area previously.

Forming questions with verbs with dependent prepositions is also practised:
What are you looking at?
Who did you talk to?
Common mistakes
*At what are you looking?
*What are you looking?

Vocabulary

This follows on from the reading about the suffragettes. Students have to sort a group of words according to whether they can apply to men, women, or both.

Everyday English

It has been said that a mastery of question tags, short answers, and reply questions is essential to sound natural in spoken English, as they are used so much as fillers, lubricators, and invitations to enter conversation. However, they are notoriously difficult to master. In this unit, question tags with a falling intonation are introduced, not really with the expectation that students will begin to use them, but so they can begin to recognize them, and begin to be aware of their role as a discourse feature.

Only the falling question tag is introduced, which serves to invite agreement with the speaker. It would be too much for this level student to also introduce the rising question tag, which is more of a genuine inquiry for information.

Notes on the Unit

PRESENTATION (SB page 71)

Used to

T.28a

In preparation for this unit ask your students to find out from their families anything they can about the lives of their parents, grandparents, etc. in earlier decades. Some photographs would be very interesting.

1   Introduction: Ask your students if they know anything at all about the 1920s, and talk a little bit with them about the pictures around the text. Ask them to read the text. The language is quite simple, but if there are problems with vocabulary, deal with them quickly, with a quick translation or explanation.

Note
This is a Presentation text for **used to**, but in fact there is only one example of the structure in it. This is because we want students to look at the examples of **used to** in exercise 2, study the rules about when it is used, and then return to the text when they are able to work out which sentences could be formed with **used to** and which must remain in the Past Simple.

---

2   As a class, read the example sentences and the explanation in the rule box.
3   Put students into pairs to do this. Ask them to make the sentences in the third person.
   Possible Answers
   a. They used to shock their parents.
      They used to do things their mothers never used to do.
      They used to cut their hair.
      They used to wear short skirts.
      They used to smoke and go dancing.
      She (Molly) used to love doing the Charleston.
      Her boyfriend used to have a Model 'T' Ford.

They used to go for picnics.
The roads didn't use to be busy.
There didn't use to be traffic jams.
They used to go to the pictures twice a week.
It only used to cost sixpence.
Molly's favourite stars used to be Charlie Chaplin and Greta Garbo.
The films used to be silent.
They used to listen to the radio a lot.

   b. I once won a prize for that!
      My father bought a car in 1925.
      He paid £150 for it!
      I saw my first 'talking' picture in 1927.
      The BBC started in 1922.

Note
It is very important to point out to your students that a text would *not* contain so many examples of **used to** as it would sound very unnatural. Once the context is clear, there is no need to repeat the structure constantly. A natural use of **used to** in the text could be as follows:
Sample text (with **used to**)
We shocked our parents. We used to do things our mothers never did. We cut our hair, we wore short skirts, we used to smoke and go dancing. I loved doing a dance called the Charleston. I once won a prize for that. My boyfriend had a car, a Model 'T' Ford. We often used to go for picnics in the countryside. The roads weren't busy then – no traffic jams! My father bought a car in 1925, an Austin Seven. He paid £150 for it! We went to the pictures twice a week, and it only cost sixpence. My favourite stars were Charlie Chaplin and Greta Garbo – the films were silent. I saw my first 'talking' picture in 1927. Also, we used to listen to the radio a lot (the BBC started in 1922). I can remember it all so clearly.

---

4   T.28a   Isolate the structure and model it yourself, drill /juːstʊ/ with the whole class and then get individuals to repeat it. You could highlight at this point the difference between the /s/ in /juːstʊ/ and the /z/ in the verb *to use* /juːz/. Ask students to repeat the sentences from the tape and make sure they pronounce the weak form of *to* /tə/. Alternatively, you could simply model the sentences yourself.

PRACTICE (SB page 72)

1 Listening and speaking

T.28b

This first practice exercise switches decades and moves to the 1960s. Again you could quickly set the scene by asking your students what they know about the 1960s, and by talking about the pictures. It would be useful to point out mini-skirts, the Beatles, President Kennedy, etc. as this will give them useful signposts when they listen.

T.28b   Play the tape and ask them to work on the questions in pairs. Tell them to answer with **used to** when both **used to** and the Past Simple are possible.

Answers

1 She used to wear mini-skirts.
    She used to go dancing in discotheques.
    She used to go to pop concerts.
2 She went to a Beatles concert./She travelled to Liverpool to see the Beatles.
3 They used to listen to records. They didn't use to watch TV much.
4 They used to watch TV. They used to have a Mini(car) and they once went camping in France.
5 They used to say 'Make love not war'.
    They used to march to ban the bomb.
    There used to be student revolutions.
6 In 1968 there were student revolutions in many parts of the world.
    In 1963 President Kennedy was killed.
    In 1969 they (the Americans) landed on the moon.
    In 1961 they (the Russians) built the Berlin wall.

Ask your students when the Berlin wall came down. (1989) Conduct a feedback with the whole class. Ask individuals to give full sentences to practise the structure. You could give out copies of the tapescript and ask them to make sentences from it (perhaps for homework) in the same way as they did for Molly Harrison.

Additional material

Workbook Unit 10

Writing – exercise 12.   This is guided practice for writing a composition and the topic for the model text is 'Hippies'. It could be started in class and then completed for homework.

2 Speaking

The aim of this activity is to compare **used to** for past habit and the Present Simple for present habit in controlled oral practice. Read through the example with your students and then put them into pairs to go through the chart.

Formation of questions

What do/did you do at the weekend?
What do/did you do in the evening?
Where do/did you go on holiday?
What sports do/did you play?
What TV programmes do/did you like?
What newspapers/books/magazines do/did you read?
What kind of food do/did you like?

Conduct a feedback session with the whole class. Ask different pairs to give you examples of their questions and answers.

3 Writing

Get students to write down some sentences about their country and family. (This will go more quickly if you have already asked them to find out information from their families in preparation for starting the unit, as was suggested at the beginning of these notes.)

Put them into small groups to compare the information that they have about their country as it used to be, and to tell each other about their family history.

● Language review   (SB page 72)

Used to

Read the language review with your class. Put them into pairs or small groups to do the translations. Discuss how the idea of past habit is conveyed in their language(s).

▶ **Grammar reference: page 128.**

Ask students to read this at home, perhaps before they do some of the Workbook exercises for homework (see below).

Additional material

Workbook Unit 10
These exercises could be done in class to give further practice, for homework, or in a later class, to revise.
Used to – exercises 1–4.

PRESENTATION   (SB page 73)

Question forms (2)

T.29

Two kinds of questions are practised:
– questions which end with a preposition because the verb has a dependent preposition, for example:
    What are you listening to?
    Who are you looking at?

Who are you writing to?
What are you writing about?
– subject questions, where the question words *who* or *what* are
  the subject of the question, for example:
  What is making that noise?
  Who saw Tom?
  Who likes ice-cream?
  Who lives near the school?
These differ from object questions, where the question words are
the object of the verb, for example: *Who did Tom see?*
The dialogue is the means of presentation and contains examples
of both types of question.

1 | T.29 | Play the tape and ask your students to read and
listen at the same time. There should be no vocabulary
problems with the dialogue.

● Grammar questions   **(SB page 73)**

Read through the first part of each grammar question with your
students. You could ask them to give you some more examples
or you could give them yourself (see above).
Then put them into pairs to find the examples from the dialogue.
Answers
– Questions with verbs with a dependent preposition
  Who did you talk to?
  What did you talk about?
  Who did you dance with?
– Subject questions
  Who told you that?
  Who saw them?
  What happened in the restaurant?
Go through and check the answers with the whole class.

2 Play the dialogue again and ask your students to pay
particular attention to the pronunciation. Ask students to act
out the dialogue in their pairs, taking parts and reading aloud
to each other. Let them practise for a few minutes, then get
one pair to do it for the whole class.

PRACTICE   **(SB page 73)**

Students can stay in their pairs to do these exercises.

1 Grammar

Ask your students to go through the first five only. They should
be able to do these quite quickly. Check the answers with the
whole class.
Answers
a. Who does this pen belong to?
b. What are you thinking about?
c. What did you dream about last night?
d. Which countries have you been to?
e. Who did she get married to?

Now ask them to do the next five. You may need to demonstrate
exactly what is required here – someone, etc. is replaced by the
question word. You could demonstrate with this example:
Someone saw Ann. Who saw Ann?
Ann saw someone. Who did Ann see?

Answers
f. Who does John love?
g. Who loves John?
h. Who did Peter have an argument with?
i. What happened at the party?
j. Who phoned last night?
Doing this part of the exercise should prepare students for what
they have to do in the following exercise.

2 Speaking and listening

This is an information gap activity and should be good fun as
well as providing practice in question formation.
Each student looks at a different incomplete version of the love
story. By asking each other questions they can complete their
version.
Ask the As to look quickly through the story on this page and
ask the Bs to turn to page 119 and do the same with their story.
Read through the example with them to demonstrate what is
required.
Students take it in turns to ask the questions. Go round and
monitor the pairs and check that they are making the correct
questions as they work through the story.

A Love Story
Answers

Student A's questions to B	*Student B's questions to A*
Who does George love?	How often does George phone
What does he send her every	Lily?
week?	What did George write for
What was the poem about?	Lily?
Who was she talking to?	Where did George see Lily?
Who did James kiss?	Who gave Lily some flowers?
Who hit James?	Who did Lily see?
Where did the policeman take	Who saw George?
George (to)?	Who drove Lily home?
Who did Lily get married to?	What did George write?
What was the novel called?	

Complete story
George loves Lily.
George phones Lily every day.
He sends her flowers every week.
George wrote a poem for Lily.
The poem was about her blue eyes and red lips.
One day George saw Lily in the park.
She was talking to James.
James gave Lily some flowers.
James kissed Lily.
Suddenly Lily saw George.
George hit James.
A policeman saw George.
The policeman took George to the police station.
James drove Lily home.
Lily got married to James.
George wrote a novel.
It was called 'Death in the Park'.

Round off the lesson by asking some students to read a few lines
aloud of the completed story.

● Language review   (SB page 73)

Subject questions

Read the review all together. Put the students into small groups to translate the sentences.

▶ **Grammar reference: page 128.**

Ask students to read this at home, perhaps before they do some of the Workbook exercises for homework (see below).

Additional material

Workbook Unit 10

These exercises could be done in class to give further practice, for homework, or in a later class to revise.
Subject questions – exercise 5.
Subject and object questions – exercise 6.
Questions with a preposition at the end – exercise 7.

Pronunciation book Unit 10

Connected speech – Strong form prepositions at the end of sentences – exercise 2.

SKILLS DEVELOPMENT

● Reading and speaking   (SB page 74)

Pre-reading task

1 Discuss the pictures on the page with your students. Ask questions:
   – *Who are these women?*
   – *What are they doing?*
   – *What do they want?*
   Read the introduction to the article as a class. Read it aloud to them if you like. The aim of this short introduction is to set the scene for the longer text and establish the meaning of *suffragette.*

2 These general knowledge questions also aim to set the scene via a short discussion about the answers. Tell your students that you do not necessarily expect them to know the answers, but encourage intelligent guesses. Put them into pairs and give them a few minutes to discuss. Then go to the class to get feedback on their ideas. If there is controversy, allow the flow of suggestions and ideas for a little while before you give the correct answers.

   Answers
   a. New Zealand (Swiss women did not get the vote until 1971.)
   b. 1893
   c. (If you think your students will not readily know the answer to this, ask them to research it prior to the lesson. In a multinational class it will be interesting to compare the dates.)

Reading and vocabulary

1 and 2   Tell your class to read the article through quite quickly at this stage because they will have more time to study it in detail later. The idea here is to encourage speed of reading with minimal pausing to check unknown vocabulary, hence the restriction to four words.
   When they check with their partner they should be interested to see if they have looked up the same four words, where they have not they can 'teach' the other the new word(s).

3 Ask them to discuss this question with the same partner. It should provide some check of their overall understanding of the article.

Answers

To die for has two meanings:
– the literal meaning as in *He died for his country.*
– a non-literal meaning: to want something very much, as in
   I'm dying for a drink.
   The children are dying for Christmas to come.

Therefore the title of the article 'Dying for the Vote' is a play on words and can be interpreted in two ways:
– the women gave their lives to get the vote (as indeed they did).
– the women wanted the vote very much indeed (which is also true).

Check that the whole class understands the two interpretations of the title.

Comprehension check

Ask students to go through these multi-choice questions on their own at first and then to check their answers with their partners.

Answers

1 a. They demanded other things as well as the right to vote, e.g. better education for girls.

2 b. Because Parliament took no notice of all their letters and petitions and she wanted more publicity for the suffragettes.

3 c. They used to do things that were against the law, e.g. paint on walls, break shop windows, and chain themselves to railings.

4 a. She ran in front of the King's horse on Derby Day and was killed. (The Derby, pronounced /dɑːbɪ/, is a famous horse race in Britain. English Kings and Queens often own racehorses.)

5 c. Some Members of Parliament changed their minds before the war. Women did men's jobs during the war, but only after the war did they get the vote.

Check through the answers in feedback with the whole class. Don't just get the letter of the answer, ask for further explanation:
– *Why is a. (etc.) right?*
– *Why are b. and c. (etc.) not the right answer?*

Discussion

You could ask the students to work on these questions in small groups rather than pairs for this. Tell them that at least one of them should take some notes which they can refer to in the full class discussion.

In the feedback, ask for ideas about each of the questions in turn. There might be just a few ideas for 1 and 3, but 2 usually produces both ideas and argument between the sexes in the class!

● Vocabulary   (SB page 75)

Male and female words

This vocabulary activity can stand in its own right, but it was designed as an appropriate follow-on to the previous reading text, either immediately or in the next lesson.

Read through the introduction to the activity with your class. It may be worth pointing out to your students that although the English language does not have nouns of different genders, there are still words that can only apply to one sex.

1 Students could do this activity in pairs or small groups. It is expected that many of the words will already be familiar and the activity serves to revise these. Ask your students to look up unfamiliar words in their dictionary and to try to work out the pronunciation.

Answers

Male	Female	Both
landlord	heroine	musician
actor	bikini	teenager
bull	niece	cook
king	skirt	professor
duke	duchess	pilot
guy	queen	dentist
nephew	knickers	model
uncle	bra	pyjamas
hero	cow	scientist
underpants	aunt	architect
swimming	widow	judge
trunks	blouse	cousin
widower	actress	athlete
	landlady	tourist
		boots

Go through the exercise with the whole class. Work briefly on the pronunciation of some of the words as you go. The following might need some practice, perhaps a quick chorus drill:

guy /gaɪ/
heroine/hero /ˈherəʊɪn/, /ˈhɪərəʊ/
blouse /blaʊz/
pilot /ˈpaɪlət/
pyjamas /pəˈdʒɑːməz/
architect /ˈɑːkɪtekt/
cousin /ˈkʌzn/
athlete /ˈæθliːt/

2 Do this exercise quite quickly as a class. You read aloud the sentences and pause at the gap for the students to offer their suggestions.

Answers

a. nephew   d. an athlete   g. a widow
b. heroine   e. landlord   h. a dentist
c. pyjamas   f. underpants

3 Now put the students into pairs to write some similar descriptive sentences – about three or four per pair. Then nominate individuals to read aloud the sentences, pausing at the gap as you did, so that the others can offer the answer.

Additional material

Pronunciation book Unit 10
Intonation and sentence stress – intonation when giving lists – exercise 3.

● Listening and speaking   (SB page 76)

T.30

This is a jigsaw listening activity so you need two tapes, two tape recorders and ideally two rooms, so that the class can divide into groups and listen to their tapes.

Note
Here is some background information to the tape content.

T.30a   *Bill Cole*
– Bill Cole is a Cockney/a Londoner and speaks with a typical Cockney/London accent.
– A Cockney is the name given to someone born in or near the centre of London within the sound of the bells of Bow /bəʊ/ Church. Londoners say 'I'm a true Cockney – I was born within the sound of Bow Bells.'
– The East End of London is traditionally the working class end of the city with its own culture and way of life. The West End is for the rich – with theatres, night clubs, smart restaurants and shops.
– Fish and chip shops are still popular throughout Britain. These are takeaway cafés (not shops!) where you can buy a cheap meal of fish in batter and chips – traditionally these were always wrapped up in newspaper. Nowadays, they usually sell other things such as chicken and hamburgers as well as fish.
– Covent Garden was a famous fruit and vegetable market in the centre of London. George Bernard Shaw's Eliza Doolittle sold flowers there. The buildings still exist but now it is a tourist area of shops and restaurants.
– The word *vegetables* is often abbreviated to *veg.* /vedʒ/.
– *Ma* /mɑː/ is a colloquial word for *mother*. *Pa* /pɑː/ is *father*.
– Sixpence is 'old money' worth two and a half pence in today's money!
– Bill Cole could buy *pie and peas twice* = two meals of pie (meat in gravy with pastry on the top) and peas for sixpence in the 1920s!

T.30b   *Camilla, Duchess of Lochmar*
– Camilla is from an aristocratic background. The way she speaks reflects this. Her accent would be considered very upper class, and possibly a little old-fashioned these days.

Procedure
Divide the class clearly into two groups, A and B.
By way of a brief introduction tell them why Bill Cole and the Duchess are interesting. They are *exactly* the same age, but they have very different backgrounds and have had very different lives.
Then tell them that each group will hear the story of only one of the characters but after they have answered the questions they

will team up with someone from the other group and swap information so that in the end everyone will know about both Bill and the Duchess.

> **Note**
> Remember that clear instructions are vital for the success of a jigsaw activity. In a monolingual situation you could give the instructions and background in L1.

T.30 a and b

Ask the class to listen to the tape and answer the comprehension questions in their groups.

Comprehension check
Don't worry if your students do not answer in the amount of detail given below. It is enough for them to get some of the main points. You can elaborate points with them during the feedback.
Answers
Bill Cole
1 On May 7th, 1919.
2 He lived in the East End of London at number 18 India Street next to the river. His family had two rooms above a fish and chip shop. The rooms smelt of fish.
3 Yes, he had one brother and two sisters.
4 His father worked in the fruit and vegetable market at Covent Garden; his mother was a cleaner, she worked in offices and hospitals. Only his youngest sister is still alive.
5 No. He sometimes didn't go to school and he stayed with his father all day. He left school when he was twelve.
6 When he stayed with his father at the market all day. He loved the noise, colour, etc. of the market and also the taste of the pie and peas at lunchtime.
7 He was twelve. He had to help his mother look after his younger brother and sisters, so he left school and started work at the market.
8 He worked first at the market and then as a taxi-driver.

Camilla, Duchess of Lochmar
1 On May 7th, 1919.
2 At the family home, Foxton House, in Leicestershire. It has beautiful gardens; the rose garden was beautiful in June and the smell of the roses came right into the house.
3 Yes, she had three older brothers.
4 Two brothers were in the army, one was at Oxford University. Her mother and father used to spoil her, especially her father – he used to call her his 'little princess'.
5 No, she didn't have much education. She didn't go to school, she had a governess. Her mother thought it more important for a girl to learn to dance, go to parties, and look pretty.
6 The two years before she married the Duke – all the dances and parties.
7 He died when she was sixteen. It was a terrible time for her and her mother. Her mother wanted her to find a good husband.
8 She has never had a job. She only knew one girl who did have one.

When they have completed the questions tell each person from Group A to find someone from Group B, and in that pair (it may be necessary to have one group of three) to go through the

questions together, telling each other about their character. Allow as much time as they need for this and go round listening but only interrupting to ask them about the people. Don't be too strict about correcting language mistakes as this is a fluency activity.
Bring the whole class together for a final check of the answers. Go through the questions comparing answers for both characters. Don't go through one character at a time. Ask your students if they would now like to hear the other tape. At this stage of the lesson you could give out photocopies of the tapescripts for them to read and listen at the same time.
At the end ask them who they think has had the most interesting life and why.

● Everday English   (SB page 76)

T.31

Question tags

Practice in this section is restricted to question tags with falling intonation, which invites agreement. See the notes on page 76 of the Student's Book.

> **Note**
> Question tags are a problem for learners of English not only because of the intonation but also because in many languages the same conversational effect is achieved by a fixed standard phrase, e.g. *n' est-ce pas?* (French), *nicht wahr?* (German). There is not the complication of changes of form as there is with question tags in English.

1   T.31   Say nothing to your class about the grammar area of the lesson. Simply tell them:
Here are two similar conversations in a restaurant.
Listen to them and tell me at the end any differences you hear.
Play the tapes and invite suggestions from the whole class.
Differences
– The first one is longer.
– It sounds a bit more natural, polite, and conversational.
– There are lots of question tags: *wasn't it? didn't we?* etc.
Once you've established this last point, move on to 2.

2 Read through the explanation together with the whole class. Practise saying the two examples with falling intonation. Also point out the rule that *if the sentence is positive the question tag is negative*, as in the two examples. Conversely *if the sentence is negative the question tag is positive*. You could write these examples on the blackboard and practise them.
That film was very interesting, wasn't it?
She doesn't look very well, does she?
Play the first conversation again and ask your students to write down all the question tags they hear.
Answers
wasn't it?   didn't we?   have we?   isn't it?   don't they?

Put them into pairs to see if they can remember the parts of the conversation that went with the tag.
The fish was wonderful, *wasn't it?*   Yes, it was.

We finished it, *didn't we?*   Mm, (Yes).
We haven't been here for ages, *have we?*   No, we haven't.
It's very reasonable, *isn't it?*   Yes, it is.
And the waiters really look after you, *don't they?*   Yes, they do.
Now play it again for your students to check, or move straight to 3.

3 Give out the tapescript of the first conversation and ask your students to check their answers and then in pairs practise the conversation together. You could either get some pairs to act it out to the whole class or record some of them saying it and play that back to the class comparing it with T.31.

4 Ask your class what they know about English weather – they will inevitably say that it is awful! Tell them that because the weather in England changes such a lot it is a very popular topic of conversation!
(There is an English joke you might like to tell them which illustrates how changeable the weather is:
If you don't like English weather, wait five minutes!)
Ask them to fill in the question tags in the Good Weather and Bad Weather conversations.

Answers

Good Weather	Bad Weather
A Good Morning! It's another lovely day, *isn't it?*	**A** Good morning! It isn't very warm today, *is it?*
B It certainly is. It wasn't as warm as this yesterday, *was it?*	**B** It certainly isn't. It hasn't been as cold as this for ages, *has it?*
A No, it wasn't. It rained yesterday evening, *didn't it?*	**A** That's true. We've had some lovely weather recently, *haven't we?*
B Yes. The sunshine makes you feel good, *doesn't it?*	**B** Mm. Ah, well. Mustn't complain.
A You're absolutely right.	

Check through with the whole class. Then ask various pairs to come to the front of the class and role play meeting on the street and having a typical weather conversation. Ask your students to improvise and not just memorize the conversations, and encourage them to be funny by stressing how very important (!) such conversations are when you are in England!

Don't forget!

Workbook Unit 10
There is an exercise on question tags – exercise 8.
There is a vocabulary exercise on the different spellings of words which rhyme – exercise 9.
There is a writing exercise on correcting mistakes – exercise 10.

Pronunciation book Unit 10
There is an exercise on all the diphthongs – exercise 1.

Word list
Make sure that your students complete the Word list for Unit 10 by writing in the translations.

Video
Section 7 – Report: *BBC World Service*
This video section supplements Units 9 and 10 of the Student's Book. It is a short documentary about the development of BBC World Service radio.

Progress test
There is a Progress test for Units 6–10 on page 150 of the Teacher's Book.

UNIT 11

Passives – Notices

Introduction to the Unit

The unit is called 'Read all about it' and the theme is the history of some internationally well-known products such as Coca-Cola, Nylon, the Volkswagen Beetle, and Concorde. These topics fit the grammatical area of the unit (passives) and provide many opportunities for practice.

The Skills Development section contains readings on a selection of non-topical newspaper articles. These should ideally be supplemented with more topical articles from English newspapers, if it is possible to get hold of these.

Notes on the Language Input

Grammar

Remember that it is sometimes a good idea to remind yourself of the grammar in each unit before you prepare your lessons. One way you can do this is to read the appropriate Grammar reference section at the back of the Student's Book.

Passives

The unit introduces four passives: Present Simple passive, Past Simple passive, Present Perfect passive and Future Simple passive. They are introduced together rather than dealt with one at a time. However, in the Presentation section, the approach to the formation of the passive is carefully staged, beginning with revision of different tenses of the verb *to be* and then revising past participles. Finally students see examples of the full passive in context. With such a staged approach, students at this level can cope with studying and practising four passive tenses at one time, especially as the tense use is the same as for the active, and your students should already be familiar with this.

It is worth reminding yourself that English generally makes more use of the passive voice than many other languages where the equivalent of *one* is used to avoid it – for example *on* in French and *man* in German. In English, *one* is used to replace the personal pronouns *I* and *we*, and it can sound very formal and distant. It is a feature of the speech of the Royal Family, e.g. *One has so many duties, one gets very tired* (!).

They is sometimes used to replace the passive in English. It is less formal.
They make good cars in Sweden./Good cars are made in Sweden.

There are other examples in Practice 2, Grammar, on page 78 of the Student's Book.

Vocabulary

This activity is the third in *Headway Pre-Intermediate* on words that go together (collocation). The other two are in the vocabulary sections of Units 3 and 8.

In the first exercise in this unit students have to say which nouns go with which verbs. In the second exercise they have to say which prepositions go with which verbs.

It is important to introduce students to the idea of collocation quite early in their learning of English. It is a language with many synonyms or near synonyms, and so it is important for students to develop an awareness of which words go together.

Everyday English

This is an exercise on recognizing notices in common locations around Britain.

Notes on the Unit

PRESENTATION   (SB page 77)

Passives

1 This exercise is the first stage in teaching the formation of the passive.

Ask your students to complete the sentences on their own. Emphasize that they must only use the verb *to be* in the correct tense. Ask them to name the tenses.
Answers
a. is   (Present Simple)
b. were   was   (Past Simple)
c. has been   have never been   (Present Perfect Simple)
d. will be   (Future Simple)
Ask your students to check their answers with a partner, and then conduct a full-class feedback.

82

2 This is the second stage in teaching the formation of the passive. There are two main aims to this exercise:
  – to remind students of the formation of regular and irregular past participles.
  – to check that students understand the meaning and know the form of these particular verbs, because they appear in the passive in subsequent activities and exercises throughout the unit. *Invent* and *produce* might be new words for your students, the others should be familiar.

  Ask your students to work in pairs. Tell them that not all the verbs are irregular. When they have finished ask them to check the irregular verbs in the irregular verb list on page 141 of the Student's Book.

  When you go through the exercise with the whole class, ask them first to tell you which verbs are regular. Then go quickly through the irregular ones.

  Answers

sell	sold	sold
give	gave	given
buy	bought	bought
produce	produced	produced (The verb form has the stress on the second syllable.) (regular)
drink	drank	drunk
build	built	built
write	wrote	written
grow	grew	grown
steal	stole	stolen
invent	invented	invented (regular)

3 The previous two exercises have worked on the form of the passive, which is the verb **to be** (in various tenses) and the past participle. Now the students see examples of full passives in the context of an article about the history of Coca-Cola. To introduce the topic ask your students a few general questions about Coca-Cola:
  – *How many of you like to drink Coca-Cola?*
  – *Do you know where it comes from?*
  – *Can you tell the difference between Coke and Pepsi?*
  – *Do you know any advertisements for Coke?*
  Ask them to read the article. For the time being don't focus attention on the passives. Ask your students simply to read and understand. They should have no difficulty with the vocabulary.

  > **Note**
  > 1 gallon = 4.5 litres
  > 1.6 billion gallons = 7.2 billion litres

● Grammar questions   (SB page 78)

After the reading, go through the grammar questions with the whole class. The aim of these questions is to establish that the passive is used when the main interest and focus is on the object of the sentence not the subject.

Answers
– Coca-Cola is the main interest of the text. Therefore it is the subject of many of the sentences in the text. Dr John Pemberton and Frank Robinson are only interesting because of their relation to the central theme of Coca-Cola.

– No, we don't know exactly who sells it. This isn't important. The amount that is sold is what's important.
Because of the above the passive is used. Read the rule box.

4 Read the first line with your students and complete the rule with the whole class:
  Answers
  The passive is formed with the auxiliary verb **to be** and the past participle.
  Ask your students to read the text again and underline every example of the passive.

  Coca-Cola is enjoyed all over the world. 1.6 gallons are sold every year, in over one hundred and sixty countries. The drink was invented by Dr John Pemberton in Atlanta, on May 8, 1886, but it was given the name Coca-Cola by his partner, Frank Robinson. In the first year, only nine drinks a day were sold.

  The business was bought by a man called Asa Candler in 1888, and the first factory was opened in Dallas, Texas, in 1895. Coca-Cola is still made there. Billions of bottles and cans have been produced since 1895.
  Diet coke has been made since 1982, and over the years many clever advertisements have been used to sell the product. It is certain that Coca-Cola will be drunk far into the twenty-first century.

PRACTICE   (SB page 78)

1 Writing and speaking

1 Ask your students to do this on their own. They might prefer to do it on a separate piece of paper, rather than in their books.

  Answers

Present Simple	Past Simple	Present Perfect	*Will* future
is enjoyed	was invented	have been produced	will be drunk
are sold	was given	has been made	
is (still) made	were sold	have been used	
	was bought		
	was opened		

  Ask them to check their answers with a partner. Then go through with the whole class. You could write them in columns (as above) on the blackboard as you go.

2 Ask your students to stay in their pairs to do this exercise. Students take it in turns to complete a sentence and then check in the text. Go round the pairs, helping and correcting. Go through the exercise with the whole class, asking individuals to give sentences (see answers in the text above).

3 Ask students to continue working in pairs. Go round and check that they are forming the questions correctly. Then conduct feedback with the whole class.

Answers

How much Coca-Cola is sold every year?

When was Coca-Cola invented?

How much Coca-Cola was sold in the first year?

Where was the first factory opened?

How long has Diet Coke been made?

2 Grammar

This exercise is to make students aware of how the active and passive forms of different tenses differ. You could do this exercise as a class to consolidate the work so far on the passive.

Answers

Active	Passive
b. They *grow* rice in China.	a. VW cars *are made* in Germany.
d. Thieves *stole* two pictures from the museum last night.	c. The telephone *was invented* by Bell in 1876.
f. They *have sold* the picture for £3,000.	e. Three new factories *have been built* this year.
h. *Did* they *make* many cars last year?	g. 10,000 cars *will be made* next year.
	i. The television *wasn't invented* by Bell.

3 Grammar and reading

This is an exercise in recognizing when to use an active or a passive verb form, and putting it into the appropriate tense. The text is about the invention of nylon. To introduce the topic, ask students to look at the pictures and name the objects made of nylon.

Answers

parachute, carpet, tights

Then ask:

– *Are you wearing anything that is made of nylon? What?*

– *Are there any things in this room made of nylon?*

Ask students to work on the exercise in pairs. Tell them to check any unknown vocabulary in their dictionary.

Answers

a. was invented

b. worked

c. was introduced

d. became

e. was used

f. is found

g. has played

h. will be manufactured

Go through the answers as a class.

4 Writing

This exercise could be done in class or for homework with some other exercises from the Workbook.

Read through the examples as a class. Point out that when they have to give **B**'s reply, a short answer isn't enough. They should also add a sentence, giving more information. Students can do this exercise in pairs if you decide to do it in class.

Answers

a. **B** Yes, it is. It is sold in over one hundred and sixty countries.

b. **A** Was Coca-Cola invented by Frank Robinson/Asa Candler?

c. **B** No, it hasn't. It's been made since 1982.

d. **B** No, it wasn't. It was invented before the Second World War, in the early thirties.

e. **A** How much nylon will be made/manufactured next year?

● Language review   (SB page 79)

The passive

Read the Language review all together. Put students into small groups to translate the sentences.

▶ **Grammar reference: page 129.**

Ask students to read this at home, perhaps before they do some of the Workbook exercises for homework (see below).

Additional material

Workbook Unit 11

These exercises could be done for homework or in a later class to revise.

The passive – exercises 1–6 (Exercise 5 could equally well be done in conjunction with the Everyday English section on page 83 of the Student's Book.)

Exercise 6 could be done after the newspaper stories on page 80 of the Student's Book.

Pronunciation book Unit 11

Connected Speech

Word linking in a text about the invention of the bowler hat – exercise 2.

Weak form auxiliaries and passives in a newspaper article – exercise 3. This exercise could also be done after the reading activity on page 80 of the Student's Book.

SKILLS DEVELOPMENT

● Reading and speaking   (SB page 80)

In preparation for this lesson try to get hold of some recent English newspapers. Looking at them would be a useful way of following up this activity.

Newspaper stories

To introduce the topic, ask your students to bring to class newspapers in their own language if they can.

Tell them to look quickly through and say which articles they think seem interesting, ask:

– *Which articles do you want to read? Why?* (But read them later, not now!)

– *Which parts of the newspaper do you find most interesting?*

– *Which do you not find interesting? Sports? Business? News comment?* etc.

Now read the introduction to the reading as a class.

Pre-reading task

Ask students to read the headlines. Check that they understand all the vocabulary.

> **Note**
> The expression to be *alive and kicking* means to be *healthy and active*.

Students could do exercises 1 and 2 in pairs, working with a dictionary.

1 Ask your students to discuss this with their partner. Encourage them to say not only *which* stories they think will be interesting but *why*.

2 They will need to check the meaning of some of these words in their dictionary in order to discuss which words might go with which headline. Some of the words clearly fit one headline only, but others could go with more than one.

Sample Answers

fit (adj) – (1) because it means healthy and the article is about health.

graceful (adj) – (2) because perhaps it describes how Concorde flies.

honesty (n) – (3) because perhaps the reward was for an honest action.

lottery (n) – this could be (4). Perhaps the vet won the money, but it could also be (3).

mansion (n) – this could be (3). Perhaps the person who won the money bought a mansion, or it could be (4). Perhaps the vet bought one.

to operate (on sb) (v) – This could be (3), an operation on an animal, but it is more likely to be (1) an operation on the man's heart.

stable (n) – (4) because of the connection with animals.

speed (n) – (2) because Concorde is a fast plane.

spinster (n) – (4) a spinster might have no family to leave money to.

> **Note**
> The word *spinster* is not generally used nowadays about an unmarried woman because it is derogatory and old-fashioned. The term *single woman* is more usual.

to train (v) – (1) perhaps the heart man is trying to keep fit.

transplant (n) – (1) perhaps the man was given a new heart.

wallet (n) – (3) perhaps the reward was for finding a wallet.

will (n) – (4) perhaps the vet was left money in someone's will.

(to be) worth (adj) – perhaps (3) or (4) because they are about money.

Bring the class together and go through the possibilities; at this stage don't tell your students if their ideas are right or wrong, just discuss what could be possible and why.

3 Ask your students to work on their own. Choose *one* headline only and write *one* other question to go with the example question for their article.

Reading

Ask your students to read their chosen article and answer questions 1–3 in the comprehension check on their own.

Comprehension check

Get your students to do questions 1 and 2 and then conduct some feedback with the whole class before they move on to 3.

Answers

1 1 HEART MAN ALIVE AND KICKING
    fit, to operate, to train, transplant
   2 CONCORDE'S BIRTHDAY
    graceful, speed
   3 MILLION DOLLAR REWARD
    honesty, lottery, wallet, worth
   4 £3 MILLION FOR A VET
    mansion, stable, spinster, will, worth

2 **Answers to example questions in Pre-reading task 3**
  Why did the man need a new heart?
  Because he had heart disease and he couldn't work.
  How old is Concorde?
  Nearly 25 years old.
  What did the person do to get a million dollars?
  He found and returned a winning lottery ticket and was given a reward for his honesty.
  Why did the vet get £3 million?
  Because he helped an old spinster and she left him the money in her will.

  Ask for some examples of your students' own questions and discuss the answers. Ask:
  – *Did anyone write a question that was **not** answered in their article?*

3 Take care with the instructions here. Make it very clear to your students that only four of the sixteen questions go with their story and they must only answer these questions.
  You could ask them to look quickly through the first time and decide which are their questions, then go back and answer them.
  Answers (The number of the article is in brackets.)
  a. (1) Because it is exactly one year since he was given a new heart.
  b. (2) No. Concorde was developed by Britain and France together.
  c. (4) He is lucky because an old spinster left him her money, her house, and her stables, worth £3 million.
  d. (3) Because he found a wallet with a winning lottery ticket and he was given a $1 million reward.
  e. (1) Because he wants to raise money for the hospital's transplant programme.
  f. (2) Over 5,000 hours.
  g. (4) Because she did not leave them her money. They say that she was senile and did not know what she was doing.
  h. (3) He posted the wallet back to Mr Dupont (but he kept the lottery ticket).
  i. (1) He can work, look after his two sons, and climb the stairs.
  j. (4) No, they didn't. They were shocked. They couldn't believe it.
  k. (3) No, he didn't. He sat and thought about it for two hours.
  l. (1) He can play with his children. He can play football and snooker, go jogging and swimming with them.
  m. (2) Because New York is five hours behind London and

Concorde takes only 3 hours 25 minutes to fly between London and New York.

n. (4) They hope to make the mansion beautiful again.

o. (3) When he was shown the lottery ticket and the newspaper.

p. (2) She is the oldest passenger to fly in Concorde. She was 99 years old!

4 The following two activities (4 and 5) will hopefully lead to some free speaking practice as students discuss their articles. Ask them to stand up if possible and find another/other student(s) who has/have read the same article and check through the four answers. If they are alone in reading that article, check through with that student yourself.

5 Now ask each student to find someone who has read a different article. Ask them to tell each other a little about it. This should not be at length or in too much detail. Encourage them to give the main points only. Then ask them to circulate and find out a little about each of the articles. Get them to ask each time: *Why did you choose that article?*
Bring the class together and check through all the answers.

6 At this point the activity moves away from fluency practice of reading and speaking and focuses on specific language. Ask your students to underline examples of passive verb forms in all four articles and then show a partner the examples they have found.
Answers
1 ... he was operated on ... and given a new heart.
   So far eleven people have been given new hearts.
   I hope more people will be helped by the hospital.
2 Concorde was developed by both France and Britain.
   It was given over 5,000 hours of testing.
   Concorde is much used by business people ...
   Each Concorde is built at a cost of £55 million.
   Twenty have been built so far.
3 ... he was given $1.2 million as a reward.
   The door was opened not by Mr Dupont, but by his son, Yves ...
   ... until he was shown the lottery ticket ...
4 Vet Peter Pocock has been left a fortune by a spinster ...
   Miss Margaret de Beaumont was helped in other ways by Mr Pocock.
   ... the mansion will be made beautiful again.
   It has not been looked after well for many years.
   ... the beauty of the buildings and garden can still be seen.

Note
My boys are very pleased in 1.   *They were shocked* in 4.
Your students will no doubt pick out these two sentences as examples of the passive. In a way this is correct but in fact these sentences, despite being passive in form, contain examples of past participles used as adjectives.
Point this out to your students and give them credit for finding them. You could remind them very quickly of other such past participle adjectives with which they are already familiar: *interested, worried, tired*. (There is an exercise on these adjectives in the Vocabulary section of Unit 12, Student's Book page 90.)

Further reading and speaking
The aim of this activity is not to encourage detailed reading of English newspapers but to point out quite gently that if you are interested in an article you can usually get something from it even with a limited knowledge of the language.
Hopefully, you will have managed to get hold of some recent English newspapers for this part of the lesson.
Put the class into small groups and ask each group to choose a newspaper and then to look through it together and pick out one or two articles that they think might be interesting. (If your classroom is big enough they could gather round the newspapers on the floor.) Tell them not to worry about words that they do not know, and just get some information from the articles. Go round the groups after a while and ask them to show you the articles they have chosen and tell you a little about them.
Conduct a feedback/discussion with the whole class. Point out the different/same types of articles chosen and ask each group to tell the others a little about them.
You might be able to encourage some keen students to continue buying an English newspaper or magazine. It is one way of developing language ability outside the classroom.

Additional material
You could use either/both of the following two exercises in conjunction with this reading activity, if you have not used them previously to practise passives.

Workbook Unit 11
Newspaper articles – exercise 6.

Pronunciation book Unit 11
Weak form auxiliaries and passive verbs in a newspaper article – exercise 3.

● Vocabulary   (SB page 82)

Words that go together

The aim of this exercise is to remind students of the role of dictionaries in giving information about words that go together. Ask your students to work in pairs.

1 **Nouns and verbs that go together**
The verbs in this exercise have been chosen because they should all be familiar to the students, but they are often incorrectly used in relation to some nouns.
Take care to make clear to your students that the verb in the middle sometimes does not go with *one* of the nouns surrounding it and sometimes it does not go with *two*. This varies.
Tell your students to check the nouns in their dictionaries first. This is more likely to tell them which verbs go with them than vice versa.
Answers
steal – can go with *£1,000*, *a wallet*, and *ear-rings* but it cannot go with *a bank* or *a post office*. (You can rob a bank or a post office but not steal it!)
win – can go with *a competition*, *a war*, *£10,000*, *a football match* but it cannot go with *John McEnroe*. (You can win a prize or a game, not a person.)

catch – can go with *a fish, a bus, a train, a cold, a thief* but it cannot go with *a car*. (You can only catch public transport.)

wear – can go with *a seat belt, ear-rings, a watch, a uniform* but it cannot go with *a briefcase* or *an umbrella*. (You carry or hold these.)

tell – can go with *a lie, the truth, a joke, a story* but it cannot go with *a poem*. (You write or recite a poem.)

play – can go with *the piano, tennis, cards* but it cannot go with *swimming* or *a competition*. (You go swimming and enter a competition.)

Go round and check the pairwork and help with any difficulties in using the dictionaries.
Then bring the whole class together to check through the exercise.
You can have fun and reinforce some of the right answers by miming the wrong answers.
For example you can mime somebody trying to 'pick up' a bank or a post office and 'steal' it!; somebody 'winning' John McEnroe, taking him home to put on the mantelpiece!; trying to catch a car as if it were a ball; and perhaps 'wearing' a briefcase or an umbrella on their head!

Practice
Now ask the same pairs of students to write two more examples for each verb. Go round and check as they do this. Then ask several students to read aloud their sentences for the others to comment on.

2 Words and prepositions that go together
Ask your students to work on their own using their dictionaries only if absolutely necessary. Encourage them to do the exercise quickly and then to check their answers with their partner.

Answers

a. at	e. on	i. in, with
b. on	f. on	j. on
c. from	g. with	k. by
d. in	h. to	l. to

Remind your students of the list of words + preposition on page 142 of the Student's Book. Ask them to check their answers from the list. You can tell them that these need to be learnt by heart because there are no real rules!

● Listening and speaking (SB page 82)

T.32

The world's most loved car
This listening is based on a radio programme. It contains not only some information on the history of the car, but also two verses of a very jolly little song about the joys of owning a Beetle!

Pre-listening task
1 Ask your students if they recognize the car in the pictures.
Ask:
– *Do you have a special name for this car in your language?*
– *In English it is called a Beetle. Do you know the meaning of 'beetle'?*
– *Which country do Volkswagen cars come from?*

Note
In some languages this car is called a *ladybird* but in English it is called a Beetle. A beetle is an insect which is often black and shiny. A ladybird is a red insect with black spots.
Your students may mention the British pop group of the sixties and seventies with a similar name, The Beatles, but notice that the spelling is different in this case. The Beetle car with human qualities is from a series of films made by Walt Disney.
It/He is called Herbie. *Herbie goes to Hollywood* is one of the titles.

2 This exercise aims to teach/check some vocabulary necessary to understand the radio programme.
Put students into pairs to do the exercise. Remind them that the verbs need to be put into the correct tense. You could mention that one verb will need to be in the passive.

Answers
a. This church *was designed* by Wren in 1670.
b. He's a big *fan* of Tina Turner.
c. She's a very *reliable* friend. She's always there when you need her.
d. 'Did you talk to Pat much?'
   'No, we just *chatted* for a few minutes.'
e. Her uncle's a *jolly* man. He's always laughing.
f. That's Penny over there. Look, she's *waving* at us.

Check through the answers quickly with the whole class.

Listening

T.32

You could do this listening in two parts with your class, depending on how well you think they will manage it.

Play the tape up to the end of the first verse of the song.
Ask your students to work in pairs and make sentences about the Beetle using only the first five of the words in exercise 2. In other words, with all the words except *to wave*.
You do *not* want your students to reproduce exact sentences from the tape but to use the words about the car to show that they have understood the gist of the information given.

Possible answers
The Beetle is not very comfortable, but it's always *reliable* even in rain and snow.
It's a *jolly* friend.
The man *chats* to his car as he drives it. He says 'Well done!'
The Beetle *was designed* in 1934 by Ferdinand Porsche.
British and American soldiers were the first *fans* of the car.

Go round the pairs and check the sentences. Then ask several students to read aloud examples for the others in the class to comment on.
Ask:
– *What does Volkswagen mean?* (It means 'people's car', a car designed for people.)

Comprehension check
Ask your students to do numbers 1–6 only of the true/false exercise on their own. They then check their answers with their partner.

Answers

1 False (They are not very comfortable. People like them because they are reliable.)
2 True (His car is a reliable, jolly friend. He talks to it.)
3 False (His friends who own Beetles say that the car can't be improved.)
4 False (He was asked to design the car in 1934. It was built in 1938.)
5 False (They loved the car. They were its first fans.)
6 True

Go through the answers with the whole class.

Now play the tape to the end and repeat the procedure with questions 7–10.

Answers

7 False (Baber opened the first VW garage in Britain in the 1950s.)
8 True (The magazine was called *Beetling*.)
9 True
10 False (Beetles are still made in South America but they have not been made in Europe since 1974.)

Don't forget to ask them to make a sentence with *to wave*. Address the whole class and ask for examples.

Possible answer

At first people who owned Beetles used to wave to each other when they were driving.

At this point ask your students if they would like to hear the whole tape again. You could give them copies of the tapescript so that they can read and listen at the same time.

What do you think?

1 The message of the song is simply that the car is happy in its new home. They are a familiar sight in many countries.
Ask:
– *Can you remember any lines or just words from the song?*
– *Can you remember the tune? Look at the tapescript. Can you sing it?*
You could play the song parts of the tape again and encourage your students to join in, if they enjoy singing!

2/3 The aim here is to have a short personalized discussion. Put the class into small groups to discuss the questions first. Go round the groups and encourage ideas, perhaps by saying which is your favourite car and why. Generally respond to points being made in the groups.

> **Note**
> In Britain, the Mini and the Morris Minor are probably loved by many people in the same way as Beetles.

Finally, pull the class together and share some of the points made in their group discussions.

Possible homework

Ask the class to underline all the examples of passive forms in the tapescript.

● Everyday English (SB page 83)

T.33

Notices

Introduce the topic by asking your students for examples of any typical notices in their country. Ask which ones might be difficult for foreigners visiting there to understand.

1 Put students into pairs or small groups to do this.
Answers
1 A bank   b.
2 Outside a cinema   m.
3 A drinks machine   k.
4 A bus   e.
5 An airport   h.
6 A pub   f.
7 The Underground   c.
8 A park   l.
9 A zoo   j.
10 A hotel   d.
11 A railway station   a.
12 A public toilet   g. (or k.)
13 A motorway   i.
Check through the answers with the whole class.

> **Note**
> f. People under 18 are not allowed to buy alcohol in Britain.
> g. The opposite of *engaged* is *vacant*.
> a. Edinburgh is in Scotland. York and Newcastle are in the north of England and trains often stop there on their way to Scotland.
> c. The Victoria Line is just one of the lines on the London Underground. Some of the other lines are: the Jubilee Line, the Bakerloo Line, the Piccadilly Line, the Northern Line.

2 T.33 These five dialogues take place in one of the places above.
Play the dialogues one at a time and after each ask your students:
– *Where are the people?*
– *Who are the people?*
– *How can you tell where they are? What are they talking about?*
Answers
1 In a hotel or café. A waitress and a customer. He is asking for a typically English afternoon tea: A pot (a teapot) of tea for two. Ham sandwiches and scones with jam and cream.

> **Note**
> Your students will probably not know what *scones* /skɒnz/ are. They are small, not very sweet cakes or buns which are traditionally eaten with thick, fresh cream and strawberry or raspberry jam on the top.

2 In a bank. A cashier and a customer. She is getting some money out of the bank.

> **Note**
> *Tens* and *fives* is a short way of saying *ten pound notes* and *five pound notes*.

3 Next to a drinks machine. The man is angry because the machine is out of order and he can't get his money back. The woman is not surprised because these machines are often broken.

4 At a railway station. The station announcer is apologizing because the train is late.

> **Note**
> British Rail is the name of the British railway system. It is a common joke that the trains are always late whenever the weather isn't perfect, which is quite often in Britain! The announcer apologizes for the *severe weather conditions*. This usually means lots of snow.

5 In a pub. A barman and a young girl. The barman is asking for means of identification because the girl does not look old enough (18) to buy alcohol.

> **Note**
> British people do not have identity cards, so to prove your age you would need, for example, a driving licence, a passport, or a student card. However, it is not very common to be asked your age, although there are notices about under-age drinking in most pubs.

3 Put the students into pairs and ask them to choose two other places from the list and write very short dialogues typical for those places.
Ask the pairs to read their dialogues aloud, taking different parts. Tell the rest of the class to listen and try to guess where they are taking place.

> **Additional material**
> **Workbook Unit 11**
> Exercise 5 contains more notices and could be used after the Everyday English section.

Don't forget!

Workbook Unit 11
Exercise 7 is a vocabulary exercise which practises homonyms (words with more than one meaning).
There are two exercises on writing – 8 and 9. Students are guided towards writing a short review of a book they have read or a film they have seen.

Pronunciation book Unit 11
There is an exercise on the sounds /e/, /æ/ and /ʌ/ – exercise 1.

Word list
Make sure your students complete the Word list for Unit 11 by writing in the translations.

Video
Section 8 – Situation: *Lost Property*
This video section supplements Unit 11 of the Student's Book. In this situation, Paola loses her bag and goes to the police station to report it.

Section 9, given at the end of Unit 12, also supplements Unit 11 and is particularly suitable for use after listening to the radio programme about the Volkswagen Beetle.

UNIT 12

Verb patterns (2) – Apostrophes – Time

Introduction to the Unit

The theme of this unit is adventure. In the Presentation section, students read about one man's encounter with a tiger, and study several verb patterns. Apostrophes to show contracted forms and possession are also practised. In the Skills Development section, there is a jigsaw reading activity about national heroes, and an interview with a man who claims he has met aliens from another planet.

Notes on the Language Input

Grammar

Verb patterns

This is the second presentation section that deals with verb patterns. They were also dealt with in Unit 5. This unit focuses on **ask/tell someone to do, make/let someone do**, and then several verbs followed by either the infinitive or **-ing**.

These verb patterns do not present students with many problems of concept. They need to perceive that **tell** is used in two ways, **tell** as in **say** and **tell** as in *order someone to do something*. **Make** and **let** form a contrasting pair, **make** having the idea of compulsion, and **let** having the idea of permission.

However, students often make mistakes of form, as they inevitably confuse those verbs that are followed by an infinitive with **to** and those that are followed by an infinitive without **to** and once **-ing** forms have been looked at, students begin to put **-ing** where it doesn't belong!
Common mistakes
*He asked her dance.
*He asked her dancing.
*She makes me to do my homework.
*They let me to stay up late.

Start is one of the few verbs that can be followed by either the infinitive or the **-ing** form with no change of meaning. However,

English doesn't like two **-ing** forms together, so in a continuous tense form, we use the infinitive.
It's starting to rain. (*Not* *It's starting raining.)

We also deal with adjectives followed by the infinitive (*It's easy to learn English.*) and the infinitive to express purpose (*I went to the shops to buy a paper.*) Students often translate this second item from their own language and insert **for**, which is wrong in English.
Common mistake
*I went to the shops for to buy a paper.

Apostrophes

The correct use of apostrophes is an area of the language that many native English users have problems with. The rules are not particularly difficult, but one sees mistakes in all sorts of situations such as notices, menus, advertisements, and even the quality press. People usually remember to use them in contracted forms such as *he's* and *I've*, but they confuse *its* and *it's* and *the boy's room* and *the boys' room*. An example of a very common mistake is
*three week's holiday.
Given this situation, it is no surprise that students of English also experience difficulty with apostrophes, although their problem is more understandable.

Vocabulary

There is a second exercise on adverbs. In Unit 7 function adverbs were practised; in this unit adverbs of manner are revised.

Participle adjectives such as **bored/boring**, **surprised/surprising** are also practised. These pairs of words are often confused.
Common mistakes
*I am very interesting in art.
*It was an embarrassed situation.

Everyday English

As in many languages, there are different ways of telling the time in English. Several of these are practised in this section.

Notes on the Unit

PRESENTATION (SB page 84)

Verb patterns and apostrophes

Introduction: Ask students what animals you can find in very hot countries such as India and Nepal. Try to elicit the following animals:

tigers   elephants   deer   snakes

Ask the following questions:
– *Which of these are dangerous?*
– *What can they do to you?*

1   Read the introduction as a class. Before students read, check they understand the following items of vocabulary:
   guide   equipment   to protect   wildlife   to bleed
   lightning
   Students read the text about Tony Russell.

2   In pairs, students answer the questions. The questions are designed to elicit examples of the target language of the unit, much of which students will have come across before but which perhaps they have not been formally introduced to.
   Answers
   a. To work in a hospital.
   b. He thinks it's important to see as much of a country as you can.
   c. No. It's difficult to travel around Nepal.
   d. No. They let him have a few days' holiday.
   e. He asked a Nepalese guide to go with him.
   f. He made him wear shoes and trousers to protect him from snakes.
   g. To get a better view.
   h. Tony managed to pull Kamal away from the tiger.

● Grammar questions

– Read the first question as a class. Students find the two examples.
   Answers
   I asked . . . Kamal Rai to go with me.
   Kamal told me to be very quiet.

– Read the second Grammar question as a class. Students find the four examples.
   Answers
   The hospital let me have a few days' holiday.
   Kamal made me wear shoes and trousers . . .
   One of our elephants . . . made it go back . . .
   we . . . escaped to let the tiger eat its lunch.
   If you make someone do something, it is like saying *You must!*
   If you let someone do something, it is like saying *You can if you want.*

– Read the third Grammar question as a class. Students find the verbs.
   Answers
   I decided to go into the jungle . . . (followed by an infinitive)
   We started preparing . . . (**-ing** form)
   I started to feel . . . (infinitive)

we were trying to find . . . (infinitive)
I managed to pull . . . (infinitive)

– Read the fourth Grammar question as a class. Students find the four examples.
   Answers
   it's important to see . . .
   it is difficult to travel . . .
   it is unusual to find . . .
   it was impossible to sleep . . .

– Read the last Grammar question as a class. Students find the four examples.
   Answers
   I went to Nepal . . . *to work* in a hospital.
   Kamal made me wear shoes and trousers *to protect* me . . .
   We climbed on the elephants' backs *to get* a better view . . .
   we . . . escaped *to let* the tiger eat its lunch . . .

PRACTICE (SB page 85)

1 Grammar

1   Students work in pairs to fill the gaps.
   Answers
   a. I let them watch TV
   b. It makes me feel ill
   c. They let me do
   d. they made me work hard
   e. The ending made me cry.
   f. My parents make/made me practise
   g. My brother lets me borrow
   Ask students for some suggestions regarding teachers they like/liked and don't/didn't like!

2   Students rewrite the sentences using *tell* or *ask*.
   Answers
   a. I asked her to lend me some money.
   b. The teacher told me to do my homework again.
   c. I asked her to write to me soon.
   d. The doctor told Peter to do more exercise.
   e. She told me to drive more carefully.
   Ask students for suggestions regarding what their parents **tell/told/ask/asked** them to do.

3   Students choose the correct form of the verb. Encourage them to use the list of verb patterns on page 143 of the Student's Book.
   Answers
   a. buy   d. think   g. to snow
   b. to stop   e. to understand
   c. to find   f. to do

2 Speaking

Students work in pairs to ask and answer questions. This is for very controlled practice of the infinitive of purpose.
Sample answers
To buy stamps.   To buy petrol.
To buy a book.   To buy a paper.
To borrow a book.   To buy some meat.
To book a holiday.   To buy some beer.

3 Apostrophes

1 Read the explanation as a class. Students find examples of apostrophes from the text.

Answers

Where letters are left out	Possession
it's	a few days' holiday
	the elephants' backs
	the tiger's lunch
	the animal's throat
	Kamal's leg

2 Students correct the mistakes. All the phrases except the last contain mistakes.

Corrections

Kamal's leg
It's raining.
two days' holiday
my parents' house
a boys' school

3 Ask students to put apostrophes where necessary in the sentences.

Answers

a. My children's favourite game is chasing Wally the cat. It's not a game I like, and the cat certainly doesn't like it. It hides under Kate's bed, or runs up its favourite tree, where the children can't get it.

b. 'Have you seen today's newspaper?'
'No, I haven't. Why?'
'We're going on holiday to America in a few days' time, and I wondered what the weather's been like.'

4 Speaking

Students look at the pictures and word prompts to help them retell the story about Tony Russell. This is an accuracy-based activity, not a fluency-based one. As all the target language is contained in the text, this activity should provide an opportunity to practise and revise it.

Ask students first to do it in pairs. Go round and correct. Finally, ask one or two students to retell the story to the class. You could begin the next lesson by asking for the story to be told once more.

Sample answer

Tony Russell went to Nepal to work in a hospital. The hospital let him have a few days' holiday, and so he decided to go to the jungle. He asked Kamal Rai, a guide, to come with him. They started to prepare at 6 o'clock in the morning. Kamal made Tony wear shoes and trousers to protect him from snakes.

They climbed onto the elephants' backs to get a better view. Suddenly, they saw a tiger, and Kamal told him to be quiet. He (Tony) started to feel very frightened. Just then, the tiger jumped out. Tony looked right down its throat. The tiger grabbed Kamal's leg, but Tony managed to pull Kamal away. Then the elephant ran at the tiger, and Kamal and Tony managed to escape. That night Tony found it impossible to sleep.

● Language review   (SB page 87)

Verb patterns

Read the explanation as a class. Ask students to translate the sample sentences. Encourage them to consult the list of verb patterns on page 143.

Infinitives

Read the explanation as a class. Ask students to translate the sample sentences.

▶ **Grammar reference: page 129.**

Ask students to read the Grammar reference for homework.

> **Additional material**
>
> **Workbook Unit 12**
> Verb patterns – exercises 1–4.
> Infinitives – exercises 5 and 6.
> Apostrophes – exercise 7.
>
> **Pronunciation book Unit 12**
> There is a connected speech exercise on contractions – exercise 3.

SKILLS DEVELOPMENT

● Reading and speaking   (SB page 88)

National heroes

This activity ends with an invitation to students to talk about national heroes from their country. If you want to do this after the reading, it would be a good idea to ask students to think about this and possibly write down some ideas beforehand, so that they have had a chance to gather their thoughts.

Pre-reading task

Read the introduction and discuss the questions as a class. Don't worry if you don't get much response from students. There is no reason why they should have heard of either Robin Hood or King Arthur, except via the Disney cartoons!

> **Note**
> The pictures of King Arthur show swords.
> The pictures of Robin Hood show bows and arrows.

Vocabulary

Students use their dictionaries to match a line in A with a line in B. The aim is to pre-teach certain vocabulary items.

Answers

When you bring up children, you look after them and educate them until they are grown up.
A battle is a fight between soldiers, armies, etc.
If you defeat your enemy, you win a victory over them in a battle.

If you capture someone, you take them prisoner.
If you are wounded in a battle, you are badly hurt.
In medieval times, a knight was a soldier who rode a horse.
You bury someone in a hole in the ground when they are dead.
A tomb is the place where you bury someone.

Jigsaw reading

As usual with jigsaw activities, you need to be careful with your instructions, so that students know if they are A or B, and who they have to talk to at the swapping stage.

Divide students into two groups, and allot them a story to read. Students read and answer the questions. Let them use dictionaries a little if they want, but don't encourage them to overuse dictionaries. It is also important to read and try to understand despite the presence of unknown words.

Notes

The Celts (pronounced /kelts/) were an ancient northern European people. As England was successively invaded, Celts moved away from central England to places such as Wales, Cornwall, and Ireland. Cornwall is the most south-westerly county of England (i.e. bottom left!).

The Saxons were a Germanic people who invaded Britain and other parts of northern Europe in the fifth century AD.

Here is the pronunciation of some of the names:
Pendragon /pen'drægən/
Excalibur /ıks'kælıbə/
Guinevere /'gwınıvıə/
Camelot /'kæməlɒt/
Lancelot /'lɑːnsəlɒt/
Perceval /'pɜːsəvl/
Gawain /'gɑːweın/
Galahad /'gæləhæd/
Modred /'mɒdrəd/
Belvedere /'belvədıə/
Avalon /'ævəlɒn/

Nottingham is a town in the Midlands, in central England. A sheriff was an official with administrative and judicial responsibilities.

Comprehension check

When you feel that everyone is ready, ask students to find a partner from the other group to compare and swap information.

Answers

King Arthur	*Robin Hood*
1 In the twelfth century.	In the fourteenth century.
2 A Celtic leader who fought against the Saxons.	A robber who lived in Sherwood forest with a band of followers.
3 In the fifth or sixth century.	Perhaps in the twelfth century.
4 In a castle at Camelot.	In Sherwood Forest.
5 He was the leader of a group of knights. They had a lot of adventures. They used to hunt, have feasts, and sing. They behaved very correctly.	He had a band of followers. They used to spend time eating, drinking, and playing games.
6 It seems so. He had the right to be king. His knights behaved with respect, honour, and compassion, and they were all treated equally.	Probably. He was an outlaw who stole money, but he robbed the rich to give to the poor. He fought against injustice.
7 Because he became king of England at the age of fifteen, and he fought many battles. He is especially famous because of his Knights of the Round Table. He fought dragons and giants, and went to Rome to fight the emperor.	He is most famous for robbing the rich to give to the poor. He tried to help ordinary people. He used to invite rich people to eat with him, and then ask them to pay for the meal.
8 The Saxons, many lords, the Roman Emperor, Lucius, and his nephew, Modred.	His main enemy was the Sheriff of Nottingham, who was always trying to capture Robin.
9 He was wounded in a fight with Modred. He was taken to the Isle of Avalon. The legend says that he didn't die, but he lives on and will come back when his country needs him.	Some stories say that the Sheriff of Nottingham poisoned him. In his dying moments, Robin shot an arrow, and he was buried where the arrow landed.

When students have read both texts, ask them to find examples of some of the grammar taught in the Presentation section.

Answers

King Arthur
began to appear
managed to pull
went to Rome *to fight* the Emperor
Arthur told Sir Belvedere . . . to throw
Arthur was taken to the Isle of Avalon *to get* better

Robin Hood
began to appear
robbed the rich *to give* to the poor
chose to be
tried to give
inviting them to eat
someone looked in their bags *to see*
Robin asked them to pay for the meal
trying to capture
never managed to do it
asked Little John to bury him

Speaking

1 Answer question 1 as a class.
   ### Answers
   They are both legendary figures. We don't know if they really lived or not. Many stories have been written about them over the years. They were both leaders who tried to fight evil, and who seemed to spend a lot of time enjoying themselves.

2 Ask students to work in pairs or small groups to think of questions to ask you about Florence Nightingale and Amy Johnson. They will probably be able to come up with only three or four. As students have possibly never heard of them, it will be difficult to think of specific questions. When you answer their questions, avoid giving too much information away at once, thus forcing students to ask another question.

Florence Nightingale

She was born in 1820 and died in 1910. She was a British hospital reformer and she founded the nursing profession. When the Crimean War started in 1854, she volunteered to lead a team of nurses working in military hospitals. (The Crimean war was between Russia on one side and Britain, France, and the Ottoman (Turkish) Empire on the other.) She tried to improve the terrible conditions in the hospitals, and she was called the Lady with the Lamp. After the war she established the Nightingale School for Nurses in London.

Amy Johnson

She was born in 1903 and she died in 1941. She was a famous aviator (pilot of a plane). She established several long-distance records with her solo flights to Australia in 1930, to Tokyo in 1932, and to the Cape of Good Hope and back in 1936. In 1932 she married Jim Mollison, another pilot, and they flew across the Atlantic together in 1936. She was killed in an air crash near London.

3 Remember this activity will work best if you ask students to prepare their thoughts and some information beforehand. If you have a multinational class, it should lead to a very interesting discussion. One way of approaching it is to ask each member of the class to say who their (legendary) hero is, and why he/she is famous. This must be very brief. On the board, you can write the names of the students and the names of the heroes. Ask the class to think about which hero they would like to find out about. Then tell them to go and sit next to the student they want to talk to. After five minutes or so, ask them to choose again. This can go on as long as everyone is interested.

4 Answer this question as a class. It's quite a hard question, so don't worry if you don't get much response!
Possible answers
The people in legends are divided into good people and bad people. The heroes are virtuous, honest, and well-loved. They are often larger-than-life characters who become involved in daring adventures. There is often a moral behind the stories, urging us to do good and resist evil.

● Vocabulary (SB page 90)

Adverbs

1 Read the explanation as a class. The rules regarding the order of adverbs in English are extremely complicated, and it is not suggested that you explore this area with your class. (See Swan: *Practical English Usage* pages 23–5 if *you* want more information.)

English word order tends to be more rigid than some European languages, and we do not usually separate a verb and its object with an adverb.

2 Students work in pairs to fill the gaps with an adverb from the box. There are usually just one or two adverbs which are the best answer. Occasionally, several are possible, but don't allow odd combinations such as *read a letter seriously*.
Answers
a. clearly/properly
b. quickly

c. seriously/badly
d. fluently/well
e. quickly/slowly/carefully
f. hard/quickly/carefully/patiently
g. heavily
h. patiently
i. suddenly
j. slowly/carefully
k. carefully/clearly/quickly
l. well
m. properly

Additional material

Workbook Unit 12
There is an exercise on writing a story which further practises adverbs – exercise 11.

-ed and -ing adjectives

1 Ask students to look at the picture, and ask the following questions. The aim is to see how much students know about this area, and to try to elicit the rules.
– *How does she feel?* (Happy)
– *Does she like the book she is reading?* (Yes, she does.)
– *Why?* (It's interesting.)
– *What does the man think of the TV programme?* (He thinks it's boring.)
– *So how does he feel?* (Bored)
Read the explanation as a class.

2 Students work together to put one of the adjectives into each gap.
Answers
a. interesting   e. embarrassing
b. surprising   f. tired
c. tiring   g. bored
d. boring   h. interested

3 Answer question 3 as a class.

Additional material

Workbook Unit 12
There is another exercise on **-ed/-ing** adjectives – exercise 9.

● Listening (SB page 91)

T.34

Pre-listening task
Don't ask students to open their books until you have finished question 2 of this Pre-listening task. This is so that they won't be influenced by the picture of the flying saucer.

1 Discuss question 1 as a class. Depending on your students' interests, they might have a lot or little to say.

2 Ask students to draw a flying saucer. Then ask them to open the book and compare their drawing with the ones on page 91.

3 Read the introduction as a class, then put students in small groups to think of questions. There might be some very odd ones! Get the feedback, making sure that the questions are well-formed, and put the most interesting ones on the board.

Listening for information

T.34

Check that students know the following vocabulary items:
military base   weather forecast   full moon   helmet   visor
shiny   column   high-pitched noise like a scream

Students listen to the interview and put the pictures in the right order. They also have to look out for one mistake in each picture.

Play the tape once and put students in pairs to check the order. Get the feedback. If students aren't sure of the order, don't tell them the answer yet. Ask them to discuss the mistakes, then play the interview again to check both the order and the mistakes.

Answers
Order
a–7   b–5   c–4   d–1   e–3   f–2   g–8   h–6
Mistakes
a. Mr Burton was next to the river when the ship took off, but in the picture he is near the ship.
b. He said he didn't see any controls, but in the picture there are controls.
c. He said there were round windows all the way round the ship, but in this picture there are none.
d. He said there were no clouds, but in this picture there are clouds.
e. He said the first form walked through the wall, but in the picture it is climbing over the wall.
f. He said they both had spaceguns, but in the picture they don't have guns.
g. He said he told no one other than the person from the Ministry of Defence, but in the picture there are journalists and a photographer.
h. He said the light was red, but in the picture it is blue.

Comprehension check
1 Answer this question as a class, referring to the questions on the board.
2 Students do this question in pairs.
    Answers
    He first saw the space ship at one o'clock in the morning.
    He saw a bright light coming towards him at about three hundred feet.
    There was a full moon, so he could see the space ship clearly.
    The two forms stood about five feet away from him.
    They stopped and looked at him for ten or fifteen seconds.
    Their suits were green.
    When they spoke, it sounded like a machine talking, not a person.
    The walls, the floor, and the ceiling inside the space ship were all black.
    The forms told him to stand under the red light.
    He stood under the light for about five minutes, then they told him to turn round. After another five minutes, they told him he could go.
    The space ship took off at about two o'clock.

3 In pairs, students retell the story. You might decide to do this for accuracy purposes, and correct any mistakes accordingly, or for fluency purposes, and not correct.

What do you think?
1 Read this as a class. Ask students in pairs to compare the common ideas about UFOs with Mr Burton's experiences.
    Answers
    – The space ship that Mr Burton saw was round. He said it took off straight into the sky, so perhaps it did fly fast, but he said it made a noise like a scream.
    – He said it was very shiny, but he didn't mention any bright lights.
    – He saw it at night, and it was near a military base.
    – The aliens he saw were small, and they wore tight, one-piece uniforms. He didn't say if they had large heads, and he couldn't see their faces because they wore helmets. They had space guns, but they weren't violent.

2 and 3   Discuss these questions as a class. Again, depending on the interests of your students, this discussion might go on for a good while. You could bring in any current and/or local stories about UFOs, strange happenings, etc.

Speaking
Students work in groups of four to write a short story about an encounter with an alien. You might decide to do this on another day if your class is getting tired of talking about UFOs!

Don't underestimate the amount of time necessary to do this activity thoroughly. Students need time to consider the task, organize themselves, decide who's going to do what, swap ideas and finally write. You might find they have little to say at first, but then they start to get very involved.

Get the feedback. Students could write up their story for homework.

● Everyday English   (SB page 92)

Time

T.35

Ask students what the time is!
1 Read the explanation as a class. Drill the ways of telling the time.

2 Read this together.

3   T.35   Students listen and write down the times they hear. Tell them to write the numbers (3.15), not the words (quarter past three). After the first listening, ask students to compare their answers in pairs, then play the tape again to check.
    Answers

1 3.15	5 11.05	9 6.35
2 9.55	6 14.28/2.28	10 7.45
3 9.50	7 19.40	11 21.30
4 10.25	8 12.15	12 12.30

4 Students practise saying the time shown on the clocks in different ways.
    Answers
    1 seven fifteen/quarter past seven

2 four forty/twenty to five
3 three eighteen/eighteen minutes past three
4 four minutes to nine/eight fifty-six
5 twenty-one thirty/nine thirty in the evening/half past nine
6 five past six in the morning/six oh five (This is unusual. It sounds like a timetable.)
7 ten forty-five at night/quarter to eleven/twenty-two forty-five
8 twenty-five to eight/seven thirty-five in the evening/nineteen thirty-five
9 fourteen forty-two/two forty-two in the afternoon/eighteen minutes to three
10 nine minutes past four/sixteen oh nine/four oh nine (This is unusual.)

5 Students work alone to think of questions to ask each other. When they have four or five, they ask and answer across the room.

To practise this area further, keep asking your class to tell you the time in later lessons!

Don't forget!

Workbook Unit 12
There is a vocabulary exercise on noun formation – exercise 8.
There is a writing exercise on correcting mistakes – exercise 10.

Pronunciation book Unit 12
There is an exercise on the sounds /e/ and /eɪ/ – exercise 1.
There is a word focus exercise on four-syllable words – exercise 2.

Word list
Make sure your students complete the Word list for Unit 12 by writing in the translations.

Video
Section 9 – Report: *The Mini*
This video section supplements Units 11 and 12 of the Student's Book. It is a short documentary about the history and development of the Mini – Britain's most successful car.

Stop and Check   (WB page 64)

It's time to revise the work so far!
A suggestion for approaching the *Stop and Check* section in the Workbook is at the end of Unit 3 of this Teacher's Book.

UNIT 13

Second Conditional – Might – Social expressions

Introduction to the Unit

The title of this unit is 'Dreams and Reality'. There are two Presentation sections. In the first, the dreams of two children, set against the reality of their day-to-day life, provide the context to introduce and highlight the unreality and improbability in the use of the Second Conditional. In the second, twins of different characters, one decisive, one indecisive about the future, are used to introduce **might**.

The Skills Development section contains a dream game which is supposed to help you understand your own character, and a listening where two people of mixed nationality talk about how this has affected their lives.

Notes on the Language Input

Grammar

Remember to remind yourself of the grammar in the unit before you prepare your lessons. A quick way of doing this is to read the appropriate Grammar reference section at the back of the Student's Book.

The Second Conditional

The First Conditional was introduced in Unit 9.

The concept of the conditionals does not seem to cause students as much difficulty as the formation. There are two common problems with this area:

1 The tenses used in the main clause and **if** clause do not seem logical.
2 The complicated structural patterns are difficult for students to manipulate and get their tongues around.

Where the Second Conditional is concerned, the use of a past tense in the **if** clause to express an unreal present or improbable future often strikes students as strange and illogical, especially as in many languages unreality is expressed by separate subjunctive verb forms.

Common mistake

*If I would live in the country, I would have a dog.

The subjunctive has largely disappeared from English, but one last remnant is the use of **were** in all persons of the verb **to be** in the Second Conditional, for example:

*If I **were** rich, I'd buy a new car.*
*If I **were** you, I'd go to the doctor.*
*If he **were** here, he'd know what to do.*

However, nowadays this too seems to be disappearing, and it is equally acceptable to say:

*If I **was** rich, . . .* etc.

The contraction of **would** to **'d** can also be a problem, not only in terms of pronunciation but also because **'d** can also be a contraction for the auxiliary **had** (there is an exercise on this later, in Unit 15, Student's Book page 112, after the Past Perfect has been introduced).

Might

The use of **might** is very common in English but much avoided by learners of English, who often prefer to use *maybe/perhaps + will* to express lack of certainty about the future, for example:

Maybe she will come.
Perhaps I will play tennis this afternoon.

These are not incorrect but it sounds much more natural to say:

She might come.
I might play tennis this afternoon.

We are not suggesting that your students will immediately start using **might** after studying this unit, but we hope their awareness of it will be raised and **might** could eventually become part of their repertoire!

Vocabulary

Students will already be familiar with some multi-word verbs. There are so many in English that it is impossible to study the language for even a short time and not come across some of the more common ones, for example: *put on, take off* (a coat, etc.), *get on, get off* (a bus, etc.).

In the vocabulary section there is a gently-staged introduction to the different types of multi-word verbs. There are four exercises which move from literal use of these verbs to non-literal use and finally to problems of word order.

Everyday English

Some very common social expressions are practised. They are the kind that occur very frequently in any day-to-day English conversation.

Notes on the Unit

PRESENTATION   (SB page 93)

Second Conditional

1 Tell your students to look at the picture of Tanya, and to read the short text about her life as it really is. Check that your students understand *block of flats* and *budgie* and ask them a few questions about Tanya, for example:
– *Where does she live?*
– *What does her Mum do?*
– *What pets does she have?*
– *Does she wear a uniform?*
– *Which tense is used in the text? Why?*

Now ask your students to look quickly at the 'dream' text and ask:
– *What would Tanya like to be?*
– *Is she a princess?*
– *Is it probable that she will be princess?*
Use the questions to establish that she is dreaming about being a princess, it is not real and not probable, unlike the first text.
Now ask your class to read the 'dream' text more carefully and then ask them to work with a partner and compare the verb forms in the two texts.

● Grammar questions   (SB page 93)

Go through these with the whole class to establish the form and use of the Second Conditional.
Answers
– The Present Simple.
– No she doesn't live in a palace, she lives in a block of flats. The palace is a dream. **lived** is Past Simple.
– This is a dream; her grandmother looks after her.
  Also ask here:
  What is 'd short for?
– The Second Conditional is formed with **if** + the Past Simple tense, the auxiliary verb **would** + the infinitive without **to**.

2 This exercise is very controlled so as to give students practice at manipulating the structures involved. First model some of the sentences yourself, breaking them into two halves to do it. You could do it as a chorus drill and then ask individuals to repeat:
If I were a princess,
I'd live in a palace.
If I lived in a palace,
I'd have servants.
I wouldn't go to school.

> **Note**
> Take care with the pronunciation of the following:
> *were*. It is weak /wə/, but if it is followed by a vowel, the *r* is pronounced /wər/.
> *wouldn't* /wʊ(d)nt/. The grouping of the consonants can be difficult for many students, and the /d/ sound almost disappears.

Now ask them to work in pairs and take it in turns to practise saying the sentences in Tanya's 'dream' text.

3 Check the vocabulary before asking your students to read the texts about Graham.
chauffeur, *(to play) polo*, and *peacocks* might not be familiar. Ask your students to work on their own, and then check their answers with a partner.
Answers
If were a prince, I'd (would) live in a castle. I *wouldn't live* in a cottage. My Dad *would be* king, and my Mum *wouldn't work* in a pub. A chauffeur *would drive/take* me to school. I *would play* polo on a white horse. I *would have* peacocks in my garden. I *wouldn't have* chickens.
Go through the answers with the whole class.

4 Do the first part of this exercise a.–e. with the whole class, asking several individuals to give you the answers.

> **Note**
> Short positive answers cannot be contracted.
> *Yes, she'd* is wrong. *Yes, she would* is right.
> This should not really be a problem to students, as they will already be familiar with the short answer in
> *Would you like a coffee? Yes, I would./No, I wouldn't.*

Answers
a. Her Mum/mother would.
b. No, she wouldn't.
c. No, she wouldn't. (She'd have a governess.)
d. Yes, she would. (She'd have a white horse.)
e. She'd wear a long dress and a gold crown.

Put the students into pairs and ask them to go through the first part of the exercise again (a.–e.). Then they do the second part (f.–j.), asking and answering the questions orally. Some students might want to write out the questions and answers as well. This is fine; but ask them to do that after the oral work.
If Graham were a prince is the condition behind all the questions.
Answers
f. Would he live in a cottage?
   No, he wouldn't. (He'd live in a castle.)
g. Would his mother work in a pub?
   No, she wouldn't.
h. Who would take him to school?
   A chauffeur (would).
i. What sport would he play?
   (He'd play) polo.
j. Would he have chickens?
   No, he wouldn't. (He'd have peacocks.)
Go round and check and help the pairs before conducting a full class feedback.

PRACTICE (SB page 94)

1 Grammar

These are very controlled exercises to give further practice. It is a good idea to vary doing them as written and spoken.

1 Ask students to do this orally in pairs (there is a similar exercise in the Workbook that they could write for homework). Ask them to make the most natural sounding sentences.

Answers

If I found some money in the street, I'd keep it.

If I were president of my country, I'd build more schools and hospitals.

If I were taller, I'd try to get a job as a policeman.

If I knew the answer, I'd tell you.

If I had a lot of money, I'd buy a big house.

If I had a car, I'd give you a lift.

If I didn't eat cakes and ice-cream/so much, I'd lose weight.

If I didn't smoke so much, I'd feel better.

> **Note**
> It is important to point out to students that the sentence parts can be reversed and the main clause can equally well come before the **if** clause, for example:
> *I'd lose weight if I didn't eat so much.*
> *I'd give you a lift if I had a car.*
> Notice that there is no comma when this happens.

2 Ask students to do this on their own and then compare with a partner before you check through the exercise with the whole class.

Answers

a. If I *were* rich, I'*d travel* round the world.

b. I don't like Hollywood. I *wouldn't live* there if I *were* a film star.

c. I *would go* to work if I *didn't feel* so ill, but I feel awful.

d. What *would* you *do* if your baby *fell* into the water?

e. If I *had* more free time, I *wouldn't waste* it. I'*d learn* another language.

3 Ask everyone in the class to write down one way of finishing each sentence. Then ask different students to read them out and compare their ideas.

Sample Answers

a. . . . I'd have a party/I'd give it away/I wouldn't spend it all.

b. . . . I wouldn't be in this class/my teacher would faint!

c. . . . I'd go to the beach/I'd play tennis/I wouldn't have to study.

> **Note**
> Take care with answers to **c.** because the idea lends itself to the production of continuous as well as simple sentences, for example:
> *. . . I'd be lying on the beach.* (at this moment)
> Don't be tempted to go into this. Restrict the lesson to simple sentences.

2 Speaking

The aim here is for some less controlled speaking practice. It will probably be quite a short activity.

Put the students into pairs or small groups to discuss the situations, but don't worry if there is only a limited response. Students are often reluctant to exercise their imagination at these moments. One or two ideas for each situation is fine. It will be a bonus if discussion ensues.

Sample ideas

I wouldn't tell my mother, I'd wear the sweater, then I'd take it off when I was away from home.

I would say that I was allergic to that food. I'd ask for some bread and butter.

I wouldn't talk to him, I'd go to my neighbour's house and I'd ring the police.

I don't know what I would do. If the thief were old or poor, perhaps I wouldn't do anything.

Bring the class together to share some of the ideas.

● Language review (SB page 94)

Second Conditional

First ask everyone to turn to page 67 and read the review of the First Conditional, and then compare that with the review of the Second Conditional and notice the difference between a possible and real condition in the first and an impossible and unreal condition in the second.

Put students into small groups to translate the sentences. These aim to highlight differences between L1 and English. This will be especially apparent with those languages that have a subjunctive mood for expressing unreality.

▶ **Grammar reference: page 130.**

Ask students to read this at home perhaps before they do some of the Workbook exercises for homework (see below).

> **Additional material**
>
> **Workbook Unit 13**
> These exercises could be done in class as further practice, for homework, or in a later class to revise.
>
> The Second Conditional – exercises 1–5.

> **Note**
> At this point you might like to take a break from grammar and move forward to the Reading and speaking activity on page 96, before doing the grammar presentation of **might** on page 95.

PRESENTATION (SB page 95)

Might

1 This introduction to **might** also provides a good opportunity to revise the Present Continuous and **going to** for future plans and arrangements.

Alan and Mike are twins with very different personalities: Alan is decisive and already has clear plans for his future. Mike is indecisive and has some ideas but is not sure what he wants to do.

Ask your students to look at the pictures of the two boys. Say:
– *They are twins, but do they look the same or different?*
– *How do they look different?*

Read the introduction aloud to your students and then get them to read first about Alan.
Pause at this point and ask some questions about him:
– *What's he doing/going to do in the summer? October? After university?*

Now ask your students to read about Mike and then in pairs to answer the Grammar questions.

● Grammar questions   (SB page 95)

Answer the Grammar questions as a class.
Answers
– Alan is sure, Mike isn't sure.
– Alan uses the Present Continuous and the *going to* future because his plans are already made.
– Mike uses *might*.
Ask your students what **might** *expresses*. (an uncertain future action)
Ask for examples of sentences with **might** from the text.

2 Students remain in their pairs to do this very controlled practice, which also aims to illustrate that **might**, like all modal verbs, remains the same in all persons.
Answers
a. Alan is going to university to study business and marketing.
b. After university, he's going to work in the City with his father.
c. Mike might go to university but he isn't sure.
d. He might travel around the Far East.
e. He might become a teacher.
f. He might do a course to teach English.
Check through the answers with the whole class.

PRACTICE   (SB page 96)

1 Speaking

This aims to give further controlled practice of **might**.
Read aloud the example question and answer with your students.
Answers
a. A What sort of car are you going to buy?
    B I don't know/I'm not sure. I might buy a Ford, or I might buy a Honda.
b. A Where are you going on holiday?
    B I'm not sure. I/we might go to America, or we might go to India.
c. A What colour are you going to paint the bedroom?
    B I don't know. I might paint it blue, or I might paint it yellow.

d. A What are you going to have?
    B I'm not sure. I might have the steak, or I might have the fish.
e. A What are you going to do on/for your birthday?
    B I don't know. I might go to the theatre, or I might invite a few friends round.
Go through the sentences, getting pairs of students to act out the questions and answers to the whole class.

Finally there is a short and freer personalized activity. Students take it in turn to ask their partner:
What are you doing/going to do after the lesson? etc.
If the partner is sure the answer is:
I'm going to . . . or *I'm . . .ing . . .*
If the partner is not sure the answer is:
I'm not sure/I don't know. I might . . .

2 Grammar

These two exercises bring together all the grammar points in this unit.
1 You could do this as a quick oral reinforcement activity with the whole class, or you could ask your students to work on their own and underline the correct answers, then check with a partner before you conduct a feedback session.
Answers
a. *We're having* lamb. It's in the oven.
b. *It'll be ready* before your TV programme.
c. . . . he *might be* late. It depends on the traffic.
d. I don't know yet. *I might go* into town.

2 Ask students to do this in pairs.
Answers
a. If I *had* a car, I'd give you a lift.
b. They *might* call the new baby Victoria, but they aren't sure yet.
c. My sister would visit us more often if she *didn't* live so far away.
d. I *might* play tennis tomorrow, but I'm not sure.
e. If I *was/were* younger, I'd (*would*) learn to play the piano, but I'm too old now.
Check through the answers with the whole class. For b., d., and e. ask:
– *Why is it wrong?*

● Language review   (SB page 96)

Might

Read this all together and translate the sentence.

▶ **Grammar reference: page 130.**

Ask students to read this at home before doing some of the Workbook exercises for homework (see below).

Additional material

Workbook Unit 13
These exercises could be done for homework, or in a later class to revise.

Might – exercises 6–8.

SKILLS DEVELOPMENT

● Reading and speaking (SB page 96)

The dream game

Pre-reading task

These personalized questions are designed to set the scene for
the activity and to promote a short discussion.

Divide the class into small groups. You could introduce the task
by answering the questions yourself first and telling them a little
about your dreams. Then ask the students to work through the
three questions in their groups and to make a note of any
interesting points or ideas. Go round the groups and note
anything interesting that you hear, so that you can draw attention
to it when you have the feedback.

Conduct a short feedback session with the whole class and tell
them they are going to play a game which is designed to help
them know themselves better!

Playing the dream game

Ask the students to remain in their small groups. Tell them that
they can use their dictionaries to check unfamiliar words, but
there should not be very many of these.

1 Ask them to read and discuss the introduction. There should
   be few difficulties with vocabulary here.

> **Note**
> In some languages the word *fantasy* is the same as
> *dream*. In English a fantasy is a product of the
> imagination when awake not asleep.

After a short while, ask the whole class a few questions, for
example:

– *Do you know people who seem to remember dreams well?*
– *Did you know that we dream every one and a half hours
  throughout the night? Do you believe this?*
– *Do you ever behave badly in dreams?*
– *Do your dreams 'melt' when you wake?*
– *Do you think that images in dreams have special meaning?*

2 Now ask the students to play the game. They take it in turns
   to read aloud the six questions. They write down their ideas
   and then compare them.
   Before moving on to 3, bring the class together for some
   feedback on the different answers to the questions.

3 Students read the interpretation and try to analyse their
   answers. They should say if they think it is a true description
   of their personality. Go round the groups and encourage ideas
   if necessary.

4 Bring the whole class together and ask for opinions on the
   interpretations. Ask:
   – *Do you agree with the interpretation of yourself? Why?*
   – *Do you agree with the interpretation of the others in your
     group? Why?*
   If you have played the dream game yourself, you could at this
   point tell your class how you answered the questions and ask
   if they agree with the interpretation of you, their teacher!

> **Additional material**
> **Workbook Unit 13**
> Vocabulary – exercise 9. This is an activity that practises
> vocabulary such as *go to sleep*, *snore*, *set the alarm*, *wake
> up*, and *get up*. It might be a nice idea to do this after all
> the discussion about dreams – if you can keep awake!

● Vocabulary (SB page 98)

Multi-word verbs

(sometimes called phrasal or prepositional verbs)

Students will have already met quite a few multi-word verbs
because they are so common in English. These four exercises are
staged in such a way as to illustrate some of the different types
of multi-word verbs and to show that they can have both literal
and non-literal (idiomatic) meaning.

> **Note**
> Here for your information is a description of the types. We
> do not suggest that you pass on this information to your
> students, but it is useful to remind yourself of the types so
> that you can deal with any queries that arise.
> There are four types:
>
> Type 1 – verb + adverb (no direct object)
> *The plane **took off**.*
> *We **sat down**.*
> (This type is not highlighted for students in these exercises
> although examples appear.)
>
> Type 2 – verb + adverb + direct object
> *He **put on** his hat/**put** his hat **on**. He **put** it **on**.*
> *She **looked up** the word/**looked** the word **up**. She **looked** it
> **up**.*
> *I **turned off** the light/**turned** the light **off**. I **turned** it **off**.*
> The adverb can change position, but not if the object is a
> pronoun.
> (These are highlighted in exercise 3.)
>
> Type 3 – verb + preposition + object
> *He **fell down** the stairs. He **fell down** them.*
> *She's **looking for** her purse. She's **looking for** it.*
> *He **looked after** the baby. He **looked after** her.*
> The preposition cannot change position.
> (These are highlighted in exercise 4.)
>
> Type 4 – verb + adverb + preposition + object
> *Anna doesn't **get on with** her husband. She doesn't **get on
> with** him.*
> *Billy's **looking forward to** Christmas. He's **looking
> forward to** it.*
> (These also appear in exercise 4 because the adverb and
> preposition cannot change position.)

1 Read through the examples with your students to make sure
   they have an idea what is meant by a multi-word verb.
   Ask them to do this exercise on their own. Stress the point
   that the words in this exercise are used literally and therefore

they should be able to work out the answers quite logically and easily.
Tell them that one of the words is used twice.

Answers

a. on	d. up	g. back
b. down	e. away	h. out
c. down	f. off	i. round

Ask them to check their answers with a partner, and then go through the answers quickly with the whole class.

2 Read through the introduction and make clear that the difference between this exercise and the previous one is that here the multi-word verbs have a non-literal, idiomatic meaning. In other words you cannot work out the meaning logically from the parts. The two examples should illustrate this.

Ask them to work in pairs to discuss the answers and tell them that they can check their ideas in their dictionaries.

> **Note**
> Tell your students to be careful when looking up multi-word verbs, as many of them have more than one meaning. For example:
> *pick up* can also mean *get better/improve* or *give someone a lift in a car*; *bring up* can also mean *vomit*.
>
> Do not be tempted to start discussing all the uses! This would be very confusing. These exercises do not aim to 'tell all' about multi-word verbs, just to provide an introduction.

Answers

a. I saw 50p on the pavement and I *picked it up* = literal. I *picked up* Spanish quite easily = non-literal. It means to learn informally.
b. *Put out* your cigarette = non-literal. It means to extinguish. In Britain we always *put out* the milk bottles = literal.
c. I *looked up* the road = literal. She *looked up* the word = non-literal. It means to search/look for a word or a piece of information in a reference book.
d. Could you *bring up* my bag = literal. She *brought up* three children = non-literal. It means to rear or educate.

3 This and the next exercise aim to highlight and practise problems of word order with multi-word verbs.
Do all of this exercise with the whole class together.
Read aloud the introduction and the instructions for the exercise.
Go through the exercise asking individuals to change the sentences to 2 or 3. Say:
*Maria do **a.** 2, please.* Maria: *I threw his letter away.*
*Peter do **a.** 3, please.* Peter: *I threw it away.*

Answers

a. (as above)
b. 2 I took back the shoes . . .
   3 I took them back.
c. 2 Could you look the phone number up, please?
   3 Could you look it up, please?
d. 2 Don't forget to switch off the lights.
   3 Don't forget to switch them off.

e. 2 Turn down the radio!
   3 Turn it down!
As your students get the idea you can dot around between the sentences and give them a speedy manipulation drill.

4 Follow the same procedure for this exercise. Use the introduction to highlight the difference between the verbs in this exercise, where no changes of word order are possible, and the one before, where there are changes of word order.

Answers

a. 2 I'm looking for it.
b. 2 Can you look after it/him/her?
c. 2 I'm looking forward to it.
d. 2 John doesn't get on with her.

> **Additional material**
>
> **Pronunciation book Unit 13**
> Connected speech – multi-word verbs + linking – exercise 3.

● Listening   (SB page 99)

T.36a and b

People of mixed nationality

> **Note**
> You could do T.36b as a jigsaw activity if you prefer, following the procedures for jigsaw listening activities described in Unit 1 of this Teacher's Book.

Pre-listening task

1 These nationalities have been chosen because they appear in the listening texts. Ask students to do this in pairs or small groups.
   Answers

French	I'talian
'Polish	'Russian
Chi'nese	Ma'laysian
Portu'guese	West 'Indian

Check through the answers with the whole class.

> **Note**
> You could practise the pronunciation of these nationality adjectives at this point, particularly Chi'nese and Portu'guese, with the stress on the last syllable. However, if you do, do it quickly so that you can get on with the listening activity. There is a special exercise on stress in nationality adjectives in the Pronunciation book. This is cued at the end of this activity.

2 Ask your students to continue working in pairs or small groups to discuss these questions. The aim is to set the scene for the listening, so don't worry if there is only a short discussion.
   Possible ideas

Advantages   appearance, languages, food, travel, knowing two cultures, etc.
Disadvantages   attitudes of other people, confusion of identity, etc.

Go round and help the discussion if necessary but do not conduct a full class feedback at this point.

3 | T.36a |

Play the introduction to the programme and ask students to read and listen at the same time.
Now conduct some class feedback on 2. Ask for examples of friends and relatives, and any advantages and disadvantages of being of mixed nationality.

Listening and note-taking

| T.36b |

Play the tape of Amélia de Melo, the textile designer. Tell your students that the notes should be very brief, single words not sentences.

Answers about Amélia

Nationality of parents:	Father – Malaysian-Portuguese Mother – Polish
Languages she can speak:	English, Polish
Advantages:	not boring, two homes, two cultures, dancing, food, appearance (eyes)
Problems:	only one – at school, girls joked about her eyes
Life now:	married to an Englishman, lives in London, visits Malaysia often, might go to Poland (next summer)

Ask students to compare notes, and discuss their answers with a partner. (If your students have found the tape difficult, you could at this point play it again and they could check and fill out any gaps in their answers.)

Play the second part of the tape about Lionel Varley.
Repeat the procedure as for Amélia.

Answers about Lionel

Nationality of parents:	Mother – French Father – West Indian (Dominican)
Languages he can speak:	English, French
Advantages:	being bilingual, visits to France and Dominica, French food
Problems:	only one – at school, children called him (and a Chinese boy) names
Life now:	going to move to New York, married to an Italian-Russian

Get feedback on both Amélia and Lionel.

Comprehension check
Ask students to do this in pairs about both Amélia and Lionel.
Answers
1 Amélia's parents met when they were students in London. Lionel's parents also met in London.
2 Amélia lived in both London and Malaysia. Lionel lived in Bristol.
3 Lionel has visited both France and Dominica. Amélia has only been to Malaysia; she hasn't been to Poland yet.
4 Lionel went to Dominica because his father spoke about flowers and sunshine. He didn't feel at home there. He felt there were not the same opportunities (to be an architect?).

5 Because New York is very cosmopolitan.
6 She and her husband might go to Poland.
7 Amélia is married to an Englishman. Lionel is married to an Italian-Russian.
Bring the class together to go through the answers.

What do you think?

Possible answer
1 Probably not, because of all the advantages listed above.
2 and 3 These two questions will hopefully personalize the issue and generate some discussion. They should also lead to some free practice of the Second Conditional, but don't labour this! The main aim is free speaking.

Additional material

Pronunciation book Unit 13
Word Focus – word stress in countries and nationalities – exercise 2.

● Everyday English (SB page 100)

Social Expressions

| T.37 |

1 Ask students to work in pairs to do this.
   Answers
   a. A *I hear* you're going to get married soon. *Congratulations!*
      B *That's right*, next July. July 21st. Can you come to the wedding?
      A *Oh, what a pity!* That's when we're away on holiday.
      B *Never mind*, we'll send you some wedding cake.
      A That's very kind.
   b. A *Good heavens!* Look at the time! *Hurry up*, or we'll miss the train.
      B *Just a minute*, I can't find my umbrella. Do you know where it is?
      A *I've no idea*. But you won't need it. It's a lovely day.
      B *OK*, I hope you're right. Let's go.
   c. A *Good luck* in your exam!
      B *Same to you*. I hope we both pass.
      A Did you study all last night?
      B *No, of course not*. I watched TV and went to bed early. *What about you*?
      A I did the same. *See you later*, after the exam.
      B All right. Let's go for a drink.
   d. A I passed!
      B *Well done!* I failed.
      A *Bad luck!* What went wrong?
      B I'm always very nervous in exams, and this time I was very nervous *indeed*.
      A Oh, *I see*. Well, all I can say is *better luck next time*.

2 | T.37 | Play the dialogues and pause after each for students to check their answers.
   After each one ask the pairs to practise saying that dialogue together.

At the end of all four allocate a pair for each dialogue to read and act it for the whole class. Ask the other students to comment on the pronunciation. You could play the tapes again at any point to establish a good model.

Don't forget!

Workbook Unit 13
There are two exercises on writing, including one on formal and informal letters – exercises 10 and 11.

Pronunciation book Unit 13
There is an exercise which brings together all the sounds and practises the phonemic script – exercise 1.

Word list
Make sure that your students complete the Word list for Unit 13 by writing in the translations.

Video
Section 10 – Situation: *Introductions*
This video section supplements Unit 13 of the Student's Book. In it, David takes Paola to meet his parents. Students practise meeting new people and making introductions.

UNIT 14

Present Perfect (2) – Telephoning

Introduction to the Unit

The theme of this unit is giving news and expressing change. These topics lend themselves to practice of the Present Perfect Simple to express the present result of a past action. In the second Presentation, the use of the Present Perfect Continuous is examined.

In the Skills Development section, there is a reading text about changes in international air travel, and the listening activity provides further practice of the Present Perfect.

Notes on the Language Input

Grammar

Present Perfect Simple

In Unit 7 two uses of the Present Perfect Simple were practised, one to express experience and one to express unfinished past. In this unit a third use is introduced, which is to express the present result of a past action.

Your students should be familiar with the form of the Present Perfect by now, but it is most unlikely that their production of the tense is accurate. This is for the reasons mentioned in the teaching notes to Unit 7. Although a similar form of **have** + the past participle exists in many other European languages, its use in English is dictated by aspect (i.e. how the speaker sees the event), not necessarily time. The Present Perfect is probably the most difficult tense form for learners to master, and it is not an exaggeration to say that this process takes years.

However, this is not to say that nothing can be done to help! If students can be shown how the tense is used in context, and where it is *not* used, their understanding will gradually increase. There is a case for saying that you are *always* teaching the Present Perfect. When a student makes a mistake, you might decide to remind your class of the rules. If an interesting example occurs in a reading or listening text, you might decide to draw their attention to it. This is not to say that you should correct *every* mistake. Students would become very frustrated! But seeing the tense in context, again and again and again, is the only way that their familiarity with this tense will increase.

Present Perfect Continuous

Many of the above comments are true of the Present Perfect Continuous, too. This tense is sometimes introduced idiomatically in first year courses, and in this unit of *Headway Pre-Intermediate*, it is not examined in any great depth. This is because the subtleties of it are too complex for the level. There are two aspects which students have to perceive, the perfect aspect and the continuous aspect, and it is unreasonable to expect them to be able to do this immediately. As it is a continuous verb form, there are more 'bits' for students to get wrong!

Common mistakes of form

*I been learning English for three years.
*I've learn English for three years.
*I've been learn English for three years.

The concepts expressed by the Present Perfect Continuous are often expressed by either a present tense verb form in other languages, or by a form of the Present Perfect Simple. Many languages (quite sensibly!) dispense with the need to express the ideas inherent in the continuous aspect, but English has it, and where it is possible, prefers to use it. *I've been learning English for three years* sounds much more natural than *I've learned English for three years*. But *I've lived here all my life* sounds better than *I've been living here all my life*, because of the temporariness expressed by the continuous aspect.

When the Present Perfect is used to refer to an activity with a result in the present, it can be very difficult to know whether to use the simple or the continuous. *I've painted the bathroom* and *I've been painting the bathroom* refer to the same action, but mean very different things. The first refers to a completed action, but the second refers to a recent activity which may or may not be finished. The area is further complicated by the fact that, if a completed quantity is stated, the Present Perfect Simple must be used, not the Continuous. This is because of the idea of activity in progress expressed by the continuous aspect.
I've written three letters today.

Common mistakes of use

*I learn English for three years.
*I've been knowing her for a long time.
*I've been writing three letters today.
*I'm hot because I've run.

It is for the above reasons that the Present Perfect Continuous is dealt with lightly in this unit!

105

Vocabulary

There are exercises on word families and shifting stress as a word changes class (for example, from noun to verb).

Everyday English

In this section, using the telephone is practised in both formal and informal situations.

Notes on the Unit

PRESENTATION (SB page 101)

Present Perfect Simple

T.38a

> **Note**
> We suggest you ask students to read the Grammar section for homework *before* you begin the presentation. Ask them to spend five or ten minutes on it, and tell them not to worry if they don't understand it all. They won't!

1 Read the introduction as a class, and look at the pictures. Ask students how the Present Perfect is formed.

2 T.38a Read the introduction. Students listen and answer the questions. Ask them to do this in pairs before giving the answers yourself.
  Answers
  a. I've moved to Paris.
     I've found a job that I like.
     I've got engaged.
  b. He's gone to South America.
  c. She's bought a flat there.
  d. They've retired. They've bought a house on the south coast.
  e. He's lost weight.
  Drill the above sentences around the class, paying attention to contractions and sentence stress. Correct any mistakes.

● Grammar questions (SB page 102)

Answer the Grammar questions as a class.
Answers
– No, he's in London.
– Yes, he is. *I've been to Paris* expresses an experience sometime in my life. (I went to Paris and came back (home).) *He's gone to South America* expresses a past action with a result in the present. (He is not here now.)
– No. He has just finished. *Just* means a short time before.

3 Students work in pairs to talk about Tom's news.
  Answers
  He's lost weight.
  He's stopped smoking.
  He's cut off his beard.

He's bought a new car.
He's moved to London.

> **Additional idea**
> Choose five students, and ask them to look very carefully at the room and the people in it for about fifteen seconds. Send them out of the room. Ask the other students to do something to make the room different. Here are some examples:
>
> | | |
> |---|---|
> | clean the board | take off a jumper |
> | open the window | put a chair on a desk |
> | change seats | put the tape recorder on the floor |
> | turn on the light | sit the teacher in a student's chair and |
> | put on a coat | vice versa |
>
> Ask the five students to come back in. They must say what has changed.
> *You've cleaned the board.*
> *Peter has put a coat on.* etc.

PRACTICE (SB page 102)

1 Speaking

1 Students work in pairs to say what has just happened in the pictures.
  Answers
  1 They've just had a crash.
  2 The plane's just taken off.
  3 He's just woken up.
  4 They've just had a meal.
  5 He's just given her some flowers.
  6 He's just finished reading a book.
  7 She's just planted a tree.
  8 He has just cleaned the car.
  9 He's just scored a goal.
  10 She's just written a letter.
  You could drill these sentences for pronunciation practice.

2 Read the introduction as a class. Check that students understand *already* and *yet*.
  Students work in pairs to practise the sentences.
  Answers
  They've already booked the hotel for the reception.
  They haven't ordered the cake yet.
  They haven't sent out the invitations yet.
  They've already booked the church.
  They haven't decided where to go for the honeymoon yet.
  They've already ordered the flowers.
  Jean-Pierre has already hired a suit.
  Angela hasn't bought a dress yet.
  They haven't ordered the champagne yet.
  They've already bought the wedding rings.

2 Grammar

1 Students work in pairs to match a line in A with a line in B. Ask them to choose the best one.
  Answers
  Joe's happy because he's just had some good news.

Richard's sad because his girlfriend's gone away on business.
Tim's worried because his daughter hasn't come home yet
and it's after midnight.
Malcolm's excited because his wife's just had a baby.
Ken's annoyed because he's just burnt the meal.

2 Students work in pairs to complete the sentences.
   Answers
   a. Mary's crying because she has just had some bad news.
   b. John's laughing because someone has just told him a joke.
   c. My parents are furious because I have lost the car keys.
   d. I'm fed up because someone has stolen my bike.

● Language review   (SB page 103)

Present Perfect Simple

Read the Language review as a class. Ask students to translate
the sample sentences. Make sure students translate for concept,
not for form. *I've lost my wallet* and *I lost it yesterday* will
probably be translated into the same tense in your students'
language(s).

▶ **Grammar reference: page 131.**

Ask students to re-read the Grammar section for homework.

Additional material

Workbook Unit 14
Present Perfect Simple – exercises 1–4.

Note
Your students might be tired of doing accuracy work at
this point. You might decide to do some fluency work, for
example, the reading on page 105, and do the second
presentation afterwards.

PRESENTATION   (SB page 104)

Present Perfect Continuous

T.38b

Note
Ask students to read the Grammar section on the Present
Perfect Continuous for homework before beginning this
presentation.

As was explained in the Notes on the language input, the
Present Perfect Continuous is dealt with relatively lightly
in this unit. It is unrealistic to expect students to perceive
all the differences of meaning between the simple and the
continuous, and the perfect aspect will continue to present
problems.

---

1 T.38b Students read and listen to the dialogue at the same
time. You could ask students to practise it in pairs.
You could highlight the form of the Present Perfect
Continuous by writing *I've been studying* on the board and
asking the following questions:
What is the name of this tense?
How is it formed?

2 Students work in pairs to complete the sentences. Point out
that **have** changes to **has** in the third person singular. You can
anticipate that some students will get the last question wrong,
as they think that all sentences require the continuous.
   Answers
   b. He's been working . . .
   c. He's been going round . . .
   d. He's been writing . . .
   e. He has written . . .

● Grammar questions   (SB page 104)

Ask students again how the Present Perfect Simple and the
Present Perfect Continuous are formed, then ask students to do
the Grammar questions in pairs. The second question is difficult,
and you might decide to discuss it in L1 if possible.
Answers
– Sentences a.–d. have examples of the Present Perfect
  Continuous. Sentence e. contains an example of the Present
  Perfect Simple.
– Sentence d. is more interested in the activity; sentence e. is
  more interested in the quantity.
At this point, you might want to have some controlled oral
practice of the Present Perfect Continuous. Play the dialogue
(T.38b) again, and ask students to say *Stop!* when they hear an
example of the Present Perfect Continuous. Stop the tape and
drill the example around the class. Pay attention to the weak
form of **been** /bɪn/ or /bn/.

● Language review   (SB page 104)

Present Perfect Continuous

Note
The Language review comes before the Practice section in
this presentation. This is to try to give the students some
rules 'to hang on to' before they are asked to recognize
and produce the new form.

Read the explanation of the two uses as a class. If you can use L1
to translate *state* and *activity*, so much the better.
Ask students to translate the example sentences. Make sure they
translate for meaning, not form. In many European languages,
all three verb forms will be expressed by a present tense.

▶ **Grammar reference: page 131.**

Ask students to re-read the Grammar section for homework.

PRACTICE (SB page 104)

1 Grammar

1 Students work in pairs or small groups to choose the correct verb form. Do the first one as a class to serve as an example. Expect students to make mistakes with this exercise, and tell them not to worry. As you correct, remind students of the rules.

Answers

Correct forms

a. *has Angela been living* (because the activity began in the past and continues to the present)

b. *has found* (because this is a completed activity – the action of *finding* doesn't last a long time, unlike *look for*)

c. *has gone* (because he's there now)

d. *bought* (because we have a definite time – a few months ago)

e. *has she known* (because *know* is a state verb, not an activity, so it cannot go into the continuous)

f. *has been working* (because he is still working as a postman)

g. *has visited* (The continuous is not possible because the quantity (ten) is stated.)

h. *has been travelling* (The sentence is stressing the activity, not the distance travelled.)

2 Read the introduction to this exercise as a class. You might decide to do the whole exercise as a class, thus reducing error (and resultant frustration). Drill the questions as you go through.

For question e., go to a student who you know plays a particular sport.

Answers

a. have you been learning
b. have you been using
c. did you have
d. have you known
e. have you been playing
f. did you start

2 Speaking

Read the introduction and look at the example sentence as a class. Students work in pairs to make a sentence about the people.

Sample answers

2 She's got paint on her clothes because she's been painting the bathroom.

3 His back hurts because he's been digging the garden.

4 He's got dirty hands because he's been mending his car.

5 He's wet because he's been doing the washing-up.

6 They're tired because they've been playing tennis.

7 Her eyes hurt because she's been studying.

8 He's got red cheeks because he's been cooking.

9 They have no money because they've been shopping.

Additional material

Workbook Unit 14

Present Perfect Continuous – exercise 5.

Present Perfect Simple or Continuous? – exercise 6.

SKILLS DEVELOPMENT

● Reading and speaking (SB page 105)

Pre-reading task

1 You could discuss the first questions as a class, rather than immediately putting students into groups. It can be interesting to hear about other people's likes and dislikes.

Put students in groups to discuss the remaining questions. Let this go on for as long as they seem interested, then get the feedback.

2 Read the definitions together. You could ask students to translate the words to check the meaning.

Reading

Read the introduction as a class. Students read the text and fill each gap with one of the words in the box.

Allow adequate time for this. Before you have a class feedback, ask students to check their answers in pairs.

Answers

a. approaching
b. jumped
c. become
d. jammed
e. tops
f. grown
g. built
h. seen
i. operating
j. shares

Comprehension check

Students work in small groups to answer the questions. There are quite a few, so you could break up the group work after about five minutes to get the feedback, then ask students to continue.

Answers

1 a.–5   c.–2   e.–1   g.–6
   b.–3   d.–4   f.–7

2 That in the early days of international aviation, flying was very simple and unsophisticated, compared to the glamorous image presented by airlines these days.

3 The crew are all very smart. Someone welcomes you on board. You are directed to your seat. The crew sometimes bring you a newspaper, and something to eat and drink. On an international flight, they ask if you want to buy any duty-free goods. In the flight described here, the crew were not particularly well-dressed, and they showed no interest in the passengers. When the boy wanted to get off, he didn't have any steps. He had to jump down.

4 Being able to travel by plane has made the world seem a smaller place. Countries which seemed a long way away can now be reached within hours.

5 It has more international flights and passengers than any other airport. In 1989, it handled 355,000 flights, over 38 million passengers and 57 million items of luggage. It is like a city, employing 53,000 people.

6 It is a very busy place, where people from all over the world can be seen. There are also all different kinds of people, rich and poor, honest and dishonest.

7 (If the statements are false, ask students to say why.)
The writer took a plane for the first time in 1959. True
He was impressed by the crew's uniforms. False (They weren't well-dressed.)
The pilot and stewardess worked together in the cockpit. False (They were probably kissing.)

The stewardess hadn't put her make-up on properly. False (Her lipstick was smudged because she was kissing the pilot.)
The plane suddenly stopped to let a boy off. True
Since then, air travel has developed and improved. True
It has become easy to fly all over the world. True
O'Hare, Haneda, and Kilimanjaro are busy airports. False (Kilimanjaro is very quiet.)
Heathrow has more international flights than any other airport. True
It was built in 1944. False (It was *begun* in 1944, which isn't really the same as saying it was built in 1944, which suggests it was finished then. In fact, it is still being built.)
The first international flight from Heathrow was to Argentina. True
Heathrow has become successful because of its geographical position. True (The suggestion is that the statement is true, although it could be argued that this is a 'chicken and egg situation'. Perhaps Heathrow got bigger as it became more successful, not the other way round.)
It has problems because it isn't big enough. True

You could end this activity with a discussion about a memorable flight, or about where students would like to fly to and why.

● Vocabulary (SB page 108)

Word families and word stress

1   These activities take longer to do than you might think. Students have to use their dictionaries to find the new word and its stress pattern. You also need to allow time for adequate pronunciation practice. You could do exercises 1–3 in class, and ask students to do 4 and 5 for homework. Read the introduction as a class. Students work in pairs to put the words in the correct row.

> **Note**
> In some languages, the word *discussion* means an argument. You could ask your students:
> – *In a discussion, are people friendly and happy?*
> – *What's the difference between a discussion and an argument?*
> In longer words, it is important to make the main stress strong, so that in comparison, the other syllables are unstressed. The most common sound in unstressed syllables is the schwa /ə/, of which there are many in the words in the box.
> Many learners of English find it hard to pronounce the word *advertisement*. They want to put the stress on the third syllable. The situation is further confused by the stress on the verb (*advertise*) being on the first syllable.

Answers
1   argument   government
2   discussion   existence   invention   computer behaviour
3   celebration   disappearance
4   discovery   authority   advertisement   development
5   accommodation
When you have the answers, ask several students to say the words, and correct any pronunciation mistakes.

2   Students use their dictionary if necessary to write in the verbs. They will probably have to do this on a separate piece of paper.
Answers
1   'argument/'argue   'government/'govern
2   dis'cussion/dis'cuss   ex'istence/ex'ist   in'vention/in'vent   com'puter/com'puterize   be'haviour/be'have
3   cele'bration/'celebrate   disa'ppearance/disa'ppear
4   dis'covery/dis'cover   au'thority/'authorize   ad'vertisement/'advertise   de'velopment/de'velop
5   accommo'dation/a'ccommodate
Again, it would be useful to practise the pronunciation of these words. You could ask students to say them to each other in pairs. Get some feedback to check that their pronunciation is good.

3   Students put the words in the box on the correct row.
Answers
1   scientific
2   reliable
3   determined
4   comfortable   generous   valuable
5   technological

4   Students use their dictionaries to write in the noun.
Answers
1   scien'tific/'science
2   re'liable/relia'bility
3   de'termined/determi'nation
4   'comfortable/'comfort   'generous/gene'rosity   'valuable/'value
5   techno'logical/tech'nology
Get some practice of these words, paying careful attention to stress.

5   Students work in pairs to fill the gaps.
Answers
a. active   f. daily
b. acting   g. useless
c. Hopefully   h. useful
d. carefully   i. noisy
e. careless   j. famous

● Listening and speaking (SB page 108)

T.39

Phoning home
This activity takes quite a while to do, as there are several parts to it. Students first listen to one side of a telephone conversation between Justin and his mother. They only hear Justin. Then they work in pairs to imagine what his mother said. Finally they hear the complete conversation.
Because students have to think what the mother said, they need time to understand the nature of the activity. They then use the clues and their imagination to complete the conversation.
The conversation contains many examples of the Present Perfect Simple and Continuous.
This will provide students with further exposure to these two tenses, but when students are trying to imagine the mother's side of the conversation, it is not expected that they will always use

the tenses accurately. When they have heard the complete conversation, you can draw their attention to the tenses.

Read the introduction together. If you have a multinational class, ask them if students in their country usually move to another part of the country when they go to university.

Listening

1 | T.39a | Before they listen, ask students to read the statements at the top of page 109. Check that there are no problems of vocabulary. Students listen to Justin's side of the conversation.

> **Note**
> Justin refers to a Chinese takeaway. This is a meal that you buy in a Chinese restaurant and then take home to eat. It is slightly cheaper than eating in the restaurant.

Students work in pairs to decide if the statements are true or false. If they are false, ask students to say why.

Answers
a. True
b. False (It was last Thursday.)
c. False (He doesn't want to talk about it.)
d. True (But Justin thinks he has told his mother about her.)
e. True
f. False (She is studying the same course as Justin, which sounds like business studies.)
g. True
h. True
i. False (It ends on the thirteenth.)
j. True

2 If you think this activity might be too difficult for your class, you could give them a copy of the tapescript. Working from the written word would be easier than working from the spoken word. Make sure you give them the tapescript *without* the mother's words!
Students work in pairs or small groups to imagine what his mother said. Tell the class that his mother's phone number is Bedford 21698.
It is very important that you stop the tape at the right moment, so that students can work out from Justin's replies what his mother said. It doesn't matter whether they get the exact words, as long as their suggestions are logical.
Do the first four or five gaps as a class, so that students see what they have to do. Stop the tape after *It's me, Justin.* Ask *What did his mother say?* (Something like *Hello*, or *Bedford 21698.*)
Play the tape, and stop after *but I'm really tired.* Ask *What did his mother say?* (It has to be *How are you?*)
Play the tape, and stop after *I've been studying really hard.* This one is more difficult as there are several possibilities. Ask for suggestions. You could prompt with *Justin said he was tired. Perhaps his mother wants to know why. Why are you tired?* is a possibility. You could prompt with *What about a question with* **What . . . doing?** to try to get *What have you been doing?* (Students will probably offer *What are you doing?*, which isn't really appropriate.)
Play the tape, and stop after *I don't want to talk about it.* Ask
– *What did his mother say?* Students have to refer back to

Last Thursday to work out that it must be a question with *When?* Prompt if necessary with *Justin says 'We had our **first one.'** First what?* If you think students have got the idea by now, play the rest of the conversation, stopping at the following points:
I've known her for ages. (This part of what Justin says is very long. If you waited until he finished, students wouldn't remember the beginning.)
You're going to Geneva.
Oh, that's not too long.
. . . gardening and cricket.
Term ends on the thirteenth.
Thanks, Mum.
I need all the luck I can get.
Have a good time in Geneva.
If you feel your class is motivated, you could put the pairs into groups of four to compare their ideas before they listen to the complete conversation.

3 | T.39b | Students listen to both sides of the conversation, and compare their ideas. This could be done as a class. You will need to be careful when accepting or rejecting the students' suggestions. Try to correct their ideas for content and logic rather than language, as this is more of a fluency activity (both listening and speaking) than accuracy.

Roleplay

Depending on how you and your class feel after the listening activity, you might want this roleplay to last a short time or a long time, or you might decide to do it on another day. Here is a possible approach, which is best done on another day.

Photocopy the complete tapescript, 39b. (You could begin by using part of the tape as a dictation.)
Ask two students to start reading the text. Stop after *Oh – what have you been doing?* Ask students:
– *What tense is this?* Ask the two readers to carry on, and ask the rest of the class to say *Stop!* when they find an example of the Present Perfect Simple or the Continuous.

Read the introduction to this activity in the Student's Book. Put the question *What have you been doing?* on the board. Remind students that it is last Sunday evening, and ask for some possible answers.
I've been watching TV.
We've been playing football.
I've been cooking.

Be careful with the suggestions you accept. The Present Perfect Continuous will not always be the right tense.
We've just had a meal.
I went to a party last night.

Ask for some other questions you might ask, and put them on the board.
What have your parents been doing?
What did you do last night?
Did you go out?

Ask students to work in pairs to have a chat on the telephone. Finally, ask one or two pairs to have their conversation again so everyone can hear.

● Everyday English   (SB page 109)

Telephoning

| T.40 |

> **Note** You need to photocopy tapescript 40 to do this exercise, and sufficient role cards for your class. They are on page 112 of the Teacher's book.

1 Tell students the following information about phone numbers in England.
   Telephone numbers are said one by one. We don't put two together as many languages do. 71 is *seven one*, not *seventy-one*.
   0 is prounced /əʊ/.
   Two numbers the same are usually said with *double*, for example, *double three*.

   Practise the telephone numbers first as a class, then in pairs. This is to establish a correct model. Try to get a pause after each group of numbers.
   Example
   071 (pause) *927* (pause) *4863*

2 | T.40 | Students listen to the tape and answer the questions. Ask students to check their answers in pairs, then have the feedback.
   Answers
   1 Peter is speaking to John.
      John wants to borrow a squash racket.
      They know each other well.
   2 A (Swiss) girl speaks first to a telephonist, then to Ann Baker.
      The girl wants some information about English classes.
      They don't know each other.
   3 Jim speaks to a friend of Mike's.
      Jim wants to speak to Mike, but Mike isn't in.
      Jim doesn't seem to know the man he talks to.

3 Read through the expressions and sentences as a class. Drill them around the class. *Hold on. I'll connect you* is what a telephonist says when he or she is putting you through to the extension you want. *Hold on* means *Wait*.
   We say *Speaking* when someone asks to speak to, say, Mrs Black, and *you* are Mrs Black.
   Give out the tapescript and ask students to practise the dialogues in pairs.

4 There are six role cards. **A** works with **B**, **C** with **D**, and **E** with **F**. Make sure you get your sums right when you are deciding how many copies to make! Every **A** needs a **B**, every **C** needs a **D**, and every **E** needs an **F**. If you have an odd number of students, you will have to take a role yourself. Give out the cards and let students prepare on their own. Say you will give them a role card which tells them who they are and who's phoning who. On each one, there are decisions to be made. Give an example from **A**'s card: *You are at home. It's 7.00 in the evening. What are you doing? Watching TV? Reading? Doing your homework?*
   When you feel students are ready, ask the **A**s to find a **B**, the

Cs to find a **D**, and the **E**s to find an **F**. They can do the roleplay standing up. Remind them that **A**, **C** and **E** must start the conversation.
When they have finished, ask two or three pairs to do their roleplay again in front of the class so everyone can hear. It's a nice idea to put two chairs back to back when doing this, so students can't see each other's lips and have to rely on what they hear.

> **Additional material**
> **Pronunciation Book Unit 14**
> There is an intonation and stress exercise on giving phone numbers and addresses – exercise 3.

> **Don't forget!**
> **Workbook Unit 14**
> There is a vocabulary exercise which revises many of the multi-word verbs students have met in *Headway Pre-Intermediate* – exercise 7.
> There are two writing exercises – exercises 8 and 9. Students are asked to write a formal or informal letter.
>
> **Pronunciation book Unit 14**
> There is an exercise on the sound /h/ – exercise 1.
> There is a word focus exercise on words with silent letters – exercise 2.
>
> **Word list**
> Make sure your students complete the Word list for Unit 14 by writing in the translations.
>
> **Video**
> Section 11 – Report: *The Village*
> This video section supplements Unit 14 of the Student's Book. It is a short documentary showing how life has changed in rural Britain over the last 50 years.

STUDENT A

Phone number: 322 4987

Information

You're at home. It's 7.00 in the evening. You're watching TV. You've already done your homework. It was the vocabulary exercise on page 108 of *Headway Pre-Intermediate*.

Decision

What are you doing for the rest of the evening? Going out? Staying in?

The phone call

Your friend B, who's in the same class as you, is going to phone.

When the phone rings, pick it up and say your number.

STUDENT B

Information

You're at home. It's 7.00 in the evening. It's time to do tonight's English homework, but you have a problem. You've forgotten what it is, and you've left your copy of *Headway Pre-Intermediate* at school.

You're going to phone your friend A, who's in the same class.

Decision

What are you doing for the rest of the evening? If you need to borrow a copy of *Headway Pre-Intermediate*, could you go round to A's house? What time?

The phone call

Phone A. A will start the conversation. Ask *How are you?* and have a little chat before you ask about the homework. Say *I've forgotten what tonight's homework is. Do **you** know?*

STUDENT C

Phone number 899 0452

Information

You're Mr/Mrs Carr, and you're English. You live in London. Your address is 22, Hill Road, and your house is about ten minutes from Highgate tube station, which is on the Northern Line.

It's 7.00 in the evening. You're at home. Today is the 18th. Next week, on the 25th, Student D, Daniel/Denise, from France, is coming to stay at your house while he/she learns English for a month, but you don't know how he/she is travelling to London, or what time he/she expects to arrive.

Decision

Are you going to meet D if he/she comes by plane? What about if he/she comes by train?

The phone call

D is going to phone you. When the phone rings, pick it up and say your number. Ask questions such as *How are you?*, *Have you packed yet?* At the end of the conversation, say *We're looking forward to meeting you.*

STUDENT D

Information

You're French, and your name is Daniel/Denise. You live in Paris. Today is the 18th. Next week, on the 25th, you're going to England for a month to learn English. You're going to stay with Mr and Mrs Carr, who are English. They live in Highgate, which is in North London, but you don't know the exact address.

You're going to phone them to tell them how you're travelling, and what time you expect to arrive.

Decision

How are you going to travel? By plane? By boat and train?

What time does the plane/train arrive?

Do you want Mr/Mrs Carr to meet you?

If you are going to get the tube to their house, you need to ask *Which is the nearest tube station?*

The phone call

Phone C. C will start the conversation. Say *I'm phoning to tell you how I'm coming to London.* Don't forget to ask for the address.

STUDENT E

Phone number 622 9087

Information

You're at home in your flat, which you share with a girl called Marion. It's 7.00 in the evening.

Marion is out at the moment.

Decision

Where is Marion?

When will she be back?

Do you know what she's doing tonight, or not?

The phone call

Someone is going to call. When the phone rings, pick it up and say your number. If it's for Marion, Say *Can I take a message?*

STUDENT F

Information

It's 7.00 in the evening. You want to talk to a friend of yours called Marion. It's very important. You've found a second-hand car that you think she'd like to buy.

Decision

If she isn't in, are you going to leave a message?

Are you going to phone back later, or do you want Marion to phone you?

Are you in for the rest of the evening, or are you going out?

The phone call

Phone Marion. The other person starts the conversation.

Photocopiable

UNIT 15

Past Perfect – Reported statements and questions

Introduction to the Unit

The theme of this unit is love. In the first presentation, students read an extract from a popular romance, and examine the Past Perfect in relation to the Past Simple. In the second presentation, reported statements and questions are practised. The link between the Past Perfect and reported speech is that the Past Perfect is used in reporting past tense verb forms.

In the Skills Development section, students read a nineteenth-century parable, and talk about parables from their own country. This is a potentially interesting topic, especially in a multilingual group. Make sure you give your class adequate advance warning so that they have time to think of some. In the listening activity, students hear an Elvis Presley song, *The girl of my best friend*, and just for fun they are asked to write a love poem!

Notes on the Language Input

Grammar

Past Perfect

All perfect tenses (Present Perfect, Past Perfect, and Future Perfect) express the idea of an action being completed before a certain time. The Present Perfect expresses an action completed before now; the Past Perfect expresses an action which happened before another action in the past. Neither the form nor the concept of the Past Perfect present learners with any great difficulty, and there are equivalents in many European languages. There are none of the complexities of use that confront students with the Present Perfect.

However, students still need to perceive the relationship between the Past Simple and the Past Perfect, and to understand when the latter tense is needed to show one action finished before another one started. There is also the problem that **'d** is the contracted form of both **would** and **had**, and there are exercises to practise this in the Student's Book and the Pronunciation book.

Reported statements and questions

Tense usage in reported speech is relatively straightforward and logical, and comparable systems exist in many European languages. Students need to perceive the mechanics of 'one tense back'. This unit does not go into areas such as *here* changing to *there*, and *yesterday* changing to *the day before*, or any of the occasions when the verb form does *not* shift one tense back in reported speech.

In reported questions, word order can present problems. **Do/does/did** are not used, and the word order is the same as for a statement.

Common mistakes
*He asked me how did I feel.
*She asked me what did I want?
*I asked her where was she going.

Vocabulary

The two pairs of verbs **bring** and **take** and **come** and **go** are practised in the first vocabulary exercise. They are easily confused, and learners need to perceive that the correct choice depends on whether the movement is towards or away from the speaker.

Common mistakes
*I'm going to bring my books back to the library.
(Spanish student in London) *I come home next month.

The area can seem quite complicated when you meet examples such as *We're going to the cinema tonight. Do you want to come?*, but in fact the rules are being followed. It is a matter of not only where the speaker is, but where he/she *will be*.

In the second vocabulary exercise, **get** to express some sort of change is practised, for example, *get married, get wet, get lost*.

Everyday English

As this is the final activity in *Headway Pre-Intermediate*, the Everyday English section practises different ways of saying goodbye.

Notes on the Unit

PRESENTATION (SB page 110)

Past Perfect

> **Note**
> This is probably the first time your students have been formally introduced to the Past Perfect, although they may well have come across it in their reading, and it has been used occasionally in previous units of *Headway Pre-Intermediate*. You might want to present the tense yourself before beginning this unit. Here is one possible deductive approach.
> Write the following two sentences on the board.
> *When we arrived, Anna made some coffee.*
> *When we arrived, Anna had made some coffee.*
>
> Ask students the following questions:
> *What are the tenses in the first sentence?* (both Past Simple)
> *Which action happened first, **we arrived** or **Anna made** some coffee?* (we arrived)
>
> You could ask similar questions about the second sentence if you think students might know the answer, or you might choose to tell them.
> *In the second sentence, **had made** is the Past Perfect. It is used to show that one action happened before another action in the past. So in the second sentence, Anna made some coffee before we arrived.*
> *The Past Perfect is formed with the auxiliary verb **had** and the past participle.*
>
> You could put the following time-line on the board.
>
>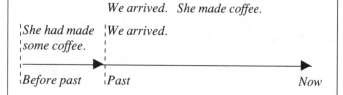
>
> We arrived.   She made coffee.
>
> |She had made |We arrived.
> |some coffee. |
>
> |Before past |Past   Now

Introduction: Ask students to look at the picture on page 110, and tell them they're going to read part of a popular romance. Ask:
What sort of things happen in such stories?
1 Ask one student to read version **A** out loud, and then another student to read version **B**. Put students in pairs to compare the two versions. They might immediately spot that in version **B** the Past Perfect is used, or they might manage something such as *the order is different*, which is fine.
2 The aim of this exercise is to show students how the Past Perfect can be used to change the order in which events are given in a story.
Read through version **A** again, and look at the box (in the right-hand column) at the same time. Draw students' attention to the column of numbers 1–8, which show that the events are given in chronological order.

Read the instructions to this exercise as a class, and do one or two of the sentences together as an example. Then put students in pairs to complete the exercise.

Answers	**B**
Marsha and Felix met.	(2)
They fell in love.	(3)
They got married.	(1)
Felix moved into Marsha's flat.	(5)
Marsha told her parents.	(4)
They were angry.	(6)
Felix met another woman.	(8)
The marriage started to go wrong.	(7)

3 Students work in pairs to write the verb forms from version **B** on the line in the box.

Answers

had met	told
had fallen	were
got married	had met
had moved	started

When you have checked the answers, drill the sentences that contain examples of the Past Perfect. Pay careful attention to the weak form of **had**. After vowel sounds it becomes /d/. After consonants, it becomes /əd/.
they'd /ðeɪd/
Felix had /fiːlɪks əd/

4 Do this exercise as a class.
Answers
a. True
b. False (He had already moved in.)
c. True
d. False (The marriage started to go wrong because he had met another woman.)

● Grammar questions (SB page 111)

Answer the Grammar questions as a class. You might have to explain *chronological order*, which is referred to in the second question.
Answers
– Past Simple
– True
– *had* + the past participle
– It expresses an action which happened before another action in the past.

PRACTICE (SB page 111)

1 Speaking

1 Students work in pairs to tell the story in the pictures. Stress the fact that they must do this first in chronological order. Ask *What tense will you use?* The answer is the Past Simple.
Sample answer
Felix packed his suitcase. Then he wrote Marsha a letter and left the flat. Marsha arrived home and saw the envelope on the mantlepiece.

Now ask students to tell the story again, beginning at picture 4.

Sample answer

When Marsha arrived home, Felix had already packed his case. He had written Marsha a letter and had left the flat. She saw the envelope on the mantlepiece.

2 Students work in pairs to make sentences from the chart. Do one or two as a class to serve as an example.

Answers

I was late for work because my alarm clock hadn't gone off.
My teacher was angry because I hadn't done the homework.
The house was in a mess because we hadn't tidied up after the party.
My leg hurt because I had fallen over playing tennis.
I was hungry because I hadn't had any breakfast.
The plants died because we had forgotten to water them.
I went to bed early because I had had a busy day.
I apologized because I had been rude the day before.

2 Grammar

Students work in pairs to discuss the difference in meaning between the verb forms.

Answers

a. *was packing*	He was in the middle of packing.
packed	He packed when/as soon as Marsha arrived home.
had packed	His suitcase was already packed when she arrived home.
b. *started*	The concert started when/as soon as we arrived.
had started	We were late!
c. *climbed*	First the police arrived, then the robber climbed out of the window.
had climbed	First the robber climbed out of the window, then the police arrived.
was climbing	He was in the middle of climbing out.

3 Listening and pronunciation

T.41

Read the introduction as a class.

T.41 Students listen to the sentences, and put a tick if the sentence contains an example of the Past Perfect.

Answers

The following are the sentences which contain an example of the Past Perfect.

a. d. g. i. j.

4 Reading and grammar

Students work in pairs to put the verbs in brackets into the correct tense. They can finish the story in class or for homework.

Answer

Marsha read Felix's letter and then she walked slowly into the kitchen. She had bought his favourite food for dinner. She threw it in the rubbish bin. Why had he done this to her? She remembered how happy they had been in the beginning. They had laughed a lot then. Marsha felt desperate.
One hour later the phone rang in the flat. It was Marsha's parents, but she didn't answer the phone. She . . .

● **Language review**

Past Perfect

Read the explanation as a class. Ask students to translate the sample sentences.

▶ **Grammar reference: page 131.**

Students read the Grammar reference for homework.

Additional material

Workbook Unit 15
Past Perfect – exercises 1–4.

Pronunciation book Unit 15
There is a connected speech exercise on the contraction **'d** – exercise 3.

Note
Your students might be tired of doing accuracy work, and might prefer to do some fluency work before beginning the second presentation. You could do the listening activity on page 117.

PRESENTATION (SB page 112)

Reported statements and questions

1 Ask students to look at the direct statements in the left-hand column. Read them out one by one, and ask students to identify the tense. Then look at the reported statements on the right and do the same. If your students ask, say that **would** is the past form of **will** only in reported speech.

Answers

Present Simple	Past Simple
Present Continuous	Past Continuous
Past Simple	Past Perfect
Present Perfect	Past Perfect
Will future	Past of *will*

● **Grammar questions** (SB page 113)

Answer the Grammar questions as a class.

Answers

– Tenses move 'one back'.
– Both the Past Simple and the Present Perfect change to the Past Perfect.

2 As a class, look at the four examples of direct and reported questions, then answer the Grammar questions.

Answers

– There is no question mark in reported questions.
– In direct questions, the subject and verb are inverted (and

– *do/does/did* are used), but in reported questions there is no inversion.

– *If*

Now ask students to complete the chart with the four reported questions. You could point out that *ask* can also have an indirect object.

She asked me how many cigarettes I smoked.

Answers

He asked me if I liked whisky.

She asked me why I was laughing.

She asked where John had gone.

He asked who Anna had met.

PRACTICE (SB page 113)

1 Grammar

Students work in pairs to report the statements and questions.

Answers

a. Jim said (that) he loved Anna.

b. Anna asked Jim if he loved her.

c. She said she was leaving on Sunday.

d. He asked her where she was going.

e. Sue said that Mr Walker had phoned before lunch, but he hadn't left a message.

f. Miss Wilson asked if there had been any messages for her.

g. He said he didn't think it would rain.

h. Mary asked Jim why he hadn't told Anna the truth.

2 Speaking

T.42

In pairs, students read the report of the interview, and then write the actual words in direct speech.

The answer can be found in the tapescript.

● Language review (SB page 114)

Reported statements

Read the explanation as a class. Ask students to translate the sample sentences.

Reported questions

Do the same.

▶ **Grammar reference: page 131.**

Students read the Grammar reference for homework.

Additional material

Workbook Unit 15

Reported speech – exercises 5–8.

SKILLS DEVELOPMENT

● Reading and speaking (SB page 114)

In the pre-reading task, students are asked to talk about a parable or fable from their own country. For this to work well, they need time to prepare. Make sure you give enough warning, so students can do some thinking and some research, if necessary.

Pre-reading task

1 Students work in groups to tell each other some parables or fables. Make sure they understand what a *moral* is, i.e. the lesson about life that a story teaches us.

2 Check that students understand the title of the story. Ask students to think of some things they could do if they had the ability to turn back the clock. They might be able to think of just one or two things, or if they get the idea, they might come out with a lot of ideas.

Reading

Students read the story up to line 30 and answer the questions. They are asked not to worry about any words they don't know, because there is an exercise on guessing meaning later.

Comprehension check

Answers

1 Once.

2 First he made his wife think that it was only because the beautiful lady had a dog that he didn't try to kiss her. Then he admitted that he had thought she was beautiful, and had had to resist temptation.

3 She was furious at his first explanation, and even more furious at his second.

Students work in pairs to work out a possible ending. Allow enough time for this. It might take a few minutes for ideas to come. Get the feedback, then ask students to read the two possible endings. See if *their* endings are similar, then answer the **What do you think?** questions.

What do you think?

Answers

1 (No set answer)

2 There are several ways of interpreting the stories. The moral of the first ending could be that the best way to deal with people is with flattery and deceit. You should tell people what they want to hear even though it is wrong. A weaker interpretation is that it is better not to hurt people sometimes by telling a 'white lie'. The moral of the second ending is that it is impossible to please some people, and so you shouldn't worry about them, and you should do what *you* want to do. The story is probably about dealing with your husband or wife rather than people in general.

Vocabulary

Read the introduction as a class. Ask students to try to work out the meanings. Some words they will know because they are similar to words in their own language, and some they will not be able to guess at all. Stress that guessing the meaning 100 per cent often isn't necessary, 50 per cent is usually enough. And of course, you can say that the best advice when you're reading and you come across a new word is to ignore it, which is what we do in our own language.

Do the first two or three as a class. If you get no response, give large hints such as the following:

regretted – He repeated the event, so it must be something to do with not liking what he had said or done.

in the light of experience – *Light* can have a metaphorical meaning of understanding or knowing, so it means *with the understanding of what he had done.*

a barn – some kind of building outside, maybe a farm building

seeking – wanting, looking for

downpour – you pour liquids, so maybe this is another word for rain, perhaps heavy rain

suspicious – not sure about, worried about, didn't believe

hurt – He is angry that his wife doesn't believe him.

to resist temptation – Temptation is wanting to do something you know you shouldn't, so maybe resist means something like *fight.*

an immoral deed – The sentence should show that *deed* means *action.*

flung – His wife was very pleased, so *flung* must mean *put* or *threw.*

● Vocabulary   (SB page 116)

Bring/take and *come/go*

1 Read the explanation as a class.

Do the first couple of the questions together, then ask students to work in pairs.

Answers
a. going   going   taking   come   bring
b. bring   going
c. come   brought
d. come   bring
e. go   take
f. going   coming   bringing   take

Get

Read the explanation and look at the pictures as a class. Ask students to fill the gaps in pairs.

Answers
a. got wet
b. getting married
c. got divorced
d. get very angry
e. getting more and more difficult
f. getting late
g. get ready
h. get worried
i. got lost

● Listening and writing   (SB page 117)

A love song

T.43

Pre-listening task
Read the introduction as a class.
1 Answer this question together. Prompt if necessary, by saying
A man is singing about his best friend's girlfriend.

Is his best friend a boy or a girl?
Why is he singing about his girlfriend?
Do you think he likes her?
Do you think he loves her?
So what is the problem?
What can the singer do about it?

2 Students look at the words in the box to identify those that rhyme. Several of the words appear in the song.

Note
End is both a noun and a verb. In the song it is used as a verb, meaning *to finish.*
Students will know the word *face* as a noun, but in the song it is used as a verb, meaning *to look at.*
Lies has two meanings, *to lie on the ground* and *to not tell the truth.* In the second meaning, *lie* can also be a noun, *to tell a lie.*
Part has two meanings. The noun means *a bit.* The verb means *to separate.*
Tears has two meanings and two pronunciations. In this context, the pronunciation is /tɪəz/ and rhymes with fears.

Answers
bad – sad
heart – part
end – friend – mend – pretend
eyes – lies
face – place
fair – hair
fears – tears
forever – never
June – moon
kiss – miss
pain – rain
talks – walks
together – weather

3 Ask students to write a poem and not to worry about the quality! Make one up yourself to give them an idea, or read this one.
I feel so sad.
My life is bad.
I'll love her forever.
I can't tell her – no, never.
I met her in June.
Under the moon.
My love will never end.
My broken heart will never mend.

4 Listen to everyone's poem!

Listening
1 Students try to put a word from the box into each gap. Help them by giving them the first one, *walks*, or mime it for them to guess. Pointing out the rhymes will help. (*Happiness* and *kiss* do not really rhyme.)

2 The singer has an American accent. Unfortunately, it is not Elvis Presley singing.
   T.43   Listen to the song. Students check that their words are the same.
   Answers
   walks   talks   pretend   hair   fair   end
   tell   hold   arms   face   kiss   mend

3 If you and your class like singing, off you go!

● Everyday English (SB page 118)

Saying goodbye

| T.44 |

1   Students work together to match a picture and a caption.
    Answers
    1–c.   2–e.   3–h.   4–g.
    5–b.   6–a.   7–d.   8–f.

2 | T.44 | Students listen to the sentences, and practice
    saying them.

Don't forget!

Workbook Unit 15
There is a vocabulary exercise on words that are often
confused, for example, *say/tell, lend/borrow* – exercise 9.
There are two writing exercises – exercises 10 and 11.
Students are given the beginning and ending of a story,
and are asked to write the middle.

Pronunciation book Unit 15
The sounds /əʊ/, /ɔː/, and /ɒ/ are practised – exercise 1.
Exercise 2 practises words that look as if they have more
syllables than they actually do when pronounced, for
example, *chocolate*.

Word list
Make sure your students complete the Word list for Unit
15 by writing in the translations.

Video
Section 12 – Situation: *Farewell*
This video section supplements Unit 15 of the Student's
Book. In this situation, Paola and David say good-bye to
his parents, and then go to Padstow harbour for an
emotional farewell scene. Students practise saying goodbye.

Progress test
There is a Progress test for Units 10–15 on page 154 of the
Teacher's Book.

Stop and Check   (WB page 78)

It's time for the final revision.
There is a suggestion for approaching the *Stop and Check*
section in the Workbook at the end of Unit 3 of this Teacher's
Book.

Tapescript section

Unit 1

Tapescript 1a

▶ The student Rob Fellows

Hello! My name's Rob Fellows. I come from Dundee, a town on the east coast of Scotland, but I'm a student at Durham University, in the north of England. I'm studying French and German, and I can speak the languages quite well. I also know a little Spanish, so I can speak four languages. I'm enjoying the course a lot, but it's very hard work!
I live in Durham Castle, because the Castle is part of the University, with about thirty other students. The course started two years ago, and I'm in my third year. After the course I'm going to work in France, but I don't know where yet.

Tapescript 1b

▶ The student Maggie Wood

My name's Maggie Wood. You spell that W-O-O-D. I come from Australia. I'm studying art, but I don't go to university. I work at home. I watch special programmes on television. I'm reading about Italian painters at the moment in Italian, which is difficult because I only speak a little Italian. The course is really interesting, but it isn't easy having a part-time job and studying!
I live near London. I came to England fifteen years ago. I'm married, and my husband's name is Dave. He's a taxi-driver. We have three children, two boys and a girl.
My course started a year ago, and it's three years long. After the course I'm going to look for a job as a librarian in a museum.

Tapescript 2a

▶ Leaving home – David Snow talking about his daughter

My daughter Jackie is living in London now. We're very worried about her, really. London is such a dangerous place for a young girl. She's only eighteen, and London's so far away. Her mother went down to see her there, but I don't like London.
I don't know why she went there. I think she has some friends there. She says she wants to be a dancer, and she's doing a sort of course, a ballet course or something, but dancing isn't a real job, and you don't earn much money being a dancer.
She's living in a flat in north London – with her boyfriend, I think, and we don't like that at all. We've never met the boyfriend – Tony, his name is. He doesn't have a job.
I think she's earning some extra money working as a dancer in a theatre or club in the centre of London, but I'm not sure. I hope it's a nice place. I do worry about her. London is such a big place. I'm sure she wants to come home, really. She phones home sometimes, but not very often, and when we phone her she's always out. We *are* her parents, and I know we're important to her, but it still makes me sad.

Tapescript 2b

▶ Leaving home – Jackie Snow talking about her life in London

I came to London two months ago because I want to be a professional dancer, and the best schools of dance are here in London. I'm doing a course at the National Dance School, which is very hard work, but I'm really enjoying it. The course is expensive, but I work with a theatre group at the weekend. We teach dance to groups of children. I'm living with another girl in a flat in north London. It's small, but it's comfortable. My boyfriend, Tony, lives in the same street with his parents. They're very kind, and often cook meals for me.
I know my parents are worried about me living in London, but it isn't dangerous at all if you're careful. It's so exciting here, there's so much to do and see. It was difficult in the beginning, especially getting to know the Underground, and I didn't know many people, but it's fine now. I have a lot of good friends. I love my Mum and Dad very much, but I don't want to live at home for the rest of my life. I phone home every Sunday, and when I go to a museum or art gallery, I always send them a postcard. Mum reads them, but I don't know if Dad does.

Tapescript 3

▶ Social English

Hello, Jane!
Hi, Peter!

How are you?
Fine, thanks.

See you tomorrow!
Bye!

Good night!
Sleep well!

Good morning!
Good morning!

Cheers!
Good health!

Excuse me!
Yes. Can I help you?

(Someone sneezes) Bless you!
Thanks.

Have a good weekend!
Thanks! Same to you!

Thank you very much indeed.
Not at all. Don't mention it.

Make yourself at home.
That's very kind. Thank you.

Unit 2

Tapescript 4

▶ An interview with Emma

I = Interviewer
E = Emma
I Hello, Emma. Thank you for agreeing to do this interview, especially as I believe you're studying for your exams at the moment.
E Yes, I am. But I'm happy to do the interview.
I Now, the questions. First of all, where do you come from?
E Oxford, in England.
I And where do you live?
E At home with my mother. You see, my parents are divorced.
I Oh! I'm sorry about that. Erm . . .have you got any brothers or sisters?
E Yes, I have. I've got a brother.
I Is he older than you?
E No, he's younger. He's twelve.
I And what's he doing at the moment?
E Well, he's either playing football or watching TV. That's what he always does after school.
I And where does your father live?
E He lives in Scotland, near Edinburgh.
I How often do you see him?
E Well, we see him quite often. We spend every school holiday with him.
I Now a final question, Emma. What do you do in your free time?
E I listen to music, especially pop music.
I That's great, Emma. I've got all the information I need. Thank you very much.

Tapescript 5

▶ Life in a Japanese school

P = Presenter
G = Graham Grant
P Hello and welcome to this week's *Worldly Wise*, the programme that looks at the world we live in. Today we have with us Graham Grant. Graham is now back working in England, teaching Japanese, after two years teaching English in Japan. We want to find out from him about life in a Japanese school.

Graham – we all know that education is important in every country, but they say that in Japan it is even more important. Is this true?

G Well – yes – I think it *is* true, erm ... for lots of reasons, but I think there is one main reason.

P What is that?

G I think it's the Japanese attitude to jobs.

P Surely a good job is important to most people?

G Yes, of course, but in er ... this country, er ... Britain, for example, I think many people expect to, and ... er ... perhaps want to, try more than one job in their lives. You can try lots of things until you find the right job. In Japan it's different. Most jobs are for life. People usually stay with the same company from the time they leave school or university until they retire. So the children must do well at school to get a good job when they leave, because after that it's too late.

P Doesn't this mean that they have to work hard?

G Yes, it does. The hard work starts at twelve when they leave primary school and move to junior high school.

P What happens there?

G Well, the atmosphere is different from primary school. It's less relaxed and more competitive. There are about forty pupils in each class, and discipline is quite strict. The pupils sit in rows, and before each lesson they stand up and bow to the teacher, just as all Japanese people bow to each other when they meet. Politeness and respect are very important in Japan. The teacher talks and the children listen and take notes. They don't ask questions. It's considered rude to question a teacher.

P It sounds different to many English schools.

G Yes, it is. And another difference is that they go to school on Saturday too, so they have six days of school a week. They also go to special extra schools in the evening, so they're busy most of the time. And they have three or four hours' homework every night.

P Phew! They must love the holidays!

G Yes, they do, but they don't have much holiday. They go back to school because that's when they have club activities – sports clubs, art clubs, English clubs.

P This is all really interesting, Graham, but it's time for a final and important question. Do they like school?

G Well, that's a question I often asked them and they all said the same. 'Yes, we like school because we have no time to be bored, and we love all the club activities.'

P How very interesting! I think English schools could learn something from Japan. Thank you for talking to us, Graham. I must ring home now and check that my daughter is doing her homework and isn't watching television!

Tapescript 6a

▶ Numbers

a. Sixteen
b. Fifty
c. There are eighteen people outside.
d. I paid ninety pounds for this coat.
e. I read thirteen books on holiday.

Tapescript 6b

▶ Dictation of numbers and prices

1 A How old is she?
  B Mmm ... I think she's about er ... sixty-two.
2 A You live in Station Road, don't you?
  B That's right.
  A What number?
  B One hundred and eighty-two.
3 A How many students are there in the class?
  B About fourteen.
4   There are about two hundred and twenty Spanish pesetas to the pound.
5 A How much does he earn?
  B Six hundred and fourteen pounds a week.
6 A How much is a double room, please?
  B Eighty-seven pounds a night.
7 A And breakfast?
  B Six pounds fifty.
8   My grandfather was a hundred and six when he died.
9   I had a phone bill today – two hundred and twenty-seven pounds!
10 I'm reading a very long book – eight hundred and seventy pages.
11 I'm half way through it. I'm on page four hundred and thirty-five.
12 A I like your shoes.
  B Thank you.
  A How much were they?
  B Nineteen pounds.

Unit 3

Tapescript 7

▶ The couple who survived at sea

Bill and Simone Butler, a couple from New York, spent sixty days in a life-raft in the seas of Central America after their yacht sank. Three weeks after they left Panama, they met some sharks, which hit the side of the boat until it sank. Bill and Simone had two life-rafts, so they jumped into the bigger one. For twenty days they had tins of food, fruit, and bottles of water. They caught fish every day and cooked it in different ways. Then they lost the line, but Bill managed to catch fish in a cup.

One or two ships passed them, but no one stopped. Then suddenly a fishing boat saw them, and Bill and Simone jumped into it. The captain of the boat took them to Panama. Their drama was over.

Tapescript 8

▶ An interview with a biographer

P = **Presenter**
LP = **Lucy Parker, the biographer**

P Today in *Bookworld* we have an interview with Lucy Parker who has written a biography of Ian Fleming, the author of the internationally famous James Bond spy novels.
Welcome Lucy.
I think the thing that many people want to know is: 'How much is Ian Fleming, the author, like the hero of his books, James Bond?'

LP A lot, I think. We can see a lot of James Bond in Ian Fleming's life.

P Well – let's begin at the beginning – when he was a child.

LP Well – he was born on May 28th, 1908 in England. His family were rich. His grandfather was a millionaire banker and his father a Member of Parliament.

P Was he close to his family?

LP Well – his father was killed in the First World War, when Ian was only nine. He had three brothers, and he was quite close to them, but he was different from them.

P How was he different?

LP Well – they all went to Eton. His brothers liked it. He hated it. He hated the army too. He didn't want to be a soldier. He was good at languages, so he went to study in Geneva in 1930. Then the next year, he wanted to join the Foreign Office, but didn't pass the exams. He went back home, and he was living with his mother again, feeling very bored, when he got a job as a journalist. He worked in London, Berlin, and Moscow. Then he worked as a stockbroker, and he was doing this when the Second World War started. That's when he started working in the world of spies.

P What did he do?

LP Well – he joined Naval Intelligence and had a lot of contact with MI5 and the Secret Service. He went on secret missions to North Africa, Lisbon, and America.

P Ah – that sounds like James Bond. What about his life when he wasn't working?

LP Well, he was a good-looking man. He loved money and had an expensive way of life. He always dressed very carefully. He had a lot of girlfriends. He didn't marry until he was forty-three. He drank a lot – gin, Martini, vodka – and he smoked sixty cigarettes a day. Probably as a result of this, he had a bad heart from quite a young age.

P Mmm . . . I see. But what about his writing – when did that start?

LP After the war. He went to Jamaica and loved it and decided to buy some land by the sea and build a house. He called it *Goldeneye*. And in Jamaica in 1952, three very important things happened: he got married, he had a son, and he started writing about James Bond. His first book was *Casino Royale*, then his second book was *Live and Let Die*, in 1954.

P Yes, and I believe there were twelve more James Bond books after that.

LP Yes, indeed – fourteen altogether before his death in 1964. His last book was *The Man with the Golden Gun*.

P Did he ever meet Sean Connery, who played James Bond in the first films?

LP Yes, he did. He helped choose Sean Connery for *Dr No*, but he died while they were making the second Bond film, *From Russia with Love*.

P How sad, but at least he knew his books were successful.

LP Oh, yes – 40 million sold at the time of his death.

P Amazing. Thank you very much, Lucy. It's very interesting to hear about the man who created James Bond.

Tapescript 9

▶ Saying the date

the fourth of June
June the fourth

the twenty-fifth of August
August the twenty-fifth

the thirty-first of July
July the thirty-first

the first of March
March the first

the third of February
February the third

the twenty-first of January, nineteen eighty-eight
the second of December, nineteen seventy-six
the fifth of April, nineteen eighty
the eleventh of June, nineteen sixty-five
the eighteenth of October, nineteen eighty-nine

Unit 4

Tapescript 10

▶ Ben and Sam in the kitchen

B = Ben
S = Sam

B Now, have we got everything we need?

S Well, let's see. There are some onions and potatoes, but there aren't any mushrooms and, of course, there isn't any minced beef.

B Are there any carrots?

S A few. But we don't need many, so that's OK.

B How much milk is there?

S Only a little. And there isn't any butter, and we haven't got much cheese.

B Well, we don't need much cheese. Is there anything else?

S No, not for Shepherd's Pie. We've got some salt and pepper, and there's a lot of flour. Would you like me to help with the shopping?

B Yes, please.

Tapescript 11

▶ Five radio advertisements

M = Man
W = Woman
V = Voice

1 M Er . . . Excuse me! Miss!
  W Yes, love?
  M What's on the menu today?
  W Well, let me see. We've got pie and chips and chop and chips and steak and chips and plaice and chips and skate and chips and cod and chips and egg and beans and chips.
  M I see. You mean you've got pie . . .
  W and chips
  M and chop . . .
  W and chips . . .
  M and steak . . .
  W and chips . . .
  M and plaice . . .
  W and chips . . .
  M and skate . . .
  W and chips . . .
  M and cod . . .
  W and chips . . .
  M and egg . . .
  W and beans and chips.
  V Everyone loves chips, but not all the time. That's why Ross have brought out Oven Crunchies – real pieces of potato you can bake in the oven, fry, or grill. Delicious with anything, they're a welcome change from chips.
  M Now you can give those chips a rest. Oven Crunchies are the very best. They're new from Ross, and they will make you sing. Buy them, try them with

anything.
  W You mean that Oven Crunchies are so good?
  M Oh, yes.
  W Why's that?
  M 'Cos they're from Ross.
  V Oven Crunchies from Ross – the name that stands out in the freezer.
  M They're absolutely new . . .
  V }
  W } . . . from Ross.

2   **Railway announcement** We apologize for the cancellation of this service.
  Bus conductor Sorry! Full up!
  Man Give us a break, will you? Ah! That's better! Look at that wonderful seafood! And the wine!
  Voice This short break has been brought to you by P & O European ferries. From day-trips at ten pounds fifty return, to five-day returns by foot, coach, or by car. P & O will cruise you from Dover to the Continent for a welcome break. See your local travel agent for more details. Right! Back to reality!

3 (Singing) And though I'm not a great romancer, I know that I'm bound to answer when you propose, 'Anything goes.' It's the hottest show in town. (Singing) I get no kick from champagne. It's the tops. It's Elaine Page in *Anything Goes*. (Singing) Mere alcohol doesn't thrill me at all. So tell me why should it be true . . . *Anything Goes*, London's most glamorous hit musical, featuring the unforgettable songs of Cole Porter. (Singing) . . . that I get a kick out of you. Book your seats now at Prince Edward Theatre or at your local ticket agent. The cast album is now available from all good record shops.

4 A car fanatic in America wanted a few extras in his 1982 Cadillac, such as a TV, video, three telephones, a bar that seats twenty, solar deck, and a swimming pool. So he gave it eighteen wheels and stretched it . . . to a massive seventy-one feet eleven inches. If you're looking for something new, with a little more leg room, you can meet a car made for you at the London Motor Show Motor Fair, at Earl's Court, on now until Sunday 29.

5   (Singing) Can't beat it. The feeling you get from a Coca-Cola. Can't beat the real thing. (Various voices) When you . . . buy . . . Coca-Cola . . . you get . . . free . . . meal.
  Man What they're trying to say is that

when you buy the special Coca-Cola twelve-packs, as long as a grown-up eats as well, you'll get a free kid's meal at Little Chef, Happy Eater, Welcome Break, or Harvesters.

Children But that's what we said! (Singing) Can't beat the feeling.

Tapescript 12

▶ Polite requests and offers

1 A Can I have a book of stamps, please?
  B Do you want first class or second?

2 A We'd like two cheeseburgers and one Big Mac, all with fries, please.
  B Would you like anything to drink with that?

3 A Could you tell me where the shoe department is, please?
  B Yes, of course. It's on the third floor.

4 A Have you got any Sunsilk shampoo for greasy hair?
  B I'll check, but I think we only have it for dry.

5 A Excuse me. Can you tell me where platform six is?
  B It's over there. Come with me. I'll show you.

6 A I'd like a large, brown, sliced loaf, please.
  B I'm afraid we only have white left.

7 A Can I take this bag as hand luggage?
  B Yes, that's fine. I'll give you a label for it.

8 A Could I have another plastic bag? I've got so much to carry.
  B Here you are. We don't charge for them.

Unit 5

Tapescript 13

▶ Jenny and Chris

J Would you like a game of tennis next Thursday?
C I can't, I'm afraid. I'm going to Bristol.
J What for?
C I have an interview for a job as manager of a record shop.
J I didn't know you wanted to move.
C Well, my parents are going to retire to Bath next year, and I want to be near them.
J How are you getting to Bristol?
C I have a bit of a problem, actually. My car isn't working at the moment. I'm thinking of getting a taxi to the station, and then getting a train.
J I'll give you a lift to the station. Don't worry about a taxi.

C Really?
J Mmm.
C OK. Then I'll get a taxi home.
J Well, what time is your train back?
C It gets in at twenty-one fifteen – what's that? – quarter past nine in the evening.
J It's all right. I'll pick you up as well. It's no trouble.
C That's great! Thanks a lot, Jenny.

Tapescript 14

▶ How different students organize their vocabulary learning

1 I have a little notebook. It's an address book with the letters of the alphabet, and I write the new words in two or three times a week. I write the English word first, then the translation, and a short sentence as an example. I try to learn ten new words a day.

2 I have a little notebook. I always have it with me. I try to fill one page a day. Sometimes I put words in groups, like fruit – all kinds of fruit, you know? Or colours, or clothes, or things and the shops where you buy them. I have some grammar pages, where I write irregular verbs, or a page for prepositions. I think prepositions are difficult, you know – *on* Sunday, *in* the morning, listen *to* a concert – but you say *phone someone*. In my language we say 'phone to someone'.

3 I stick little bits of paper all over my house! Sometimes I write what the thing is, er … On the mirror, I have *mirror*, on the door handle, I have *door handle*. Yeah, I know, it's funny. My friends think 'What's the matter with her?' but I like it. And sometimes I write the words that are new, from the last lesson, and I put the word on the … on the kitchen door and I see it every two minutes!

4 I write the new words on a little piece of paper, with the English on the one side and the Turkish on the other side. I write the English word in a sentence so I know how to use it, and what words it's used with. Then in my left pocket, I have the new words, and in the day, when I'm having a break or travelling on the bus, I take out the new words, and if I remember them they go into my right pocket. If I don't remember them, they go into my left pocket again.

5 I am very lazy! I don't do anything special at all! But I read a lot. I always have an English book in my bag. There are a lot of simple books, you know? Stories in easy English, they have questions at the back and they explain some difficult words, but I just enjoy the story and I think I learn new words and I don't know I learn new words, but I see a word six, maybe seven times, and then I know it! And the stories are good!

6 I have a picture dictionary, which is good for learning words in groups, you know,

jobs, the names for all the things in a car, like er … *steering wheel*, *brake*. But I don't know how to pronounce the words.

7 I have a little cassette recorder, and after the lesson I record onto the tape the sentences that have the new words. Then when I am driving I can listen to them.

8 I like to look up words in my dictionary. Especially, I like to find different parts of speech for the same word, mm … *act*, *actor*, *actress*, adjective *active*, adverb *actively*, noun *action*. That I think is very useful – see! *Use*, *useful*, *useless*! A word family!
  And something else! I always put a mark with my pencil next to the word I look up. Then, if I look up the same word again, I think 'Ah! This word, I must learn it this time!'

Tapescript 15

▶ Henry's family

My wife's name is Elizabeth, that's E-L-I-Z-A-B-E-T-H. I have three children, two girls and a boy. The oldest girl is Megan. You spell that M-E-G-A-N. Then there's Katie. That's K-A-T-I-E. And the little one's name is James. J-A-M-E-S.

My father's name is Harold. You spell that H-A-R-O-L-D. My mother's name is Elsie. E-L-S-I-E. I have a sister called Tricia. T-R-I-C-I-A.

Now my wife's family. My father-in-law's name is Thomas. T-H-O-M-A-S, and my mother-in-law's name is Jessica. And you spell that J-E-double S-I-C-A. And that's everyone!

Unit 6

Tapescript 16a

▶ World travels

F = Friend
T = Tina

F You're so lucky Tina. You travel so much with the orchestra. Where did you go last year?
T We went to New York first, then Tokyo and Rome. But it's hard work, you know.
F I'm sure it is. I'd just love to travel to all those places. Tell me about them. What are they like?
T Well, New York's always very exciting. It's busy day and night – but the streets! They're so dirty! We went there last February and it was very cold. It snowed the whole time.
F And you went to Tokyo next? What's that like?

T Yes, we flew there at the beginning of March. It's another very busy city. It's very crowded. The streets are clean, but in the centre it can get quite polluted. We had big audiences, they loved the music, and I love Japanese food, so we had a good time.

F And last of all, Rome. I want to go there in the summer. Tell me about Rome. What's it like?

T Well, we were there in May. It was beautiful. The weather was perfect and not too hot. It's a noisy city and expensive, but it's got all those beautiful old buildings. It's so interesting.

F And the food! I can't wait to try real Italian food.

Tapescript 16b

▶ Which is the most exciting?

T I had a wonderful tour, but it's always nice to come home. It's interesting to compare the cities – Tokyo's exciting, but, for a musician, London is more exciting than Tokyo, and, of course, New York is the most exciting of all.

London is, of course, much older than New York, but it isn't as old as Rome. Rome is the oldest city I visited. London doesn't have as many old buildings as Rome, but it has more than both New York and Tokyo. Cities are interesting, but walking round them is very tiring. You need places to sit down. New York has Central Park. It has more parks than Tokyo, but London has the most parks. There are five in the city centre.

Tapescript 16c

▶ London is older than New York

London is older than New York, but it isn't as old as Rome.

I'm not as tall as you.
But I'm taller than Ann.

It's not as cold today as it was yesterday.
But it's colder than it was last week.

This book is more interesting than I thought.
But it isn't as interesting as the one I read last week.

Tapescript 17

▶ Synonyms in conversation

a. 'Mary's family is very rich.'
'Well, I knew her uncle was wealthy.'

b. 'Look at all these new buildings!'
'Yes, this city's much more modern than I expected!'

c. 'Her boyfriend's really good-looking.'
'Well, he's certainly one of the most handsome men in the room!'

d. 'Wasn't that film wonderful!'
'Yes, it was marvellous.'

e. 'George doesn't earn much money, but he's so kind.'
'I know. He's very generous to both his family and his friends.'

f. 'Her bedroom's really untidy again!'
'Is it? I told her it was messy yesterday, and she promised to clean it.'

g. 'Was Sarah angry when you told her?'
'Yes, she looked really annoyed.'

h. 'I'm bored with this lesson!'
'I know. I'm really fed up with it, too!'

Tapescript 18

▶ Living in Madrid

I = Interviewer
K = Kate Leigh

I Kate, you've lived in Spain for a long time now, haven't you?

K Mm. About eight years.

I So you know it well enough to compare living in Spain and living in London?

K Well, I can compare living in Madrid with living in London . . .

I Ah, yes, all right . . .

K . . . not quite the same thing.

I So what are the main differences?

K I think the first one is the time of day that things happen. People get up later, and start work later. I start at ten, and lunchtime is much longer. Everything closes for about three hours. Then, at five, people go back to work.

I And what time do they finish?

K About seven or eight. Then they go out, and they go to bed incredibly late – about one or two in the morning.

I Do they have a siesta?

K No, not in Madrid. Well, only in summer, because in summer work hours change because it's *so* hot. Everyone works from eight thirty to three, then has lunch, then a siesta, and then goes out.

I So office hours change?

K Everything changes, on the first of June.

I For how long?

K Until the fifteenth of September.

I How did you find the differences of time when you first went out?

K Very difficult, because I was hungry all the time! I wanted to eat at about eight o'clock, but eating is very different in Spain. People eat all day. They have snacks in the morning, maybe an omelette and a beer, and then have their main meal at lunchtime, and then *tapas*, which are lots of little dishes, in the evening.

I So that's what you do now?

K Oh, yes. I like it. The Spanish think that the English eat very little!

I And what about the people?

K Well, this is the second big difference. People live in the streets, they live much more outdoors, so you see them more, and it's easier to get to know them.

I So you think it's true that the English are cold?

K No, but they live differently. Madrid is a lot smaller than London, and people live in the centre. It's not like London where people live in houses in the suburbs. In Madrid people live in flats in the centre, so it's natural to be out on the streets most of the time.

I And how do you find living in Madrid?

K I think it's nicer. It's a lot cheaper, and shops are open longer. I find it safer. I can be out in the streets at all hours, and there's never any problem. The family is still very important. I think people are more caring to other people, if you see what I mean.

I Mm. Anything else about the people?

K Er . . . They are terrible drivers! There are a lot more accidents – road accidents. And this is strange, because the public transport system is very good and very cheap, but people like to use *their* car.

I There's an Underground, isn't there?

K Mm, with a flat rate fare, so you get ten tickets for about two pounds.

I That's very good. Are you thinking of coming back to England?

K Er . . . sometime, but not yet! The weather's much better, and I like living in a southern European atmosphere!

Tapescript 19

▶ Directions

When you come out of school, turn left. Walk past the library and through the park until you get to the cinema. Turn left and you'll find the bus station. Take a number 16 and get off at Blackwood – that's B-L-A-C-K-W-O-O-D. Go under the bridge and turn right. Go to the end of the road and turn left. My house is the fourth on the right. It's the one with the red door.

Unit 7

Tapescript 20

▶ How long?

T = Tony
A = Ann

T Where do you live, Ann?

A In a house near Brighton.

T How long have you lived there?

A For three years.

T Why did you move?

A The house we had before was too small. We needed somewhere bigger.

T What do you do, Ann?
A I work in a bank.
T How long have you worked there?
A For eight years.
T What did you do before that?
A I worked for a travel agent.

Tapescript 21

▶ Interview with a musician

I = Interviewer
P = Paul Carrack

I How long have you been in the music business, Paul?
P For about twenty years, I guess. I've never had another job, er . . . no, never. I've only been a musician.
I And how old were you when you started playing?
P It was when I was just a kid, I er . . . taught myself to play. I tried a few instruments . . . first the drums – that was when I was only five. After that it was the piano, and then later keyboards.
I Do you play any other instruments?
P Only the guitar. I play the guitar sometimes. That's all.
I When did you start playing professionally?
P While I was still at school. I left school at sixteen. I was playing in a band, working on Saturday evenings in pubs and clubs. When I left school, my only ambition was to be in a pop group.
I And which groups have you played with over the years?
P Let me see – I'll try and remember. I've played with Roxy Music, and The Smiths, er . . . I've given concerts with them. And then I've made records with the Pretenders and Madness – and of course Ace, I mustn't forget Ace.
I Why is Ace so important to you?
P Well, I had my first hit record with Ace, er . . . that was in 1974. The song was called *How long?* and it was a big hit all over the world.
I And now you're with Mike and the Mechanics. How long have you played with them?
P Since 1985. We've made a couple of records and we've done two tours of America. I'm the singer – the vocalist. Mike plays the guitar.
I Do you travel a lot?
P Well, er . . . I often think that I've travelled all over the world, but I haven't really. I've worked a lot in Europe er . . . Germany, France, Italy, and then of course in America. I always wanted to work in America. I was really pleased when some of my records were successful there. But . . . erm . . . there are lots of places I haven't been to yet . . . er . . . Eastern Europe, Japan, South America . . . I'd love to play in these places.

I Paul – you've obviously made a lot of records. Do you know exactly how many?
P That's a difficult question, erm . . .
I Well about how many?
P Oh, I don't know. Perhaps about twenty . . . yeah, probably about twenty.
I And have you always worked with groups? Have you ever made a record on your own?
P Yes, last summer. I made it in the summer and it came out in October. It's called *Groove Approved*.
I And is it doing well?
P Erm . . . quite well, especially in America. My records are often played on radio there – more than here in Britain. People have heard of me there . . . erm . . . I'm not a superstar – of course I'm not – but people know my name and then they buy my albums!
I And so this has been a busy year for you?
P Yes. Yes, I've had a very busy year. I've toured the States twice with Mike and the Mechanics and . . . I've made my own album . . . and I've done a tour of Germany . . . So yeah, a busy year, but a good one.
I And something you've forgotten!
P What's that?
I You've had a number one record. You were top of the pops in February!
P That's right! It was called *The Living Years*. It was number one in Britain *and* in America!

Unit 8

Tapescript 22a

▶ Opening a restaurant

M = Man
K = Kathy

M I hear you're going to open a restaurant. Is that right?
K Mm. That's right.
M With your husband?
K Yes. It's something we've always wanted to do.
M Well, good luck. I wouldn't like to do it.
K Why not?
M If you run a restaurant, you have to work very long hours.
K You work late, it's true, but you don't have to get up so early in the morning.
M And another thing. You have to work in the evenings and at the weekends, when everyone else is enjoying themselves!
K Well, I like cooking and entertaining, so that's all right. In the shop, there was no variety. If you have a restaurant, you don't have to do the same thing every day. Every day is different!
M I think you're taking quite a risk.
K Well, we'll see. I want to be my own boss.

Then you don't have to work for someone else. And I hated the uniform in the shop!
M I'll be your first customer!

Tapescript 22b

▶ Pronunciation of *have to*

have to
don't have to
Do you have to?
You have to work long hours.
You have to work at the weekends.
You don't have to get up early.
You don't have to work for someone else.
Do you have to wear a uniform?
Do you have to work outside?

Tapescript 23

▶ Holidays in January

1 In January it is very, very hot all day and all night! So you only need light clothes, not even a jumper. The most important thing is your swimming costume, because we spend most of the time on the beach. You can go surfing and windsurfing, but we like just to sit on the beach and talk, and watch all the beautiful people walking by! But you shouldn't take anything valuable to the beach or someone will steal it! As for money, well, we have very high inflation, so it's best to take dollars and change money daily.
Restaurants are quite cheap. You can get a good meal for about two dollars. Our speciality is *feijoada*, which is black beans and different kinds of meat. It is served on Saturdays, and of course the fish and seafood are great because we're next to the sea! You must try a *caipirinha*, which is a drink made of rum and lime, but don't drink it too quickly! It's very strong! The fruit juices are fantastic.
In the evening, go to the piano bars and listen to some jazz or samba. We have some of the best live music in the world. And of course you must go up the Sugar Loaf Mountain at sunset! It's amazing!
2 It's usually quite mild in January, and it doesn't often rain, so you don't have to bring warm clothes. But you'll need a light coat and jumper as it can get cool in the evening. There are some wonderful museums, especially the Museum of Islamic Art, and the mosques are beautiful. If you want to see the Pyramids, it's best to go on horseback, and I think you should go in the early morning or late afternoon.
Bring travellers' cheques with you. You can change them very easily, but you have to change money *in* the country, because you can't take any money *out* of the country.
The best place to try the local food is in the city centre. You could try some *koftas* or

kebabs, which are meat, usually lamb, or *falafel*, which is a kind of bean ball mixed with herbs, and fried until it's crispy.

To drink, one of the nicest things is mint tea, especially if it is hot. It is very refreshing.

If you have time, you really should go on a Nile cruise. There are all sorts of places to choose from, and you can visit places that are difficult to get to by land.

3 Well, in January it can be very cold with snow everywhere! But high in the mountains the sky is usually blue, and it's warm enough to have lunch outside. You should bring warm clothes and some strong waterproof shoes.

Most people go skiing every weekend, and if there's no snow you can still go walking in the mountains. A lot of the towns are very pretty. They look exactly the same today as they did four hundred years ago!

You must try *fondue*, which is cheese melted in a pot, and you put pieces of bread on a long fork to get it out ... mm! It's very, very good.

If the weather's good, you can go for a boat trip on the lake. Then you can really see how beautiful the mountains are!

Tapescript 24

▶ Invitations

A= Alice
J = Jane

1 A Hello, Jane! How are you?
   J Fine, thanks. And you?
   A OK ... Jane, what are you doing tomorrow night? Would you like to go to the cinema? Kate and I are going to see *The Moon Man*.
   J I can't, I'm afraid. I have to finish my project by Friday, and it's nowhere near ready.
   A What a pity! Never mind.
   J Thanks for the invitation.
   A That's OK.

B= Barbara
T = Tony

2 B Hello, Tony. How are you?
   T Very well, thanks. And you?
   B Fine. Listen, Tony. What are you doing on Saturday evening?
   T Er ... Nothing special. Why?
   B Would you like to go out for a meal?
   T That would be lovely! Where do you want to go?
   B Well, I like Italian food, as you know ...
   T Mm, me too!
   B How about going to Giovanni's?
   T Great! Shall we meet there?
   B Yes, why not? What time shall we meet?
   T Eight o'clock?
   B Yes, that's fine.
   T Lovely. See you then.

D = David
A = Alice

3 D Hello, Alice. Are you all right?
   A Yes, thanks. How about you?
   D Mm, fine. Alice, I was wondering, are you free tomorrow evening? Some friends are coming round to my house for a drink. Would you like to come?
   A That's very kind, David, but I'm going to the cinema with Kate. Sorry.
   D That's all right. Another time.
   A That would be lovely.

Unit 9

Tapescript 25

▶ Jenny and Mark

J If I don't go out so much, I'll do more work.
  If I do more work, I'll pass my exams.
  If I pass my exams, I'll go to university.
  If I go to university, I'll study medicine.
M If I stop smoking, I'll have more money.
  If I have more money, I'll save some every week.
  If I save some every week, I'll be rich when I'm thirty.
  If I'm rich when I'm thirty, I'll have my own business.

Tapescript 26

▶ How 'green' are you?

I = Interviewer
J = John Baines

I John, I know that you're interested in all things to do with the environment and the need to protect it ...
J Right.
I Can you tell me some of the things you've changed in your lifestyle to become a 'green' person?
J Oh, yes. I could erm ... I could think of one or two things that I've tried to do over the last couple of years. I think it's a couple of years since I got my bicycle out of the garage and repaired it, and now I use it as much as possible. I use my car less. I try to do ten per cent fewer miles every year, so last year I drove eleven thousand miles, and this year I'm going to try to do only ten thousand.
I So does this mean that you travel less?
J This doesn't mean I travel less, this means I walk more often. When I do my shopping, I always walk now. I use public transport when I can, usually going by train.
I I'm sure your car runs on unleaded petrol.
J Yes, it does. It's cheaper, and it keeps the air cleaner.

I So that's transport. What about in the home? What's different in the kitchen?
J Well, I save as much as I can, I don't throw it away. I have different bags for different things. One bag has all the cans going into it, from the cat food to the beer. The second bag has all the papers going into it, and the third bag has bottles, from er ... olive oil bottles to wine bottles to lemonade bottles. But the milk bottles still go on the doorstep so that they can be re-used.
I And what do you do with these bags?
J I take them to places where they can be recycled. There's a place in the village where you can take them.
I And have you changed any of the things you buy?
J Yes. I get washing-up liquid and washing powder that doesn't harm the environment ...
I But does it get your clothes as white?
J I don't think my washing was ever ... very white, actually. No, it's fine.
I We were talking about food. I know you've become a vegetarian. Is this part of being 'green', or something totally different?
J Erm ... yes and no. Looking after animals, I think, is as important as looking after the environment. I mean, they're part of it. So I prefer not to kill animals to eat them. Animals eat food that people could eat. But if people want to eat meat, that's their decision.
I Mm. I think it's true that people all over the world are becoming more aware of the need to look after the planet. If we don't look after it, what will happen ... do you think?
J If we don't become more friendly to the environment, then the environment will make it more difficult for us, so that our life will not be as comfortable. I think we'll survive ...
I Oh, good!
J ... but these are very important times.

Tapescript 27a

▶ Travelling

Here's your ticket and boarding card.
Do you have any hand luggage?
It leaves from platform eight.
Can I have a day return, please?
Would you like smoking or non-smoking?

Tapescript 27b

▶ At the check-in desk

A Hello. Can I see your passport and ticket, please?
B Here you are.
A Thank you. Do you have just the one case?
B Yes.
A Do you have any hand luggage?
B Just this one case.

125

A That's fine. Would you like smoking or non-smoking?
B Non-smoking, please.
A Right. Here's your ticket and boarding card.
B Thanks.
A Your flight will board at gate 14 in about an hour's time. Have a good trip!
B Thanks. Bye.

Tapescript 27c

▶ **At the railway ticket office**

A Good morning. Can I help you?
B Yes, please. I want to go to Edinburgh. When's the next train?
A Let me see. There's one at 10.42. You change at Doncaster. And there's another at 11.15.
B Is that direct, or do I have to change?
A That's direct.
B What time does it arrive?
A Which one? The 10.42 or the 11.15?
B Er . . . the 11.15.
A It gets in at . . . 14.40.
B Right. I'll have a return ticket, then, please.
A When are you coming back? Are you coming back today?
B No, tomorrow.
A Ah, so you can't have a day return. You need a period return. That'll be £78.40.
B Can I pay by credit card?
A Yes, certainly.
B Here you are.
A Thank you.
B Which platform does it leave from?
A Platform 3.
B Thanks.
A Goodbye.

Unit 10

Tapescript 28a

▶ **Memories – Molly Harrison**

I can remember it all so clearly! I used to go dancing every Saturday. We used to go for picnics.
The roads didn't use to be busy. We used to go to the pictures twice a week.
It used to cost sixpence.

Tapescript 28b

▶ **Memories – Linda Carr**

We shocked our parents. We used to do things that they never did. We wore mini-skirts, we went dancing at discotheques, and we went to pop concerts. I got tickets for a Beatles concert in 1965, and I travelled all the way to Liverpool to see them.

My parents bought me a record player for my fourteenth birthday. My friends and I listened to records nearly every night. We didn't watch TV much then, but our parents did.
Our family had a Mini, and once we went camping in France in it.
When we were students we wanted to change the world. We said 'Make love not war'. We often marched to ban the bomb. In 1968 there were student revolutions in many parts of the world. So many things happened in the 60s: President Kennedy was killed in 1963, they landed on the moon in '69, and the Berlin wall – they built that in er . . . let me see . . . I think that was 1961. Well, I'm pleased some things change!

Tapescript 29

▶ **Questions**

A Who did you talk to at the party last night?
B Oh, Jenny and Tom, but Jenny mainly.
A What did you talk about?
B She was telling me about her new job.
A Who did you dance with?
B No one. By the way, did you know that Belinda is going out with Steve?
A No. Who told you that?
B Tom did. Someone saw them together in a restaurant.
A Who saw them?
B Annie did.
A Huh! You can't believe Annie!
B Well, you don't know what Annie said.
A Why? What happened in the restaurant?
B Well, when Annie saw them, they were very surprised, and then they . . .

Tapescript 30a

▶ **Bill Cole talks about when he was young**

I was born in 1919, er . . . May 7th, 1919. I was the eldest of four. I had one brother and two sisters – just the youngest sister is still alive. I'm a true Cockney. We lived in the East End of London. We had two rooms above a fish and chip shop. Number 18 India Street it was, next to the river. The rooms always smelt of fish. We didn't have much money, but we ate well – not only fish and chips. Dad worked in the fruit and vegetable market at Covent Garden. He used to bring home all kinds of fruit and veg. Ma was a cleaner, and she worked in offices and hospitals.
Dad used to start work at four o'clock in the morning and, from when I was seven, it was my job, before school, to run to the market with his breakfast. I used to love doing that. Best of all were the days when he said: 'Don't go to school today, son. Stay with me. You'll learn more about life here. But don't tell your Ma!'
He was right – the noise, the men and women shouting and laughing, the colour, the smells –

it was wonderful. At lunchtime we got pie and peas twice, for sixpence. I can still taste that pie and peas – best taste in the world!
Then Dad died when I was twelve. I had to help Ma look after the little ones. So I left school and started to work full-time in the market. I did it for ten years. After that I was a taxi-driver. It's been a good life.

Tapescript 30b

▶ **Camilla, Duchess of Lochmar, talks about when she was young**

I was born on May 7th, 1919, at the family home, Foxton House, in Leicestershire. Our family has lived there for generations. We have the most beautiful gardens. People used to travel miles to see our rose garden in June. The smell of the roses came right into the house. I was the youngest child and the only girl. I had three older brothers . . . much older. They weren't there while I was growing up. Two were in the army and one was at Oxford University. Of course, my mother and father used to spoil me, my father especially. He used to call me his 'little princess'. He died when I was sixteen. It was a terrible time for mother and me. Fortunately, I was at home with her. I never went to school. I had a governess for a few years, so I didn't have much education. My mother thought it was more important for a girl to learn to dance, to go to parties, and look pretty. She wanted me to find a good husband after my father died. My best memories are the two years before I married – all those dances and parties. I loved it. But I met and married the Duke when I was twenty. A good marriage is important. I only knew one girl who got a job. Poor girls these days, they all have to find jobs! I can't imagine that they have as much fun as we used to have!

Tapescript 31

▶ **In a restaurant**

1 A Did you have a nice meal?
  B Yes, I did. The fish was wonderful, wasn't it?
  A Yes, it was. There was so much, but we finished it, didn't we?
  B Mm. I do like it here. We haven't been here for ages, have we?
  A No, we haven't. It has a nice atmosphere, and it's very reasonable, isn't it?
  B Yes, it is. And the waiters really look after you, don't they?
  A Yes, they do. Shall we go home now?
  B OK. Let's go.

2 A Did you have a nice meal?
  B Yes. The fish was wonderful.
  A There was so much, but we finished it.
  B I do like it here. We haven't been here for ages.

A It has a nice atmosphere, and it's very reasonable.

B And the waiters really look after you.

A Shall we go home now?

B OK. Let's go.

Unit 11

Tapescript 32

▶ The world's most loved car

P = Presenter

P This week in *Worldly Wise* we talk to people about the world's most loved car – the Volkswagen Beetle. Why do so many people love it so much?

Man They're noisy – ugly really, but so full of character. They're not very comfortable, but they're totally reliable. Mine's my friend – a reliable, always jolly friend. In rain, in snow he'll get me there, and we chat as we go along the roads together – 'Well done!' I say. 'Don't you worry about that big Volvo.' Over the years I've asked my Beetle-owning friends why they bought a Beetle . . . er . . . and they say that there are some things in life that can never be improved and the Beetle is like that!

P How did it all start? Well, *Volkswagen* means 'people's car'. And in 1934, Ferdinand Porsche was asked by the German Government to design exactly that – a car for the people. A factory was built, and the first distinctive-looking cars were ready in 1938. Then, of course, there was a problem – the Second World War!
After the war a British officer, Major Ivan Hurst, was put in charge of the Volkswagen factory. Another officer, Michael McEnvoy, remembered the car from before the war and he thought it would be good for American and British soldiers in Germany. So the first fans of the car were *not* the Germans, but British and American soldiers. And some of them loved it so much that they took their cars back home!

SONG We found a wonderful bargain,
A little Beetle Volkswagen.
He came all the way from Germany
To settle here in this country.
(Chorus)
He said: 'Ja, ja, ja!'
And he laughed: 'Tee Hee!'
He said: 'This is the place for me!'

P The first VW garage was opened in Britain in the 50s by a man called John Baber. His son, Peter, still sells VWs.

Peter My father travelled everywhere in his own VW. He used to come to my school to watch the cricket and football matches. The other boys used to call out 'Oh! Here comes Baber in his Beetle!' So when my father started a VW magazine he called it *Beetling*. Anyway, that's where we say the name came from!

P And so the Beetle got its name! At first only a few people owned them and when they met on the road they used to wave to each other. Twenty million Beetles were produced, but none have been made in Europe since 1974. However, the Beetle lives on. They are still made in South America.
A question asked by many people is: 'Will they be made again in Europe?' Surely there is a market for them – twenty million Beetle owners can't be wrong!

SONG He gives us very much pleasure,
Our little Volkswagen treasure.
When we ask if he ever felt inclined
To go back again to his home near the Rhein.
He said:
(Chorus)
'Nein, nein, nein!'
And he laughed: 'Hee, Hee.'
He said: 'This is the place for me!'
He said: 'Nein . . .' etc.

Tapescript 33

▶ Where are the dialogues taking place?

1 Waitress Good afternoon. What can I get you?

Customer We'd like a pot of tea for two, please, some ham sandwiches, and some scones with strawberry jam and cream.

Waitress Yes, of course.

2 Bank clerk . . . and how would you like the money?

Customer In tens and fives, please.

3 Man This bl. . . thing isn't working!

Woman They never work! You should know that.

Man But how can I get my money back?

4 The 7.56 from Brighton is now arriving at platform 4. British Rail would like to apologize for the late arrival of this train.

This was due to the severe weather conditions.

5 Landlord Excuse me. Are you over 18?

Young customer Yes, of course.

Landlord Have you any means of identification?

Young customer No, I haven't.

Landlord Then I'm afraid I'll have to ask you to leave.

Unit 12

Tapescript 34

▶ Unidentified flying objects

I = Interviewer

B = Mr Burton

I Mr Burton, you say that you have seen a UFO. Is that right?

B Yes, absolutely right. It happened just over a year ago.

I And where was this?

B Near my home in Aldershot, in the south of England. I live near the big military base in Aldershot.

I What time of day was it?

B It was about one o'clock in the morning. I was out fishing. The weather forecast said it was going to be a warm, clear night with no clouds, and that's perfect for fishing.

I And what happened?

B Well, I saw a bright light coming towards me at about three hundred feet, and then it started to land. It was behind some trees, but I could see it clearly because there was a full moon. Then I saw two forms coming towards me, and when they were about five feet away, they just stopped and looked at me for a good ten or fifteen seconds.

I What did they look like?

B They were quite small, about four feet tall, dressed in green suits from head to foot, and they had helmets of the same colour with a red visor, so I couldn't see their faces. They both carried space guns.

I Did they speak to you?

B Yes. The one on the right said 'Come this way, please.'

I Weren't you frightened? . . . I mean, weren't you surprised that they spoke English?

B They spoke in a funny accent. It sounded more like a machine talking than a person. No, I wasn't frightened, I don't know why. The one who spoke started to walk towards the light, and I followed him, with the other one behind me. We got to a wall and the first 'form' just walked through it! I couldn't believe it! I had to climb over it, and then we got to the spaceship.

127

I What did that look like?

B It was about forty-five feet across, and silver, very, very shiny, and there were round windows all round the side.

I Did you go inside?

B Yes, I did. There were steps going up, and we went into an octagonal room. I stood there for about ten minutes. The walls, the floor, and the ceiling were all black. I couldn't see any controls or instruments, but there was a central column going up from the floor to the ceiling, about four feet wide, right in the middle of the room.

I Were there any more of these 'forms'?

B No, just the two. Suddenly, one of them said 'Stand under the red light.' I couldn't see any red light, but then I moved to the right and I could see it up on the wall, just under the ceiling. I stood there for about five minutes, and then a voice said 'What is your age?' I said 'Seventy-four.' Then they told me to turn around. After about five more minutes one of them said 'You can go. You are too old and ill for our purposes.' So I left and went back to the river.

I Did the spaceship take off?

B Yes. I heard a very high-pitched noise, like a scream, and the thing took off straight into the sky and disappeared. I sat by the river and watched it go. This was about two o'clock.

I Then what did you do?

B Next morning I went to the police, and in the afternoon someone from the Ministry of Defence came to my house to interview me. He told me to keep quiet about the whole thing, and tell absolutely no one. I thought this was very strange, but I did as he told me.

I Why have you decided to tell people about it now?

B Because I want people to know what happened to me. I didn't use to believe in UFOs, but now I know they exist. I think governments are trying to hide something, but people have a right to know.

I Thank you, Mr Burton, very much. A fascinating story.

Tapescript 35

▶ Dictation of times

1 A What time does the football match start?
   B Quarter past three.

2 A Is it on TV tonight?
   B Yes. It's on BBC 1 at nine fifty-five.

3 A That's a shame. My favourite programme is on then.
   B What's that?
   A A documentary called *Life on Earth*. It starts at ten to ten.

4 B What time does it finish?
   A Twenty-five past ten.
   B It looks like you'll miss it if you want to watch the football.

5 The next train to leave from platform nine will be the eleven oh five to Bristol, calling at Reading and Swindon.

6 A When's the next train to Durham, please?
   B Let me see. It's the ... fourteen twenty-eight. Platform eleven.
   A Fourteen twenty-eight erm ... That's er ...
   B Twenty-eight minutes past two.

7 A I'm meeting someone on the Manchester train. What time is it due in?
   B It's running twenty minutes late, I'm afraid. It'll be in at nineteen forty, platform two.
   A Thanks.

8 The twelve fifteen flight to Dublin is now boarding at gate five. Twelve fifteen Dublin flight, gate five.

9 A Do you have any luggage, sir?
   B No, just hand luggage. What time do we start boarding?
   A At about twenty-five to seven.
   B Thanks.

10 A What time is the plane due to arrive?
   B At a quarter to eight local time.

11 A Which flight is yours?
   B BA three oh two.
   A What time does it go?
   B Twenty-one thirty.

12 A What time do you go to bed?
   B Never before midnight. Usually about half past twelve.

Unit 13

Tapescript 36a

▶ People of mixed nationality

P = Presenter
A = Amélia de Melo
L = Lionel Varley
This week in *The London Programme* – People of mixed nationality.

P In the streets of London there are people from all parts of the world. They live side by side. Sometimes they marry and have children. Many Londoners have parents of different nationality. Is this good or bad, easy or difficult for these children?
Today two people of mixed nationality tell us their stories.
First, Amélia de Melo, a textile designer.

Tapescript 36b

A My father is half Malaysian, half Portuguese. My mother is Polish ... erm ... her family came to England when she was five, just before the war. She met my father when they were both students in London. When I was a young child, ... er ... I grew up in both London and Malaysia, and we always spoke English at home. It's my first language ... er ... but my mother taught me Polish, so sometimes I spoke Polish with her. And we often had Polish food, and I learnt Polish dancing – my aunts in Poland sent me wonderful, colourful costumes to dance in. I loved them. But I loved Malaysian things too. Have you ever tried Malaysian food? It's delicious. I often cook it for myself.
I often think ... I think that if I had just one nationality, life would be quite boring. I like the mix of cultures. I only ever had one problem that I can remember. It was when I was sent to boarding school. I was twelve, and ... er ... some girls joked about the shape of my eyes. I cried and cried. I hated my eyes! But now ... now I like my eyes very much. I like to look a bit different!
Last year I got married – to an Englishman. We live in London but we often visit my parents in Malaysia. I've never been to Poland, but we might go this summer. I'd love to meet my Polish relatives.

P And now we meet Lionel Varley, who's an architect.

L My mother's French and my father's from Dominica in the West Indies. They met and married in London, but then they moved to Bristol. ... er ... my father was a dentist there. They ... er ... that is my parents – always spoke both English and French at home together, so my brother and I are bilingual. It's really useful to have two languages. We (that's me and my brother) used to spend every school holiday with our French grandmother in France. I love French food. We used to eat mainly French food at home in Bristol too ... er ... I think we didn't eat West Indian food because where we lived there were no other West Indians and you couldn't buy that type of food.
I can remember one problem – a sad time for me. It was when I first started school. I was five and everyone in the school was white, except for one Chinese boy and me, and the others called us names. I was too young to understand why, but then I made some friends, and they forgot about my colour.
My father used to talk a lot about Dominica and the West Indies. His stories were full of flowers and sunshine. So when I was sixteen, I went there. It was interesting, very interesting... er ... but I didn't feel at home, so I came back to England and studied architecture. If I lived there (in Dominica) I don't think I would have the same opportunities. Next year I'm going to move to New York. It's even more cosmopolitan than London. I know that I'll feel very comfortable there, and my wife

will too. She's Italian-Russian.

P Thank you, Lionel and thank you, Amélia. Thank you for telling us your stories.

Tapescript 37

▶ **Social expressions**

a. A I hear you're going to get married soon. Congratulations!

B That's right, next July 21st. Can you come to the wedding?

A Oh, what a pity! That's when we're away on holiday.

B Never mind, we'll send you some wedding cake.

A That's very kind.

b. A Good heavens! Look at the time! Hurry up, or we'll miss the train.

B Just a minute, I can't find my umbrella. Do you know where it is?

A I've no idea. But you won't need it. It's a lovely day.

B OK, I hope you're right. Let's go.

c. A Good luck in your exam!

B Same to you. I hope we both pass.

A Did you study all last night?

B No, of course not. I watched TV and went to bed early. What about you?

A I did the same. See you later, after the exam.

B All right. Let's go for a drink.

d. A I passed!

B Well done! I failed.

A Oh! Bad luck! What went wrong?

B I'm always very nervous in exams, and this time I was very nervous indeed.

A Oh, I see. Well, all I can say is 'better luck next time!'

Unit 14

Tapescript 38a

▶ **Angela's news**

A = Angela
T = Tom

A Tom! Hello! I haven't seen you for ages!

T Goodness! I remember you! It's erm . . . Angela, isn't it?

A That's right! You were in the class above me at school! Don't you remember?

T Yes, of course I do! How are you?

A I'm fine. We haven't seen each other for . . . oh, three years! How are you?

T Very well. Do you still live in Manchester?

A No, I've moved to Paris.

T Oh! When did you do that?

A About a year ago.

T And why did you go?

A Well, I wanted a change, and I had some friends there, and I like it very much.

T Yes. I've been to Paris. It's wonderful, isn't it?

A Mm. And I've found a job that I like. I work for a film company.

T That's great. What about Alan? Are you two still together?

A No, that ended ages ago. He's gone to South America. I'm going out with a boy called Jean-Pierre. He's French, and we've just got engaged.

T Hey, that's great! Congratulations! Are you going to stay in Paris?

A Yes. We've bought a flat there. It's small, but it'll do.

T What about your parents? How are they?

A They've retired now. They've bought a house on the south coast. Now listen! That's enough about me! What about you? You've changed! You've lost a bit of weight, haven't you?

T Yes, I have. I think I used to eat the wrong things. Well, let me see. I've just finished college . . .

Tapescript 38b

▶ **Tom's news**

T = Tom
A = Angela

T Well, I've just finished college. I've been studying archaeology. And for the last month I've been working as a postman.

A And what are you doing in London?

T I'm trying to find a job. I've been going round museums to see if they need anybody. I've been writing letters for weeks!

A Have you had many replies?

T Well, a few, but not many. I've written at least thirty letters.

A Poor old you! Look, let's go and have a cup of tea, and we can catch up on some more news.

T What a lovely idea!

Tapescript 39a

▶ **Phoning home – Justin**

M = Mother
J = Justin

M . . .

J Hello, Mum. It's me, Justin.

M . . .

J I'm fine, but I'm really tired.

M . . .

J Well, we've just started exams, so I've been staying up late . . . er . . . it was three o'clock last night . . . yeah, I've been studying really hard.

M . . .

J Last Thursday. We had our first one on Thursday morning. It was terrible. I don't want to talk about it.

M . . .

J Not a lot. I've been working too hard. Sometimes I go round to Lucinda's place and we study together.

M . . .

J You know – Lucinda – I'm sure I've told you about her. She's doing the same course as me. I've known her for ages. We often help each other with work . . . er . . . not . . . all the . . . er . . . time. Sometimes we go to the pub or cook a meal together. Today we've been testing each other on economics and marketing. That's tomorrow's exam. She's just gone out to get a Chinese takeaway.
Anyway, Mum – how are you and Dad? What have you been doing all day?

M . . .

J Packing? Oh, yes, I'd forgotten – you're going to Geneva. I hope it goes well . . . erm . . . How long are you away for?

M . . .

J Oh, that's not too long. What about Dad? How is he?

M . . .

J Typical! A typical Sunday – gardening and cricket. Tell him I'll go to a match with him when I come home.

M . . .

J In two weeks. Term ends on the thirteenth. Oh – Mum, would it be OK if Lucinda came to stay in the holiday? Erm . . . we have to do a project together.

M . . .

J Thanks, Mum. Lucinda's just come back with the food. I'll ring again before I come home. Love to Dad.

M . . .

J Thanks. I need all the luck I can get. Bye. Have a good time in Geneva!

M . . .

Tapescript 39b

▶ **Phoning home – Justin and his mother**

M = Mother
J = Justin

M Hello. Bedford 21698.

J Hello, Mum. It's me, Justin.

M Hello, love. How are you?

J I'm fine, but I'm really tired.

M Oh – what have you been doing?

J Well, we've just started exams, so I've been staying up late . . . erm . . . it was three o'clock last night . . . yeah, I've been studying really hard.

M Of course, it's exam time. When did they start?

J Last Thursday. We had our first one on Thursday morning. It was terrible. I don't want to talk about it.

M OK. What else have you been doing?

J Not a lot. I've been working too hard. Sometimes I go round to Lucinda's place and we study together.

M Lucinda? I haven't heard about her before. Who is she?

J You know – Lucinda – I'm sure I've told you about her. She's doing the same course as me. I've known her for ages. We often help each other with work . . . erm . . . not . . . all the . . . er . . . time. Sometimes we go to the pub or cook a meal together. Today we've been testing each other on economics and marketing. That's tomorrow's exam. She's just gone out to get a Chinese takeaway.
Anyway, Mum – how are you and Dad? What have you been doing all day?

M Well, I've got another business trip tomorrow, so I've been packing all day – getting ready to go.

J Packing? Oh, yes, I'd forgotten – you're going to Geneva. I hope it goes well . . . erm . . . How long are you away for?

M Only three nights. It's a conference.

J Oh, that's not too long. What about Dad? How is he?

M He's very well, but pretty tired. It would be better if he didn't have to commute to London every day. He's been gardening most of today, and watching cricket on TV.

J Typical! A typical Sunday – gardening and cricket. Tell him I'll go to a match with him when I come home.

M Oh, yes – when exactly are you coming home?

J In two weeks. Term ends on the thirteenth. Oh – Mum, would it be OK if Lucinda came to stay in the holiday? Erm . . . we have to do a project together.

M That's fine, love. She's very welcome to stay. We'd like to meet her.

J Thanks, Mum. Lucinda's just come back with the food. I'll ring again before I come home. Love to Dad.

M Bye, love. And good luck in the exams!

J Thanks. I need all the luck I can get. Bye. Have a good time in Geneva!

M Thanks. Take care of yourself and work hard. Bye.

Tapescript 40

▶ Three phone calls

1 **A** Hello. 52902.
B Hello, Peter. This is John.
A Hi, John. How are you?
B Fine, thanks. And you?
A All right. Did you have a nice weekend? You went away, didn't you?
B Yes, we went to see some friends who live in the country. It was lovely. We had a good time.
A Ah, good.
B Peter, could you do me a favour? I'm playing squash tonight, but my racket's broken. Could I borrow yours?
A Sure, that's fine.
B Thanks a lot. I'll come and get it in half

an hour, if that's OK.
A Yes. I'll be in.
B OK. Bye.
A Bye.

2 **A** Hello. International School of English.
B Hello. Could I speak to Ann Baker, please?
A Hold on. I'll connect you.

C Hello.
B Hello. Can I speak to Ann Baker, please?
C Speaking.
B Ah, hello. I saw your advertisement about English classes in a magazine. Could you send me some information, please?
C Certainly. Can I just take some details? Could you give me your name and address, please?

3 **A** Hello. 755987.
B Hello. Is that Mike?
A No. I'm afraid he's out at the moment. Can I take a message?
B Yes, please. Can you say that Jim phoned, and I'll try again later. Do you know what time he'll be back?
A In about an hour, I think.
B Thanks. Goodbye.
A Goodbye.

Unit 15

Tapescript 41

▶ Past Perfect

a. We'd stopped playing when the rain started.
b. We stopped playing when the rain started.
c. We'd play tennis if the rain stopped.
d. When I arrived, she'd left.
e. When I arrived, she left.
f. We walked ten miles, then we had a rest.
g. We had a rest when we'd walked ten miles.
h. I'd like to stop for a rest.
i. She checked that she'd turned off the television.
j. I'd known him for many years when he died.

Tapescript 42

▶ An interview with Celia Young

C = Celia Young
I = Interviewer
I Celia – why have you written another romantic novel?
C Well, I find romantic fiction easy to write, but my next novel won't be a romance. I'm hoping to write something different, possibly a detective story.
I I'm interested in the character of Felix. Is

he anyone you know from real life?
C No . . . erm . . . I'm glad I don't have a Felix in my life. I've been happily married for over fifteen years . . . erm . . . to Richard Marsh, the politician.
I You've now written five novels. When did you start writing?
C Well, I've written stories and poems all my life and I'll continue to write even when I'm an old lady!
I Celia – thank you for talking to me. I hope *Hot Lips* will be successful.

Tapescript 43

▶ A love song

The girl of my best friend
The way she walks,
The way she talks,
How long can I pretend?
Oh, I can't help it, I'm in love
With the girl of my best friend.

Her lovely hair.
Her skin so fair.
I could go on and never end.
Oh, I can't help it, I'm in love
With the girl of my best friend.

I want to tell her how I love her so,
And hold her in my arms, but then
What if she got him and told him so?
I could never face either one again.

The way they kiss.
Their happiness.
Will my aching heart ever mend?
Or will I always be in love
With the girl of my best friend?

Never end.
Will it ever end?
Please let it end . . .

Tapescript 44

▶ Saying goodbye

1 Goodbye! Have a safe journey. Send us a postcard!
2 Goodbye. It's been most interesting talking to you. We'll let you know by post.
3 Goodbye. Thank you for a lovely evening. You must come to us next time.
4 Bye-bye! Thank you very much for having me.
5 Bye! See you later. Are you doing anything tonight?
6 Goodbye! Drive carefully and call us when you get there!
7 Goodbye. Here's my number. Please get in touch if you have any problems with it.
8 Goodbye! Good luck in the future. I've really enjoyed our lessons together!

WORKBOOK KEY

UNIT 1

Exercise 1
a. Is it raining?
b. Are they at school?
c. Are they learning English?
d. Are you tired?
e. Were you at home last night?
f. Am I right?
g. Has he got blond hair?
h. Can you speak Danish?

Exercise 2
a. Does she come from France?
b. Do they live in a flat?
c. Do you take sugar in tea?
d. Do I speak English well?
e. Did you watch a film last night?
f. Did it start at 8.00?
g. Do you want to go home?
h. Does he work hard?

Exercise 3
What? – A pair of jeans.
Who? – Peter.
Where? – At home.
When? – Yesterday.
Why? – Because I wanted to.
How? – By bus.
Whose? – Mine.

Exercise 4
a. What did you buy at the shops?
   A pair of jeans.
b. Who is the teacher?
   Peter.
c. Where are your parents at the moment?
   At home.
d. When did you see her?
   Yesterday.
e. Why did you go to Italy?
   Because I wanted to.
f. How do you come to school?
   By bus.
g. Whose is that car?/Whose car is that?
   Mine.

Exercise 5
a. How
b. What
c. Where
d. Who
e. What
f. Why
g. Where
h. Which
i. When
j. Why

Exercise 6
What colour is your hair?
Or How long is your hair?
How far is it from school to your house?
How tall are you?
What sort of music do you like?
How much does a hamburger cost in your town?
How often do you go swimming?
What size shoes do you take?
How long does your English lesson last?
What newspaper do you read?
What time did you get up this morning?

Exercise 7
Sample answers
a. What's it about?
b. What sort of car is it?
c. Where did you go?
d. Is she going on holiday?
e. What does he do?
f. How many children have they got?

Exercise 8
a. 1   c. 2   e. 1   g. 2
b. 3   d. 1   f. 3

Exercise 9
Sample answers
a. Yes, I am.
b. No, he/she isn't.
c. Yes, they are.
d. No, they aren't.
e. Yes, I am.
f. No, he/she isn't.

Exercise 10
thinking   shining   getting
waiting   smoking   stopping
raining   having   running
wearing   taking   beginning

Exercise 11
Sample answers

a. I'm not sitting in class.
b. It's raining.
c. The sun is shining.
d. I'm not wearing jeans.
e. I'm going out tonight.
f. We aren't having a holiday soon.
g. My parents are working.

Exercise 12
1 musician   artist   farmer
   scientist   politician   manager
   electrician   gardener   photographer

2 The musician is playing the piano.
   The farmer is driving a tractor.
   The scientist is doing an experiment.
   The politician is making a speech.
   The electrician is mending a plug.
   The photographer is taking a picture.
   The gardener is planting some flowers.
   The manager is making a phone call.

Exercise 13
a. because it is interesting
b. quiet
c. years
d. went to Italy
e. gave me a present
f. enjoying
g. hair
h. I usually go
i. an apple
j. then I went

UNIT 2

Exercise 1
a. Stefan Edberg doesn't play football. He plays tennis.
b. The Queen doesn't live at 33, Station Road, London. She lives in Buckingham Palace.
c. Kangaroos don't come from Canada. They come from Australia.
d. The sun doesn't shine at night. It shines in the daytime.
e. In England people don't drive on the right. They drive on the left.
f. My teacher doesn't arrive late. He/She arrives early.

Exercise 2
a. Where do you usually go at the weekend?
b. What time does the bank open?
c. Where does your mother come from?
d. Which school do your children go to?
e. Where does your brother work?
f. What sort of car does your sister drive?

Exercise 3
Sample answers

a. Yes, I do.
b. No, I don't.
c. No, I don't.
d. Yes, they do.
e. Yes, he/she does.
f. Yes, it does.

Exercise 4

wants	washes	studies	goes
reads	kisses	carries	does
eats	catches	flies	
thinks	crashes	cries	

Exercise 5
Sample answers

She listens to music.
She plays tennis.
She likes John Moore.
She reads a lot.
She doesn't tidy her room.
She watches TV in her room.
She draws and paints pictures.
She uses a computer.
She rides a horse.
She does ballet.
She takes photographs.

Exercise 6
a. Do you often go to the cinema?
b. I never eat meat, because I don't like it.
c. My parents always listen to the radio in the evening.
d. How often do you have a holiday?
e. We sometimes go to a Japanese restaurant.
f. I am never late for school.

Exercise 7
Correct verbs
a. I am reading
b. I read
c. We are going
d. Nurses look after
e. Annie comes
f. She is coming
g. I speak
h. Do you want

Exercise 8
a. is	d. am	g. are	j. are
b. Do	e. does	h. Do	
c. are	f. am	i. Does	

Exercise 9
a. He's a waiter.
b. Yes, he is.
c. He's serving food.
d. He's a taxi-driver.
e. No, he isn't.
f. He's reading a newspaper.
g. She's a chef.
h. Yes, she is.
i. She's cooking.

Exercise 10
a. is	d. is	g. is	i. is
b. is	e. has	h. is	j. is
c. has	f. has		

Exercise 11
a. She has a tennis racket.
   She's got a tennis racket.
b. She has a lot of books.
   She's got a lot of books.
c. She has an untidy room.
   She's got an untidy room.
d. She doesn't have a CD player.
   She hasn't got a CD player.
e. She has a computer.
   She's got a computer.
f. She doesn't have a Walkman.
   She hasn't got a Walkman.

Exercise 12
a. Yes, she has.
b. Yes, she does.
c. No, she hasn't.
d. No, she doesn't.

Sample answers

e. Yes, I have.
f. No, I don't.
g. Yes, I have.
h. No, I don't.

Exercise 13
a. a rug	f. a chest of drawers
b. a wardrobe	g. curtains
c. an armchair	h. a cupboard
d. a sofa	i. a fireplace
e. a bookcase	j. French windows

Exercise 14
a. Does he have/Has he got
b. She's a housewife.
c. speaks Spanish
d. red
e. in London to study
f. starting my first job
g. wears
h. one younger brother
i. He likes
j. because it is raining

Exercise 15
1 a. but	c. and	e. but			
b. so	d. and	f. so			

3 a. We enjoyed the holiday, but it rained a lot.
   We enjoyed the holiday. However, it rained a lot.
   Although it rained a lot, we enjoyed the holiday.
  b. He's moving to London next month, but he doesn't like big cities.
   He's moving to London next month. However, he doesn't like big cities.
   Although he doesn't like big cities, he's moving to London next month.
  c. She isn't English, but she speaks English perfectly.
   She isn't English. However, she speaks English perfectly.
   Although she isn't English, she speaks English perfectly.

4 a. The weather was bad, so we didn't enjoy our holiday.
   We didn't enjoy our holiday because the weather was bad.
  b. We wanted to get good seats, so we arrived at the cinema early.
   We arrived at the cinema early because we wanted to get good seats.
  c. He worked hard, so he passed all his exams.
   He passed all his exams because he worked hard.
  d. He worked hard. However, he didn't pass his exams.
   Although he worked hard, he didn't pass his exams.
  e. James is very rich, so she's getting married to him.
   She's getting married to James because he's very rich.
  f. She's getting married to James. However, she doesn't love him.
   She's getting married to James although she doesn't love him.

5 a. although	e. so	h. because
b. and	f. and	i. but
c. so	g. but	j. so
d. and			

UNIT 3

Exercise 1
a. lost
b. spent
c. laughed
d. saved
e. left
f. fell
g. hurt
h. couldn't
i. found
j. took
k. needed

Exercise 2
a. Christopher Columbus didn't discover India. He discovered America.
b. Beethoven didn't come from Paris. He came from Germany.
c. Leonardo da Vinci didn't live in Brazil. He lived in Italy.
d. The Americans didn't land on the moon in the nineteenth century. They landed on the moon in the twentieth century.
e. The USA didn't win the last football World Cup. (West Germany) did.
f. I didn't have grass for dinner! I had (chicken).

Exercise 3
a. Where did you go for your last holidays?
b. Where did you stay?
c. How long did you stay there for?
d. Did you have good weather?
e. How did you travel round?
f. Did you have good food?

Exercise 4
a. Yes, he did.
b. No, he didn't.
c. No, he didn't.

Sample answers

d. Yes, I did.
e. Yes, I did.
f. No, it didn't.

Exercise 5
wanted arrived planned
helped used travelled
washed liked robbed
walked smiled
made
felt
sent
knew

Exercise 6
a. in
b. when
c. for
d. ago
e. (nothing)
f. at
g. last
h. at in
i. On
j. When
k. on
l. In
m. ago
n. (nothing)
o. at in
p. (nothing)
q. in

Exercise 7
a. Annie and Pete were dancing.
b. Sarah and Bill were sitting on the sofa.
c. Katie was choosing a record.
d. Max was drinking champagne.
e. Beth and Dave were eating crisps.
f. Justin was showing Lucinda a photograph.
g. Harry was smoking a cigar.
h. James was telling a joke.

Exercise 8
MAN GETS SHOCK
… shock while he was mending a plug at his home …
… went home. 'I was trying to mend my wife's hair-drier,' he said. 'Suddenly …'

TREE DESTROYS HOUSE
… destroying it. 'I was working in the garden at the time,' she explained. 'It was quite windy …'
'… from our tree. The earth round the bottom of the tree was moving. Suddenly …'

POST OFFICE ROBBERY
… description of the two men, because they were wearing masks, but they know …
… Charlie Carrack, who was coming home from school at the time.

MOTORIST DRIVING AT 120 MPH
… stopped him on the motorway when he was travelling at 120 miles an hour. The speed …
… 70 miles an hour. 'I know I was driving fast,' he explained to the court. 'This was …'

Exercise 9
a. while
b. during
c. for
d. for
e. During
f. while
g. for
h. During
i. while
j. for
k. During
l. While

Exercise 10
Correct verb forms
a. met — was doing
b. was paying — heard
c. turned — saw
d. was wearing
e. decided
f. were having
g. got
h. was picking — cut
i. left — said
j. finished — went

Exercise 11
a. I had supper
b. Did you have a good game of tennis?
c. Have a nice time!
d. Did you have breakfast
e. I'm going to have a bath
f. if you want to have a swim
g. Did you have a good day
h. we had a row
i. Do you want to have a look?
j. Could I have a word with you

Exercise 12
2 a. 3 b. 1 c. 5 d. 2 e. 4 f. 6

3 One hot, sunny day in July, a tramp was walking along a country road. He was chewing a piece of grass because he felt hungry. Suddenly, on the other side of the hedge, he saw a pond with a large, white duck swimming round and round on it. The tramp had a good idea. Immediately he jumped over the hedge and ran towards the duck. Soon he was sitting by the pond with a large pile of white feathers beside him. Just then he heard a shout. The farmer was coming across the field, waving his arms. Hurriedly the tramp put the duck back into the water.
The farmer was very angry. He pointed to the pond and shouted, 'What's the matter with my duck?'
'Ah!' said the tramp quietly. 'It wanted to go for a swim, and I'm looking after its clothes!'

Exercise 13
a. I studied management for three years.
b. While I was on holiday Or During my holiday
c. I fell down
d. What did you do last night?
e. When he was 19 (years old) he went
f. I lost all my money.
g. last night Or yesterday evening
h. I met my husband
i. years
j. I left university

STOP AND CHECK 1–3

Questions
a. How many children has Peter got/does Peter have?
b. What are you reading?
c. Where did they go (to) on holiday last year?
d. Which shop does she work in?
e. Why did you get up early this morning?
f. When/What time does the supermarket close?
g. How often do you go swimming?
h. Whose car did you borrow?

Tenses
a. spends
b. Are you looking
c. don't have
d. doesn't like   love
e. bought   Do you like
f. was working   started
g. comes   lives   met   was learning

Have/have got
Sample answers

1   He has/He's got a hat/a cat/a kettle/a pair
    of boots/a walking stick.
    He hasn't got/doesn't have a car/a
    house/any money.
    He has/He's got a big house, a car, a
    swimming pool, a dog, a cigar.

2   Has he got a cat? Yes, he has.
    Does he have a house? No, he doesn't.
    Does he have a walking stick? Yes, he
    does.
    Has he got any money? No, he hasn't.

Past tense forms

heard	could	broke	phoned	put
caught	lived	began	hit	tried
left	fell	made	felt	built

Prepositions

a. to   on   f. (nothing)
b. at   in   g. in
c. in   in/near   h. (nothing)
d. after   i. to
e. for   j. on/until

Vocabulary

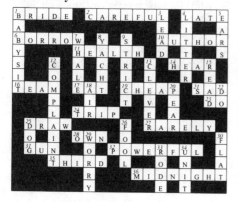

UNIT 4

Exercise 1

a. a stamp   i. a job
b. a book   j. some work
c. some petrol   k. an apple
d. a tree   l. some fruit
e. some air   m. a tomato
f. some money   n. some tomato soup
g. a pound   o. a problem
h. some music   p. some information

Exercise 2

a. paper   f. potato
b. a newspaper   g. glass
c. coffee   h. a glass
d. a coffee   i. a cake
e. a potato   j. cake

Exercise 3

a. any   f. any
b. some   g. some
c. any   h. some
d. some   i. any
e. some   any   j. any

Exercise 4

a. How many children has she got?
b. How much butter do you want?
c. How many countries did you visit?
d. How much was it?
e. How many bedrooms has it got?
f. How many people are coming?
g. How many plays did he write?
h. How much does she earn?

Exercise 5

a. There is a lot of oil.
b. The shop has a lot of bottles of water.
c. There isn't much frozen food.
d. There aren't many sweets.
e. The shopkeeper has got a lot of cheese.
f. I can see a lot of newspapers.
g. But I can't see much bread.
h. There isn't much yoghurt.
i. He hasn't got many birthday cards to
    choose from.
j. But there are a lot of grapes!
k. Why aren't there many magazines?
l. But there is a lot of rice!

Exercise 6

a. A little. I'll go to the dentist tomorrow.
b. A few. But no one that you know.
c. A little. The children ate most of it.
d. A little. Do you want some ice in it?
e. A few. You can borrow them if you want.
f. A little. I'm trying to lose weight.
g. A few. But most of them come from
    France.
h. A little. But I prefer reading.
i. A few. But most of them are bills.
j. A little. It takes them about an hour a night.

Exercise 7

a. a   a   the   the   the
b. the   the
c. a   a   a   The   the
d. a   a   an   the
e. the   the
f. an
g. the   the
h. a
i. the   the

Exercise 8

Cows eat grass.
Leaves fall off trees in autumn.
Wood floats on water.
Cats like eating fish.
Wine comes from grapes.
Birds live in trees.
Children go to school until they're 16.

Cars need oil and petrol.
Fruit is full of vitamins.

Exercise 9

a. (nothing)   (nothing)
b. the
c. (nothing)   (nothing)
d. the
e. a   (nothing)
f. the
g. (nothing)
h. a   (nothing)
i. (nothing)   the
j. the
k. (nothing)   the
l. (nothing)   a
m. (nothing)
n. the

Exercise 10

a. boys   i. churches
b. ladies   j. addresses
c. days   k. stories
d. potatoes   l. sandwiches
e. parties   m. keys
f. watches   n. videos
g. glasses   o. ways
h. cities

p. children   s. teeth
q. people   t. sheep
r. women   u. fish

Exercise 11

a. socks   f. a tie   k. a skirt
b. boots   g. a raincoat   l. a scarf
c. sandals   h. pyjamas   m. shorts
d. a belt   i. a blouse   n. a suit
e. a jacket   j. a shirt   o. tights

Exercise 12

a. came here   f. look at my photos
b. went to a pub   g. a lot of things
c. Is there enough h. There isn't any
    salt?   i. music
d. dinner   j. must go
e. information

Exercise 13

1   First name – What's your first name?
    Surname – What's your family name?
    Date of Birth – When were you born?
    Place of Birth – Where were you born?
    Permanent Address – Where do you live?
    Marital Status – Are you married or single?
    Occupation – What do you do?
    Qualifications – What degrees, diplomas,
        certificates, etc. do you have?
    Hobbies/Interests – What do you do in
        your free time?
    Tel. no. – What's your phone number?

UNIT 5

Exercise 1
a. to see
b. to hear
c. painting
d. learning/to learn
e. having/to have
f. to post
g. to get
h. to laugh/laughing
i. to do
j. to go
k. listening/to listen
l. to take
m. talking/to talk

Exercise 2
Sample answers

a. Jane is going to be a vet because she likes working with animals.
b. Malcolm wants to be a farmer because he enjoys being outside in the fresh air.
c. Suzy hopes to be a stockbroker because she wants to earn a lot of money.
d. Gill would like to do voluntary service because she wants to help children in the Third World.
e. Justin is going to do a master's degree because he enjoys being a student.
f. Janine wants to be an accountant because she likes working with numbers.
g. My father hopes to retire next year because he wants to have more free time.
h. David wants to be captain of the football team because he loves being the leader.
i. My parents are going to buy a cottage by the sea because they enjoy sailing.
j. My family is going to have a holiday in Rome because we like walking round old cities.

Exercise 3
a. What did she want to talk about?
   She wanted to talk about a problem she's having.
b. Why did you decide to do that?
   I decided to leave the job because it was boring.
c. Did you forget to tell her?
   I forgot to say exactly when.
d. What time do you want to leave the house?
   I want to leave as early as possible.
e. When did you finish reading it?
   I finished (reading) it last night.
f. What would you like to do?
   I'd like to stay at home.

Exercise 4
Would you like to watch TV? – No. There's nothing good on tonight.
Would you like something to eat? – No, thanks. I'm not hungry.
Do you like parties? – I'm afraid I don't. I think they're noisy, and there are usually too many people.
Do you like chips? – No. I think they're very bad for you.
Do you like watching TV? – Yes, especially films and cartoons.
Would you like to come to a party on Saturday? – That's lovely! What time?

Exercise 5
Correct questions

a. Do you like your teacher?
b. Do you like going for walks?
c. Would you like to go for a swim?
d. What do you like doing at the weekend?
e. What would you like to do this evening?

Exercise 6
a. What sort of books do you like reading?
   I like biographies and thrillers.
b. Would you like to be a teacher when you grow up?
c. What would she like for a present?
   Well, I know she likes cooking.
d. She likes drawing.
e. . . . she would like to run in the Olympic Games.

Exercise 7
a. I'll do the washing-up.
b. I'll pay for the coffee.
c. I'll have a lamb chop, please.
d. I'll answer it.

Exercise 8
a. He's going to fall down the hole.
b. The books are going to fall on her head.
c. She's going to buy the book/learn Japanese.
d. They are going to plant a rose.
e. He's going to build a bookcase/ bookshelves.
f. It's going to jump onto the wall.

Exercise 9
Correct verb forms

a. I'm going to buy
b. What are you going to buy
   I'll buy her a record
c. She'll do it
d. I'll tell   I won't
e. I'm going to make
f. What are you going to do
   I'm going to make
g. Why are you going to see
   my husband and I are going to start
h. I'll lend
   I'll give

Exercise 10

Health	The weather	Football
optician (*n*)	flood (*n* and *v*)	kick (*n* and *v*)
insect cream (*n*)	mist (*n*)	draw (*n* and *v*)
aspirin (*n*)	sunshine (*n*)	goal (*n*)
prescription (*n*)	snow (*n* and *v*)	win (*n* and *v*)
painful (*adj*)	foggy (*adj*)	referee
fit (*adj*)	chilly (*adj*)	(*n* and *v*)
cough (*n* and *v*)	freeze (*v*)	score (*n* and *v*)

Exercise 11
a. I'd like to go
b. took care of their cat
c. wants to go
d. buy
e. Yes, he does.
f. like to come
g. hoping
h. from Anna. She sent it from Paris.
i. eat
j. They don't want

Exercise 12
2 a. lovely
   b. terrible
   c. comfortable   small
   d. spectacular
   e. old
   f. long
   g. good

UNIT 6

Exercise 1
a. What's the countryside like?
b. What are the people like?
c. What are the towns like?
d. What is Sydney like?
e. What are the kangaroos like?
f. What are the beaches like?
g. What are the TV programmes like?

Exercise 2
a. What was the flight like?
b. What was the weather like?
c. What were the beaches like?
d. What was the food like?

Exercise 3

beautiful	more beautiful	most beautiful
new	newer	newest
lovely	lovelier	loveliest
hot	hotter	hottest
good	better	best
handsome	more handsome	most handsome
mean	meaner	meanest
generous	more generous	most generous
thin	thinner	thinnest
busy	busier	busiest
patient	more patient	most patient
young	younger	youngest
bad	worse	worst
comfortable	more comfortable	most comfortable
rude	ruder	rudest
fit	fitter	fittest

Exercise 4
a. 16
b. Robert.
c. 12
d. No, she isn't.
e. No, I'm not.
f. Graham and Abigail.

Exercise 5
a. ruder
b. the smallest
c. better
d. warmer
e. the most expensive
f. more generous
g. earlier
h. the most difficult

Exercise 6
a. as
b. as
c. than
d. as
e. than
f. as

Exercise 7
a. Bill's not as intelligent as Jill.
b. The moon isn't as hot as the sun.
c. Are you as old as your husband?
d. I can't read as quickly as you.
e. Bill didn't win as much money as Harry.
f. Is Luxembourg as big as Switzerland?
g. My work isn't as good as Eva's.
h. Cats aren't as friendly as dogs.

Exercise 9
A hill is smaller than a mountain. *Or* A mountain is bigger than a hill.
A clock is bigger than a watch.
An armchair is smaller than a sofa.
A suitcase is bigger than a briefcase.
A cottage is smaller than a castle.
A motorway is bigger than a path.
A lorry is bigger than a van.
A pond is smaller than a lake.
A boot is bigger than a shoe.
A kitten is smaller than a cat.
A jacket is smaller than a coat.
A river is bigger than a stream.
A cup is smaller than a mug.
A village is smaller than a town.
A bush is smaller than a tree.

Exercise 10
a. there is a castle
b. than
c. What would you like to eat?
d. as useful as yours
e. as many tapes as you
f. Where did you go
g. There were
h. the richest woman
i. It was very hot
j. then we went

Exercise 11
1 a. the boy who broke
b. the palace where the Sultan lives.
c. the policemen who caught
d. a watch which/that stopped
e. the pub where we met
f. the letters that/which arrived
g. the house where I was born.
h. the lady who ordered
i. the children who live
j. The clothes that come from Marks & Spencer are good quality.

2 a. which/that
b. where
c. who
d. where
e. who

STOP AND CHECK 4–6

Expressions of quantity
1 a. some   any
b. any   any
c. some
d. any   some
e. some
2 a. How much money
b. a few potatoes
c. much time
d. a lot of hotels
e. many language schools
f. I've got something
g. John lives somewhere
h. Somebody told me

Articles
a. the   the
b. The   the
c. (nothing)
d. (nothing)   a
e. an
f. (nothing)   a   a
g. a   the

Verb patterns
a. to share
b. going
c. to live
d. to find
e. to meet
f. travelling

Going to and *will*
a. I'm going to cook
b. I'm going to study
c. He'll help
d. I'll buy
e. I'm going to cut

Descriptions
1 What's the weather like? – It changes a lot.
What's Ann like? – She's very nice.
What was the film like? – OK, but boring near the end.
What does she like doing? – Horse riding.
What are her parents like? – They're a bit strict.
2 faster   fastest
funnier   funniest
more expensive   most expensive
richer   richest
hotter   hottest
more interesting   most interesting
better   best
worse   worst
easier   easiest
more important   most important

Vocabulary

UNIT 7

Exercise 1
a. have been
b. has met
c. has travelled
d. has seen
e. has hunted
f. has ridden
g. has been
h. has been
i. have been
j. have lived
k. has never been
l. has had
m. has done
n. has certainly had

Exercise 2
a. He has been to the North Pole.
He has seen polar bears.
He has never got lost.
b. They haven't had a job for six months.
They haven't had a holiday since Christmas.
They haven't been to the cinema for a year.
c. She has played since she was six.
She hasn't won a senior competition.
She has never played at Wimbledon.

Exercise 3
a. Have you ever got lost?
b. Have you ever forgotten your words?
c. Have you ever climbed Mount Everest?
d. Have you ever fallen off your ladder?
e. Have you ever had a number one record?
f. Have you ever had an electric shock?

Exercise 4
a. Yes, he has.
b. No, he hasn't.
c. Yes, they have.
d. Yes, he has.

Sample answers

e. No, I haven't.
f. Yes, I have.
g. No, he/she hasn't.
h. Yes, I have.

Exercise 5
written   found
won   visited

sold	stopped
tried	studied
read	died
played	done

Exercise 6

a. for	d. since	g. for
b. since	e. for	h. since
c. for	f. since	

Exercise 7

Correct sentences

a. did you do	d. have studied
b. have been	e. for three weeks
c. went	f. did you buy

Exercise 8

a. is	d. has been	g. lived
b. went	e. was	h. moved
c. became	f. has written	i. live

Exercise 9

a. When did he go to Oxford University?
b. When did he become a Member of Parliament?
c. How long has he been an MP?
d. When was he Defence Minister?
e. How many books has he written?
f. Has he ever written a spy story?
g. What does his wife do?
h. How many children do they have/have they got?
i. How long did they live in Oxford?
j. When did they move to London?
k. Where do they live?
l. How long have they lived in London?

Exercise 10

a. try on – jeans
  tear – jeans
  lick – ice-cream
b. wipe – the blackboard, your face
  whistle – a tune
c. carry – a suitcase, a bag
  wear – a suit
d. pour – a drink, with rain
  blow – your nose
e. use – a hammer
  waste – time, money

Exercise 11

a. My husband and I
b. my aunt who lives
c. a city in Spain
d. studied tourism for three years
e. university when I was twenty-three
f. for five years
g. did you go
h. bored
i. have you known
j. They haven't lived

Exercise 12

1.
a. that/which	f. that, which
b. (who)	g. (that/which)
c. who	h. that/which
d. (that/which)	i. (who)
e. who	

2. 2 Paragraph 1 ends ... Velvet.
  Paragraph 2 ends ... in 1962.
  Paragraph 3 ends ... the most.
  Paragraph 4 ends ... addictions.
3 where film makers
  child stars who
  first marriage, which
  the man (who) she loved the most
  Clinic, where

UNIT 8

Exercise 1

a. have to take	e. have to make
b. have to go	f. has to wear
c. have to drive	g. had to go
d. has to be	

Exercise 2

a. don't have to pay	e. don't have to iron
b. doesn't have to do	f. doesn't have to do
c. didn't have to do	g. didn't have to go
d. don't have to ask	

Exercise 3

a. Do you have to wear a uniform in your job?
b. Why did you have to buy so many books?
c. Do you have to get a visa to go to the States?
d. How often does John have to take his pills?
e. Do you have to look after this plant very carefully?

Exercise 4

Sample answers

a. Yes, he/she does.	d. Yes, I did.
b. No, I don't.	e. Yes, I do.
c. No, he doesn't.	

Exercise 5

Sample answers

I have to get up early in the morning. School starts at 8.00.
I don't have to do the cooking. My mother does it.
We have to do the washing-up. My sister and I do it.
My parents have to go to work. They work five days a week.
My mother has to do the ironing. She hates it.
My father doesn't have to work in the garden. We haven't got one.
My sister has to babysit when my parents go out.

My brother has to make his bed in the morning. He moans about it.
My grandmother has to do the shopping. She doesn't mind.
My grandfather doesn't have to get up early in the morning. He's retired.

Exercise 6

Sample answers

a. I think you should go to the dentist.
b. I think you should phone the police and tell your bank.
c. I don't think he should drive.
d. I think she should write to people instead of phoning them.
e. I think you should take them back to the shop.
f. I think they should wait.
g. I think you should tell them to buy fruit.
h. I think you should be more careful.

Exercise 7

Sample answers

a. Do you think I should go?
b. Do you think I should ask her for it?
c. Do you think I should accept?
d. Do you think I should apologize?
e. What do you think he should do?
f. Do you think I should buy it?

Exercise 8

a. should	f. don't have to
b. shouldn't	g. should
c. have to	h. don't have to
d. should	i. shouldn't
e. have to	j. should

Exercise 9

Clothes – jumper, anorak, boots, tracksuit, gloves
Food – Christmas turkey, thick soup, stew, baked potatoes
Weather – ice, mist, frost, fog, snow, grey skies
Things I like doing – going tobogganing, going for walks on bright, frosty mornings, opening Christmas presents, sitting in front of an open fire

Exercise 10

a. when it is warm
b. went to Brazil
c. doesn't have to
d. to do the shopping
e. You can't smoke
f. to my aunt's house
g. Does he have to leave
h. it is quiet
i. he made so many mistakes
j. think I should

Exercise 11

1 Dear Sir or Madam – Yours faithfully
   Robert J Fleming (formal)
   Dear Ms McDonald – Yours sincerely
   Robert Fleming (formal)
   Dear Helen – Love, Bob (informal)
   Dear Philip – Yours, Bob (informal)
   Darling Rosie – Lots of love, Bobby XXX
   (informal)

3
                              Rua Luis de Deus 18,
                              3000 Coimbra,
                              Portugal.

The Principal,
The Oxford English College,
234 Hilton Rd.,
Eastbourne BN4 3UA

                              29 March 1991.

Dear Sir or Madam,

I saw your advertisement for English classes in this month's *English Today* magazine and I am interested in coming to your school this summer.
I have studied English for three years but I have never been to England and I feel that this is now necessary, especially to improve my pronunciation. Please could you send me more information about your courses, and an application form. I would also like some information about accommodation.
I look forward to hearing from you as soon as possible.

Yours faithfully,
Ana Maria Fernandes

UNIT 9

Exercise 1

The summer will be very wet.
There will be a General Election in the autumn.
Liverpool will win the football championship.
Astronauts will land on Mars.
Scientists will find a cure for cancer.
The Prime Minister will resign because of a political scandal.
The Queen will have more grandchildren.
Thieves will steal the Mona Lisa from the Louvre.

Exercise 2

a. I won't pass them.
b. She won't lie.
c. I won't lose it.
d. We won't eat at home.
e. We won't turn it up.
f. I won't go to bed late.
g. We won't stay late.
h. I won't refuse it.

Exercise 3

Sample answers

a. Do you think you'll have a bath tonight? Perhaps.
b. How long do you think your homework will take?
   About two hours.
c. What time do you think you'll go to bed?
   About 11.00.
d. Do you think you'll go abroad next year?
   I hope so.
e. Where do you think you'll go?
   I don't know. Maybe to Japan.
f. Do you think Brazil will win the football match?

Exercise 4

Correct forms

a. I'll open it.
b. I'll buy it for you.
c. I buy *The Times*.
d. I'll have lamb.
e. We have supper at about 8.00.
f. OK. I'll answer it.

Exercise 5

a. will start
b. will try
c. If
d. succeeds
e. will be
f. will go
g. When
h. arrive
i. will join
j. As soon as
k. get
l. will have to
m. will do
n. will help
o. If
p. is
q. will make
r. When
s. get
t. will show

Exercise 6

If the sea gets warmer, the ice at the North and South Poles will melt.
If the ice melts, the sea level will rise.
If the sea level rises, there will be floods in many parts of the world.
If there are floods, many people will lose their homes and land.

Exercise 7

a. What will you do if the plane is late?
b. Where will you stay if the hotels are full?
c. Who will you talk to if you don't make any friends?
d. What will you do if you don't like the food?
e. Where will you go if the beaches are crowded?
f. What will you do if you get sunburnt?

Exercise 8

a. If
b. when
c. when
d. If
e. If
f. When
g. when
h. If

Exercise 9

a. I'll wait here until you get back.
b. Give me a ring when you hear some news.
c. After the TV programme ends, I'll do my homework.
d. Before I go to work, I'll have a bath.
e. While she's in Paris, she'll visit friends.
f. As soon as the lesson ends, I'll go home.
g. I won't leave the house until the postman calls.
h. Can you feed the cats while I'm away?
i. I'll tell you about the holiday when I get back.
j. I'll study English until I speak it perfectly.

Exercise 10

Sample answers

a. They are all books, but you read a magazine for pleasure. The others are reference books.
b. They are all musical instruments, but you blow a trumpet. The others have strings.
c. They are all forms of transport, but a bicycle doesn't have an engine (*or* has only two wheels).
d. They are all fruit, but a grapefruit is yellow. The others are red.
e. They are all animals with four legs, but an elephant is the only one with a trunk.
f. A spider is the only one that can't fly.
g. They are places to live, but a caravan is mobile.
h. They are all liquids, but petrol is the only one you can't drink.
i. They are all tools, but a spade is the only one you use in the garden.
j. They are all games, but you play chess on a board. You play the others with a ball.

Exercise 11

a. arrived in Tokyo
b. Sylvia and Ronald arrive
c. interested in
d. should do
e. When I go back
f. Yesterday she travelled by plane to New York.
g. I won't buy
h. he comes
i. We must/we'll have to
j. If you want

Exercise 12

2 Travelling by train has many advantages. First of all, there are no stressful traffic jams, and trains are fast and comfortable. Also, you can use the time in different ways, for example, you can just sit and read, or watch the world go by. You can work, or you can have a meal or a snack in the buffet car.
   However, travelling by train also has some disadvantages. For one thing it is expensive

and the trains are sometimes crowded and delayed. What is more, you have to travel at certain times and trains cannot take you from door to door. You need a bus or a taxi, for example, to take you to the railway station.

Despite the disadvantages, I prefer travelling by train to travelling by car, because I feel more relaxed when I reach my destination.

Purpose of each paragraph
1 – advantages of trains
2 – disadvantages of trains
3 – personal opinion

STOP AND CHECK 7–9

Past Simple and past participle

made/made	travelled/travelled
tried/tried	knew/known
won/won	wrote/written
drank/drunk	acted/acted
ate/eaten	spent/spent
had/had	spoke/spoken
saw/seen	
broke/broken	
read/read	

Present Perfect Simple

1. a. has written   wrote
   b. Have you ever tried
   c. I have never been   When did you go
   d. I have lived
   e. lived   moved
   f. met   have you known
2. a. for   since
   b. never
   c. for   ever
   d. since   never
3. Sample answers
   a. How long have you lived
      For ten years.
   b. Have you ever drunk
      Yes, I have.
   c. have you visited
      Five.
   d. did you go
      To Italy.
   e. did you do
      We went sightseeing.
   f. have you known
      For years and years.

Have to and *should*

a. have to
b. should
c. don't have to
d. have to
e. should
f. don't have to
g. should
h. don't have to

First Conditional and time clauses

1. a. eat   will be
   b. will fail   don't study
   c. will you do   fail
   d. will suffer   don't look after
   e. will do   finishes
   f. reads   will understand
   g. will he stay   goes
   h. will give   arrives

2. If I pass my driving test, I'll buy a car.
   You'll learn English more easily if you study a little every day.
   Will you give her these flowers when you see her?
   If they don't give him the job, I don't know what he'll do.
   I'll marry you as soon as we find somewhere to live.
   Your plants won't grow well if you don't water them.
   As soon as we get the tickets, we'll send them to you.
   If I buy the champagne, will you pay for the meal?

Vocabulary

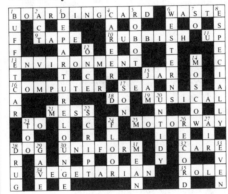

UNIT 10

Exercise 1

I was very fit when I was young. I used to do a lot of exercise.

The teachers at my school were horrible. They used to hit the pupils.

My sister's room was so messy. She never used to tidy it at all.

I had a dog when I was a kid. It used to follow me everywhere.

My family had some lovely holidays. We used to go camping all over Europe.

When I was young, we didn't have a car. We used to go everywhere by bus.

And we didn't have central heating. We used to freeze on winter mornings.

My uncle was a pilot for British Airways. He used to fly Concorde.

Exercise 2

Sample answers

a. The houses used to be cheap.
b. They used to be clean.
c. There didn't use to be any litter.
d. They used to be empty/It used to be easy to park.
e. There didn't use to be a lot of traffic.
f. It used to be quiet.
g. He used to be so cheerful!
h. He used to be so generous.
i. He used to dress so carefully.

Exercise 3

a. He never used to. He used to drive carefully.
b. She never used to. She used to be very careful with her money.
c. They never used to. They used to get on well.
d. She never used to. She used to tell the truth.
e. She never used to. She used to be the first one up in the morning.
f. It never used to. It used to work perfectly.

Exercise 4

a. 1   d. 2
b. 1   e. 1
c. 2   f. 2

Exercise 5

a. What happened at the end?
b. Who broke the vase?
c. Who comes to school by car?
d. What happened at the party?
e. Who wants an ice-cream, and who wants a lolly?
f. Which goes faster, a BMW or a Jaguar?
g. Who took my pen?
h. Who wants to watch a film, and who wants to work on the computer?

Exercise 6

a. How many people did Andrew save?
b. How many people died in the crash?
c. Who saw the helicopter crash?
d. Where did it crash?
e. How far did Andrew run to get to the scene of the accident?
f. What does Andrew's father do?
g. Who phoned for an ambulance and the fire brigade?
h. What did the Chief Fire Officer say?

Exercise 7

Sample answers

a. What are you listening to?
b. Who is she talking to?
   What is she talking about?
c. What are you thinking about?
d. What are they looking for?
e. Who is she going on holiday with?
f. Who are you going out with?

g. What was it about?
h. What did you argue about?
i. Who is he in love with?
j. Who is she getting married to?

Exercise 8

It's chilly today, isn't it? – Yes, there was a frost last night.
You don't like this food, do you? – Well, I find it a bit too salty.
You know the Browns, don't you? – Yes. They live next door to me.
This exercise isn't hard, is it? – No. It's quite easy.
You've got a car, haven't you? – Yes. A Renault.
You haven't met Henry, have you? – No. How do you do.

Exercise 9

The following are the words which are different.

a. ear   e. lower   h. pies
b. word   f. far   i. food
c. home   g. fool   j. road
d. wrong

Exercise 10

a. Where I live now there is
b. used
c. that it is always raining
d. Who told you
e. I'm looking
f. women
g. There are twenty students
h. used to go
i. to look at?
j. finished doing

Exercise 11

3 1 e.   2 d.   3 c.   4 a.   5 b.

UNIT 11

Exercise 1

a. was sold
b. was made
c. is known
d. was bought
e. has been played/was played
f. were demonstrated
g. has been kept
h. has been looked
i. were made
j. are admired

Exercise 2

a. Where has it been kept?
b. When were Stradivari's best instruments made?
c. When were the Houses of Parliament built?

d. How many people were hurt in the crash?
e. Where is champagne produced?
f. How many times has it been washed?
g. How much was she fined?
h. How much are school teachers paid?
i. How often is your post delivered?
j. Why were they given an award?

Exercise 3

Sample answers

a. President Kennedy wasn't killed in New York. He was killed in Dallas.
b. Coffee isn't grown in Scotland. It's grown in Brazil.
c. *Sunflowers* wasn't painted by Renoir. It was painted by van Gogh.
d. Walkman cassette players weren't developed by the Russians. They were developed by the Japanese.
e. The Berlin Wall wasn't knocked down in 1982. It was knocked down in 1989.
f. The 1988 Olympic games weren't held in Paris. They were held in Seoul, Korea.
g. Rolls-Royce cars aren't made in Japan. They're made in England.
h. Coca-Cola hasn't been produced for over two hundred years. It has been produced since 1895.

Exercise 4

a. No, it wasn't.   c No, it hasn't.
b. Yes, it is.   d Yes, they were.

Sample answers
e. Yes, it is.
f. No, it hasn't.

Exercise 5

a. A part-time assistant is wanted.
   They want a part-time assistant.
b. Jewellery is bought and sold.
   They buy and sell jewellery.
c. Credit cards are accepted.
   They accept credit cards.
d. Afternoon tea is served.
   They serve afternoon tea.
e. Dogs aren't allowed to go in that shop.
   They don't allow dogs to go in.

Exercise 6

MOZART MAKES RECORD
A Mozart manuscript which *was lost* for forty years *was sold* at an auction yesterday. The signed piano works *were bought* by an Austrian library for a record £880,000.

DRUGS SEIZE AT AIRPORT
A 40-year-old businessman from Birmingham *was arrested* last night at Heathrow Airport. A substance believed to be cocaine *was found* in his suitcase. He *was questioned* by customs officials before being taken to Acton Police Station.

TRAIN CRASH AT 80mph
The London-Edinburgh express *was derailed* yesterday morning as it was passing through York station. Four people *were taken* to hospital, but no one was seriously hurt. Trains *were delayed* for the rest of the day.

FELLOWS LOSES FIGHT
Former champion Larry Fellows lost his fight in Dallas last night when he *was knocked out* in the eighth round by Joe Wheeler. After the fight Joe *was crowned* heavyweight champion of the world. The fight *was stopped* in the second round when the crowd started to throw objects at the referee, who the crowd thought was being unfair to the former champion.

Exercise 7

a. Entry 3, definition 2 (b)
b. Entry 3, definition 1
c. Entry 1, definition 2
d. Entry 2
e. Entry 1, definition 2
f. Entry 1, definition 1
g. Entry 2, definition 2
h. Entry 1, definition 4
i. Entry 1, definition 1
j. Entry 3
k. Entry 4
l. Entry 2
m. Entry 3, definition 1
n. Entry 3, definition 3

Exercise 8

1 1 – d   2 – a   3 – c   4 – b
3 Present Simple

Exercise 9

a. got it?   f. Germany
b. have they been   g. made
c. man who came   h. chosen
d. ran to the end   i. did they come
e. wasn't painted   j. by Shakespeare

UNIT 12

Exercise 1

a. to decide   h. to rent
b. to go   i. (to) choose
c. visiting   j. to have
d. sightseeing   k. talking/to talk
e. playing   l. to enjoy
f. to go   m. to think
g. to find

Exercise 2

a. to start   d. pay
b. reading   e. to be
c. to do

Exercise 3

a. She wanted her children to tidy their room.
b. She refused to lend me any money.

c. I advised Jerry to look for a better job.
d. She told her children to get out of bed.
e. He asked his daughter to post a letter.
f. The teacher let the class go home early.
g. My piano teacher makes me practise for two hours every day.
h. I managed to save £1000 in six months.

Exercise 4
a. What do you want me to do?
b. What did she tell you to do?
c. What did she help to do?
d. What would you like to do tonight?
e. What did they make you do?
f. What do you hope to do after university?

Exercise 5
a. This book is easy to read.
b. It was lovely to see you last night.
c. It's easy to make mistakes when you're learning a language.
d. It's important to keep vocabulary records.
e. I'm pleased to see you've stopped smoking.
f. It's impossible to keep the house tidy with five children.
g. It's unusual to have long, hot summers in England.

Exercise 6
I went for a walk to get some fresh air.
I'm going to the library to change my books.
I went to town to do some shopping.
I phoned the theatre to find out what time the play started.
I want to borrow some money to buy a new car.
I bought some flowers to make the house smell nice.
I'm going to Paris to visit some friends.
I wrote to John to explain how to get to my house.

Exercise 7
Corrections

a. teacher's book   Maria's house
b. teachers' room
c. says it's
d. dogs
e. its
f. (no mistakes)
g. Six pounds a kilo   That's expensive
   its flavour
h. Whose   they're yours   aren't they?
i. They're
j. can't   country's

Exercise 8
courage   operation
encouragement   notice
honesty   argument
belief   decision
organization   heat

share   importance
blood   advertisement
vote

Exercise 9
a. boring
b. excited
c. worried
d. surprised
e. interesting   tiring
f. frightened
g. worrying
h. interested   tired
i. exciting
j. annoyed

Exercise 10
a. decided to leave
b. I'm sorry I'm late.
c. address
d. the bank to change
e. Jane's
f. stories
g. ate his breakfast very quickly
h. John and I went
i. a friend of mine
j. seen Ann's new car

Exercise 11
Sample answers

1 a. Unfortunately I can't
   b. went downstairs
   c. Then she went
   d. Last Thursday evening, I was sitting
   e. lying upstairs in bed
   f. we have a son called Simon, too.
   g. very interested
   h. worked hard

   Picture 1
2 a. saw a mouse
   b. screamed and jumped up on a chair
   c. she was frightened

   Picture 2
   d. up
   e. ran
   f. to get

   Picture 3
   g. couldn't find him
   h. found him under
   i. grabbed him (under her arm)
   j. ran

   Picture 4
   k. put
   l. on
   m. got up on the chair
   n. was frightened/scared
   o. jumped up/leapt onto her shoulder

STOP AND CHECK 10–12

Used to
She used to have a pet dog, but she doesn't/hasn't any more.
She didn't use to go horse-riding, but now she does.
She used to have long hair, but she doesn't any more.
She didn't use to like ballet, but now she does.
She used to love cooking, but she doesn't any more.
She didn't use to wear make-up, but now she does.
They used to go out a lot, but they don't any more.
They didn't use to watch TV, but now they do.
They used to go sailing, but they don't any more.
They didn't use to own a house, but now they do.

Questions
a. Who broke
b. Who invented
c. Who earns
d. What happened
e. Where did you go
f. Who did you talk to
g. What are you listening to?
h. What are you looking for?

Passives
Correct forms
1 a. created   e. made
   b. is called   f. have been
   c. was called   translated
   d. was given   g. have been made.

2 a. was designed   d. was made
   b. was asked   e. have been produced
   c. were taken   f. are not made

Verb patterns
1 a. He asked his children to play quietly.
   b. She asked them to be careful with the record player.
   c. He told David to stop walking on the flowers.
   d. She told Beth to pick up her litter.
   e. He told all the children to go to bed.

2 a. cry
   b. making
   c. to save
   d. learning
   e. go
   f. to explain
   g. to have

Vocabulary

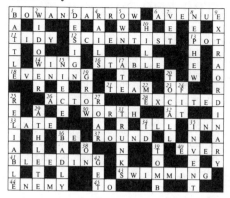

UNIT 13

Exercise 1

a. he'd wear a suit.
b. he'd have coffee and croissants.
c. he'd work in an office.
d. he'd play squash.
e. he'd go to clubs.
f. he'd go to bed at midnight.

Exercise 2

a. shares
b. were/was
c. would live
d. lived
e. would buy
f. would grow
g. travels
h. goes
i. doesn't like
j. were/was
k. would ride
l. would buy
m. loves
n. goes
o. would walk

Exercise 3

a. What would he wear?
b. What would he have for breakfast?
c. Where would he work?
d. Where would he go in the evening?
e. What time would he go to bed?

Exercise 4

a. No, she wouldn't.
b. Yes, she would.
c. No, she wouldn't.
d. Yes, she would.
e. Yes, she would.

Exercise 5

a. If he didn't work in the evening, he'd have time to play with his children.
b. If she didn't buy so many clothes, she'd have more money.
c. If I had a car, I'd give you a lift.
d. If I didn't go to bed late, I wouldn't be tired in the morning.
e. If she had a watch, she wouldn't always be late.

Exercise 6

a. We might go to Spain.
b. I might get my cheque.
c. Joe and Ellie might pop in.
d. You might lose them.
e. He might not like it.

Exercise 7

Correct forms

a. I might go   I might stay
b. I'm going to cook
c. he might not like
d. I'll phone
e. she might be

Exercise 8

Sample answers

a. She might fall off.
b. She might not pass them.
c. They might make a mess.
d. The car might break down.
e. He might need a filling.
f. She might miss the plane.

Exercise 9

Sample answers

1 feel sleepy
2 yawn
3 brush my teeth
4 get undressed
5 set the alarm clock
6 turn out the light
7 fall asleep
8 snore
9 have a dream
10 have a nightmare
11 the alarm clock goes off
12 wake up
13 get up
14 have a wash

Exercise 10

a. If you knew
b. look after it
c. I'll give
d. live with my parents
e. I had an exam
f. accommodation
g. discussed the problem
h. in a book shop
i. it might be for me
j. I was born

Exercise 11

(Other orders might be possible.)
Letter to friends
1 f.   4 h.   7 e.
2 d.   5 c.   8 i.
3 b.   6 a.   9 g.

Letter to a hotel
1 o.   4 q.   7 r.
2 m.   5 l.   8 n.
3 k.   6 j.   9 p.

UNIT 14

Exercise 1

a. haven't heard
b. have found
c. went
d. agreed
e. haven't tried
f. has been
g. has left
h. has gone
i. has fallen
j. met
k. has ever seen
l. has won
m. had to
n. got
o. has had

Exercise 2

a. been   been
b. gone
c. Gone
d. been
e. been
f. gone

Exercise 3

a. Roger hasn't bought a doll for Harriet yet.
b. But he has already ordered the turkey.
c. Helen has already made the Christmas cake.
d. But she hasn't made the mince pies yet.
e. They haven't decorated the house yet.
f. But they have already sent out their Christmas cards.

Exercise 4

a. Has Roger bought a bike for Tom yet?
   No, he hasn't.
b. Has he ordered the turkey yet?
   Yes, he has.
c. Has Helen bought Roger's present yet?
   No, she hasn't.
d. Has she sent a present to Ann in Australia yet?
   Yes, she has.
e. Have they got a Christmas tree yet?
   No, they haven't.

Exercise 5

Ann's been sunbathing. She's a bit burnt.
She's been shopping. She hasn't got any money left.
She's been working in the garden. Her back hurts.
She's been reading for hours. Her eyes hurt.
She's been watching a sad film. She's crying.
She's been waiting for hours. She's furious.
She's been doing the housework. Everything's spotless.
She's been decorating the bathroom. She's got paint in her hair.
She's been cooking. The house smells of onions and garlic.
She's been bathing the children. She's soaking wet.

Exercise 6

Correct forms

a. I've cut
b. Have you heard

c. she's been shopping
d. I've broken
e. have you had
f. They've been living

Exercise 7

a.	down	k.	looking
b.	away (out is also possible)	l.	up
c.	Put	m.	after
d.	try	n.	round
e.	down	o.	Look
f.	turn	p.	up
g.	up	q.	looking
h.	on up	r.	back
i.	out	s.	fell
j.	fill	t.	gave

Exercise 8

a. have you been
b. She's been living
c. my leg
d. I gave the cheque to John on Saturday.
e. but I don't agree
f. frightened
g. a lovely weekend
h. She's very nice.
i. stars
j. I gave it to her

Exercise 9

a. Accepting an invitation
b. Paying a bill
c. Inviting
d. Could be several – giving news, inviting, but the formal thanks and request is probably the best
e. Thank-you letter after a weekend visit
f. Giving news
g. Formal invitation
h. Accepting an invitation
i. (Thanks and) request
j. Any informal letter, but giving news is probably the best
k. Informal invitation
l. Thank-you letter after a weekend visit
m. Formal invitation
n. Thanks and request

UNIT 15

Exercise 1

I couldn't answer the questions because I hadn't revised for the exam.
I was hungry because I hadn't eaten all day.
My mother was worried because I hadn't been in touch for a long time.
I was late because I had got stuck in a traffic jam.
I was pleased because I had passed my driving test.

I was nervous during the flight because I hadn't flown in a plane before.
My father was furious because I had crashed his car.
I was tired because I had slept badly.

Exercise 2

a.	3 1 2	d.	3 1 2 (or 3 2 1)
b.	1 2	e.	2 3 4 1
c.	2 1	f.	3 4 1 2 5

Exercise 3

a. thanked   had done
b. realized   had forgotten
c. had finished   went
d. called   had just gone
e. had been   knew
f. had listened   went

Exercise 4

a. When I had read the letter, I threw it away.
b. As soon as he had passed his driving test, he bought a car.
c. I took the book back to the library when I had finished reading it.
d. I didn't go to bed until I had done my homework.
e. When I had spent all my money I went home.
f. I'd read the book before I saw the film.
g. After her children had left home, she started writing.

Exercise 5

a. Mrs Mawby said it was a quiet flat, and the neighbours were nice.
b. She told me that the rent included gas and electricity.
c. Then she said she needed £100 deposit.
d. She told me that she had decorated the living room recently.
e. She said that other people had been to see the flat.
f. She told me I would have to make up my mind soon.
g. She said that the previous occupants had looked after it very well.
h. She told me that she had replaced all the carpets.
i. She told me that I could move in immediately.
j. I told Mrs Mawby that I would give her a ring soon.

Exercise 6

a. I asked her how many bedrooms there were.
b. She asked me when I wanted to move in.
c. I asked her what sort of heating there was.
d. I asked her how often she wanted the rent.
e. I asked her how far it was to the shops.
f. She asked me what I thought of the flat.

Exercise 7

a. She asked me if I smoked.
b. I asked her if there was a phone.
c. She asked me if I had a car.
d. I asked her if I could move the furniture around.
e. I asked her if there was a fridge in the kitchen.
f. I asked her if the flat had central heating.

Exercise 8

I   What sort of music do you like, Gary?
G   I have always liked jazz. In fact, I play in a small jazz band called Sax Appeal.
I   Where does the band play?
G   We play mainly in small clubs.
I   Have you ever played a Shakespearean role?
G   Yes, I have. I played Othello in Stratford in 1989, and I enjoyed it very much.
I   Do you ever want to direct a play?
G   I hope to one day, but I don't know when it can happen because I'm so busy acting.

Exercise 9

a.	told	m.	last
b.	said	n.	latest
c.	felt	o.	quite
d.	fell	p.	quiet
e.	lend	q.	Whose
f.	borrow	r.	Who's
g.	journey	s.	foreigner
h.	travel	t.	stranger
i.	buy	u.	game
j.	paid	v.	play
k.	Listen	w.	stolen
l.	hear	x.	robbed

Exercise 10

a. She told me that
b. teacher said we
c. where I was going
d. asked me if I (no comma)
e. We are all going
f. Everything is ready
g. We'll meet outside
h. and afterwards we
i. a lot of money
j. people are

STOP AND CHECK 13–15

Second Conditional

1 a. lived   would have
   b. had   wouldn't work
   c. would go   wasn't/weren't
   d. would you do   gave
   e. were   would look
2 a. He wouldn't be fat if he didn't eat a lot of sweets.

b. She wouldn't cough if she didn't smoke.

c. If he understood Portuguese, he'd work in Brazil.

d. If they had a garden, they'd grow vegetables.

e. If I had a boat, I'd sail around the world.

Might

a. She might have a holiday or she might look for a job.

b. They might go to Spain or they might stay at home.

c. You might forget it.

d. I might be late.

e. I might stay the night or I might come back the same day.

Present Perfect Simple and Continuous

a. I haven't finished yet.

b. Have they booked the restaurant yet?

c. We've already ordered the champagne.

d. Anna's been studying hard for five hours.

e. How long has Jim been cleaning his bike?

f. I've just seen Jim.

g. We've been helping Mary since five o'clock.

h. They haven't spoken to each other for four years.

i. Nobody has sent me a letter for a long time.

j. It hasn't rained here since June.

Tenses

a. come
b. came
c. haven't met
d. started
e. have been learning
f. didn't understand
g. has improved
h. have just taken
i. pass
j. will move
k. are coming
l. haven't seen
m. have never been
n. don't speak

Reported speech

a. hadn't met
b. had just taken
c. were coming
d. hadn't seen
e. didn't speak

Vocabulary

HEADWAY

John & Liz Soars

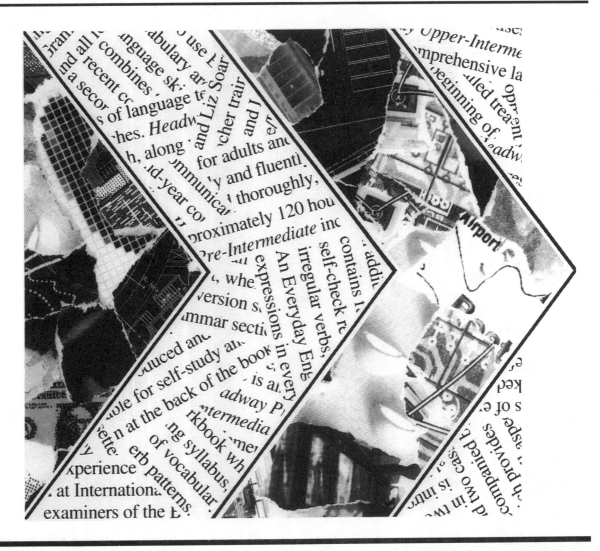

PRE-INTERMEDIATE

TEST BOOKLET

Note to the teacher

There are three tests in this booklet

Progress Test One covers the work done in Units 1–5
Progress Test Two covers the work done in Units 6–10
Progress Text Three covers the work done in Units 11–15

Each test carries with it a total possible score of 100 marks.

Oxford University Press
Walton Street, Oxford OX2 6DP

© Oxford University Press 1991

UNITS 1·5

Progress Test One

Grammar

Exercise 1   Questions and verb forms

Put the words in the right order to make a question.

Example
job learning for English your you are?
Are you learning English for your job?

a. English you start did learning when?

_____

b. tennis often play how does she?

_____

c. do doing what at you like weekend the?

_____

d. weekend do what you would to this like?

_____

e. dictionary why got you haven't a?

_____

f. much put my coffee sugar how did in you?

_____

g. phoned doing John when what you were?

_____

h. sandwiches make is who to going the?

_____

i. radio listening does enjoy to mother the your?

_____

j. live Anna where was child a did when she?

_____

Total 10

Exercise 2   Questions and tenses

Look at the chart.

Name	*Xavier*	*Mr and Mrs Ramsey*
Nationality	French	Australian
Town	London	Melbourne
Age	26	In their sixties
Family	one younger brother	no children
Occupation	chef	retired
Holiday last year	home to Paris for two weeks	two months in Scotland – visiting relatives
Holiday next year	drive to Morocco with friends	tour New Zealand for two weeks

Use the information in the chart and write the correct questions to the following answers.

Example
Where does Xavier come from?
He comes from France.

a. _____
They come from Australia.

b. _____
They live in Melbourne.

c. _____
He's 26.

d. _____
Yes, he does. He has one younger brother.

e. _____
No, they haven't got any.

f. _____
He's a chef.

147

g. _____

He went home to Paris for two weeks.

h. _____

They stayed there for two months.

i. _____

They're going to tour New Zealand.

j. _____

He's going to drive to Morocco.

Total 10

Exercise 3   Tenses and verb forms

In the following conversation put the verb in brackets into the correct tense or verb form.

Example

A   *Why ____did____ you ____go____ (go) to the seaside*
last weekend?

B   *Because we like ____sailing____ (sail).*

A   (a) _____ you _____ (know) Brian
Bailey?

B   Yes, I (b) _____ (meet) him two years ago while
I (c) _____ (work) in Germany. (d)
_____ he still _____ (live) there?

A   Yes, he does. He (e) _____ (live) in Frankfurt.
He (f) _____ (have got) a good job there but at
the moment he (g) _____ (work) in London. He's
here for a few days and I'd like (h) _____ (invite)
him and you for dinner. Can you (i) _____
(come)?

B   Yes, I hope so. I'd love (j) _____ (see) Brian
again! When I was in Germany we (k) _____
(see) each other quite often because his office was near
the school where I (l) _____ (teach) and so we
sometimes (m) _____ (have) lunch together. I
always enjoyed (n) _____ (talk) to him. I wanted
(o) _____ (write) to him but he moved and
I (p) _____ (not have) his new address.

A   Well, what about dinner on Friday?

B   That's fine. What time?

A   Is 8 o'clock OK? I (q) _____ (ring) Brian
yesterday to check the day, and I (r) _____ (ring)

him again tomorrow to check the time.

B   Well 8 o'clock is fine for me. I (s) _____ (come)
at about 8 and I (t) _____ (bring) a bottle of wine.

A   See you on Friday then!

Total 20

Exercise 4   Irregular past tenses

Here are twenty verbs. Ten are regular and ten are irregular.
Write the past tense form of the *irregular* verbs only.

buy	put
cook	speak
do	start
happen	take
have	talk
hear	visit
laugh	wait
leave	watch
listen	whisper
make	write

Total 10

Exercise 5   Countable and uncountable nouns

Underline the uncountable noun in the following pairs of
words.

Example
cheese/egg

money/pound	rice/potato	meat/hamburger
flower/flour	loaf/bread	song/music
job/homework	luggage/suitcase	food/meal
furniture/desk		

Total 5

Exercise 6   Expressions of quantity

In the following groups of sentences only one is correct.
Tick (✓) the correct one.

a.   Is there any milk? I can't see one.
Is there any milk? I can't see any.
Are there any milks? I can't see them.

b.   There's some potatoes, but only a little.
There's some potatoes, but only few.
There are some potatoes, but only a few.

c.   There's much cars parked in the street.
There are a lot of cars parked in the street.
There are lots cars parked in the street.

d. Have you got much unemployment in your town?
   Have you got the unemployment in your town?
   Have you got much unemployed people in your town?

e. Only a few people believes his story.
   Only a little people believes his story.
   Only a few people believe his story.

f. How much homeworks do you have tonight?
   How much homework do you have tonight?
   How many homeworks do you have tonight?

g. There aren't many rice and there aren't any eggs.
   There isn't much rice and there isn't any eggs.
   There isn't much rice and there aren't any eggs.

h. There was much snow last winter.
   There was a little snow last winter but not many.
   There was some snow last winter but not much.

i. How lovely! Somebody gave you some flowers.
   How lovely! Anybody gave you some flowers.
   How lovely! Somebody gave you any flowers.

j. I went anywhere very interesting for my holiday.
   I didn't go anywhere very interesting for my holiday.
   I didn't do anywhere very interesting for my holiday.

Total 10

Exercise 7   Articles

Put **a**, **an**, **the** or *nothing* into each gap in the story.

Example
I had _____ dinner with ___the___ Queen.

My Aunt Vanessa is (a) _____ artist. She lives in (b)
_____ beautiful old cottage by (c) _____ sea and she
paints (d) _____ small pictures of wild flowers and birds.
She doesn't like leaving (e) _____ cottage, but once (f)
_____ year she travels by (g) _____ train to London
and has (h) _____ tea with me at (i) _____ Savoy
Hotel. At the moment I'm quite worried about her because
she's in (j) _____ hospital, but I'm sure she'll be better
soon. I'm going to visit her next week.

Total 10

Vocabulary

Exercise 8   Which one is different?

All the words in this exercise appear in Units 1–5 of
Headway Pre-Intermediate.
They are in groups of four. Three of the words have things in
common. Underline the one word in each group that is
different.

Example
*castle cathedral cottage house (You can't live in a
cathedral.)*

a. language translator dictionary art
b. jungle village mountain field
c. handbag wallet suitcase purse
d. word processor fridge freezer cooker
e. video iron Walkman CD player
f. vacuum cleaner dishwasher lamp washing machine
g. pyjamas jumper pillow shirt
h. neck foot chest sock
i. hairdresser shopkeeper customer banker
j. tomorrow morning yesterday evening
   the day after tomorrow in two weeks' time
k. mushrooms cauliflower pineapple cabbage
l. strawberry cherry pear pea
m. knife saucepan frying pan oven
n. roast bake peel fry
o. butcher's greengrocer's chemist's baker's

Total 15

Exercise 9   Words that go together

Match a line in **A** with a line in **B**.

A	B
tell	driver
spend	work
hard	store
chewing	a bill
wear	money
take	gum
standard	a joke
taxi	of living
pay	a photograph
department	glasses

Total 10

Score

Exercise 1 _____ out of 10	
Exercise 2 _____ out of 10	
Exercise 3 _____ out of 20	
Exercise 4 _____ out of 10	
Exercise 5 _____ out of 5	**Total** _____
Exercise 6 _____ out of 10	**100**
Exercise 7 _____ out of 10	
Exercise 8 _____ out of 15	**Percentage**
Exercise 9 _____ out of 10	**Total** [___ /___ %]

UNITS 6-10

Progress Test Two

Grammar

Exercise 1   Descriptions

Below there are three dialogues. Put one of the words in the box into each gap.

worst	latest	more	as(×2)	funniest
funnier	than	friendlier	tastier	like
was	what	the	most	

A   I started a new job today, working in an office.

B   Really! How did it go?

A   It was OK. I was a bit nervous.

B   What are the other people (a) _____ ?

A   They're very nice. They seem (b) _____ than the people in my old job, and the job is much (c) _____ interesting.

B   You worked in a shop before, didn't you?

A   Yes. Working in an office is better (d) _____ working in a shop, I'll tell you! That was the (e) _____ job I've ever had. I hated it.

C   We went out for a meal to Luigi's last night – you know, that new Italian restaurant.

D   Mm, I know. What (f) _____ it like?

C   It was (g) _____ best Italian meal I've ever had, and it wasn't as expensive (h) _____ Giovanni's, so I think we'll go there again.

D   Yes. Giovanni's used to be the (i) _____ popular restaurant around here, but then it started getting very expensive.

C   And the service isn't (j) _____ good as it used to be.

D   What did you have?

C   Paul and I both had veal, but mine was cooked in wine and herbs, and it was (k) _____ than Paul's. But *he* liked it.

D   It sounds great.

E   Have you read John Harrison's (l) _____ book, *Going Round the World*?

F   No. (m) _____'s it like?

E   I think it's the (n) _____ book he's written. I laughed out loud all the way through.

F   I didn't like *The Truth and the Light*, the one that came out last year.

E   Neither did I. This one's much (o) _____ .

F   Can I borrow it?

Total 15

Exercise 2   Correct the mistakes

In the following pairs of sentences, one is correct, and in the other there is a mistake. Tick (✓) the correct one.

Example
I have watched TV last night.
I watched TV last night.   ✓

a. I have lived in Chesswood for five years.
    I live in Chesswood for five years.

b. We moved here after my daughter was born.
    We have moved here after my daughter was born.

c. Before that we have lived in London.
    Before that we lived in London.

d. I am a teacher since I left university.
    I have been a teacher since I left university.

e. I went to Bristol University in 1984.
   I have been to Bristol University in 1984.
f. We have studied English since three years.
   We have studied English for three years.
g. I never went to Russia, but I'd like to.
   I have never been to Russia, but I'd like to.

Total 7

Exercise 3   Tenses

Put the verb in brackets in the correct tense. The tenses used are the Present Simple, the Past Simple, and the Present Perfect.

Example
I _____got_____ (get) up at 7.00 this morning.

Carla Brown has a job in advertising. It's a good job, and she (a) _____ (earn) over £20,000 a year. She (b) _____ (study) marketing at college, and then (c) _____ (find) a job with a small advertising agency in Manchester. Since then she (d) _____ (change) her job several times. Now she (e) _____ (work) for Jerome and Jerome, which is a big company with offices all over the world. She (f) _____ (be) with the company for three years.

The company has clients in America, and she (g) _____ (be) there several times on business. Last year she (h) _____ (spend) six months there.

Total 8

Exercise 4   *Have to* or *should*?

Complete the sentences with a form of **have to**, **don't have to**, **should** or **shouldn't**.

Example
If you feel ill, you _____**should**_____ *go to bed.*

a. When you catch a plane, you _____ check in before you board the plane.
b. You _____ have too much hand luggage.
c. You _____ wear comfortable clothing.
d. A pilot _____ train for many years.
e. People who want to smoke _____ sit in certain seats.
f. You _____ wear your seat belt all the time. You can take it off.
g. But you _____ wear it at take-off and landing.

h. You _____ drink too much alcohol because you might be ill.
i. There is often a film on a long flight, but you _____ watch it. You can go to sleep.
j. When you've got your luggage, you _____ go through Customs.

Total 10

Exercise 5   Time clauses

Put the words in the right order.

Example
bath I when home will get have a I
I will have a bath when I get home.

a. hear if I news any you I phone will

   _____

b. pay as you I back soon can I as will

   _____

c. you feel stop better if will you smoking

   _____

d. car Peter enough when he buy a has will money

   _____

e. problem help I you have you a will if

   _____

Total 5

Exercise 6   Tenses

Put the verb in brackets in the correct tense. The tenses used are the Present Simple and the **will** future.

a. I _____ (call) you when lunch _____ (be) ready.
b. If you _____ (be) late, I _____ (go) without you.
c. If she _____ (pass) her driving test, she _____ (buy) a car.
d. I _____ (go) home as soon as I _____ (finish) work.
e. If my neighbours _____ (not stop) making a noise, I _____ (go) round and complain.

Total 5

Exercise 7 *Used to* **or the Past Simple?**

Look at the profile of the singer, Andy Goodchild. Complete the sentences, using **used to** where possible, or the Past Simple.

Example
He used to live with his parents in Leeds.
He had his first guitar when he was six.

Factfile on Andy Goodchild

Andy's highly successful solo career began in 1984. He now lives in London with his wife, Suzy, and their daughter, Trixie.
Andy tells us about his background.

1959 – 80	Lived in Leeds with my parents
1965	My first guitar!
1970 – 80	Bradford School
1971 – 75	Wrote songs with a friend called Keith
1976 – 83	Played with a band called the Forwards
1979 – 82	Played in pubs and clubs
1980	Started going out with a girl called Mandy
June 1981	Number one record, *She's mine*
1982	Toured the United States
1983	Broke up with Mandy
1984	Went solo
August 1985	Pop festival in Los Angeles

---

a. He _____ Bradford School.

b. He _____ football for the school.

c. He _____ songs with a friend called Keith.

d. He _____ with The Forwards.

e. The Forwards _____ in pubs and clubs.

f. In 1981 he _____ a number one record.

g. He _____ with a girl called Mandy.

h. The Forwards _____ the United States in 1982.

i. Andy _____ in 1984.

j. He _____ a pop festival in Los Angeles the following year.

Total 10

Exercise 8 **Questions**

Write questions about the words in italics.

Example
Somebody broke the window.
Who broke the window?

a. They are talking about *somebody*.

_____

b. Peter works for *somebody*.

_____

c. *Somebody* hit Lilly.

_____

d. *Something* smells awful!

_____

e. Jeremy lives with *someone*.

_____

f. Mike and Polly are arguing about *something*.

_____

g. Sh! I'm listening to *something*.

_____

h. *Someone* gave me £100!

_____

i. *Someone* told me Ann was getting married!

_____

j. *Something* just crept across the carpet!

_____

Total 10

Vocabulary

Exercise 9   Words that go together

Match a line in **A** with a line in **B**.

A	B
play	work
alarm	post
win	the drums
part-time	in shifts
traffic	lounge
departure	hour
sign	clock
notice	lights
rush	an award
work	board

Total 10

Exercise 10   Homophones

In the following sentences, the word in italics is the wrong homophone. The word *sounds* right, but the spelling is wrong.
Correct the spelling.

Example
*I **new** Peter when we were at school.*   ⟶ **knew**

a. I got a *check* for £50 in the post.

b. We *red* about the accident in the newspaper.

c. How much is the *fair* to Manchester?

d. Do you like my shirt? I bought it in a *sail*.

e. I didn't mean to *brake* your bike. Sorry.

Total 5

Exercise 11   Adverbs

Put one of the adverbs from the box into each gap.

too	exactly	only	even	especially

a. I'm hungry. I _____ had a piece of toast this morning.

b. I like the Impressionists, _____ Monet.

c. It is _____ three fifty-five and twenty seconds.

d. Paul plays the guitar and sings, _____ .

e. Everyone liked the curry I cooked, _____ Malcolm, who usually hates hot foot.

Total 5

Exercise 12   Opposites

Choose an adjective from the box. Write it next to its opposite.

Example
*cheap – **expensive***

generous	well-behaved	pleased	tidy	quiet
beautiful	interesting	modern	poor	miserable

a. ugly _____   f. wealthy _____
b. annoyed _____   g. happy _____
c. noisy _____   h. naughty _____
d. mean _____   i. boring _____
e. old _____   j. messy _____

Total 10

Score

Exercise 1 _____ out of 15
Exercise 2 _____ out of 7
Exercise 3 _____ out of 8
Exercise 4 _____ out of 10
Exercise 5 _____ out of 5
Exercise 6 _____ out of 5
Exercise 7 _____ out of 10
Exercise 8 _____ out of 10
Exercise 9 _____ out of 10
Exercise 10 _____ out of 5
Exercise 11 _____ out of 5
Exercise 12 _____ out of 10

Total   _____

100

**Percentage
Total**   [/ %]

UNITS 11-15

Progress Test Three

Grammar

Exercise 1 Irregular past tenses

Here are twenty verbs. Ten are regular and ten are irregular. Write in the Past Simple and Past Participle for the *irregular* verbs only.

	Past Simple	Past participle
appear		
bring		
climb		
fall		
feel		
forget		
improve		
invent		
know		
let		
lose		
manage		
pass		
pick		
speak		
start		
tell		
understand		
use		
want		

Total 10

Exercise 2 Active or passive?

Underline the correct form in the following sentences.

Example
Portuguese *speaks /is spoken* in Brazil.

a. That's the third time he *has failed/has been failed* the exam.
b. *'Hot Lips'* *wrote/was written* by Celia Young.
c. A lot of trees *cut down/were cut down* to build that house.
d. They *don't grow/aren't grown* bananas in Scotland.
e. Some pictures *have taken/have been taken* from the museum.

Total 5

Exercise 3 Passives

Put the words in the right order.

a. world   is   English   the   all   spoken   over

_____

b. since   has   nylon   1932   made   been

_____

c. Mary's   invited   I   to   wasn't   party   why?

_____

d. will   when   be   new   the   bridge   built?

_____

e. asked   car   design   were   they   to   new   a

_____

Total 5

154

Exercise 4 Second Conditional

Use each verb in **B** once only and make five sentences from the chart.

A	B	C	D	E
If I	lived earned knew had were	a dictionary you in Brazil more money Maria's address	I'd I wouldn't	go to see her. look up the word. marry George. learn Portuguese. save it.

Total 5

Exercise 5 Second Conditional and *might*

Read the text about Jane. Then complete the sentences below.

Jane's unhappy at home and unhappy at work. She has a boring job and she doesn't earn much money. Her boss says that he will perhaps give her a pay rise next month, but he isn't sure yet. She doesn't have a car and she goes to work on crowded buses every day. She doesn't have a flat, she lives in a small room above a noisy restaurant in the centre of town. She finds it difficult to sleep because the restaurant doesn't close until after midnight. She thinks that she will perhaps go and live with her friend Wendy but she isn't sure yet because she likes living on her own.

Example
Jane __**wouldn't be**__ *unhappy if she* __**lived**__ *in a quiet flat.*

a. Jane _____ happier if she _____ a more interesting job.

b. Her boss might _____ .

c. If she _____ a car, she _____ to work by bus.

d. If she _____ live above a restaurant, she _____ it easier to sleep.

e. She might _____ her friend Wendy.

Total 5

Exercise 6 Present Perfect Simple and Continuous

In the following pairs of sentences only one is correct. Tick (✓) the correct one.

a. I saw her five minutes ago.
   I've seen her five minutes ago.

b. We are here since last Saturday.
   We've been here since last Saturday.

c. How long have you known Wendy?
   How long have you been knowing Wendy?

d. We haven't made coffee yet.
   We didn't make coffee yet.

e. He is waiting to see the doctor since nine o'clock.
   He has been waiting to see the doctor since nine o'clock.

f. When did you buy your new car?
   When have you bought your new car?

g. Mary isn't home. She's been to work.
   Mary isn't home. She's gone to work.

h. I've run in the park, so I'm tired.
   I've been running in the park, so I'm tired.

i. I've run round the park three times.
   I've been running round the park three times.

j. They already had their dinner.
   They've already had their dinner.

Total 10

Exercise 7 Present Perfect Continuous

Ask questions to find out *How long . . . ?*

Example
'I'm learning English.'
'*How long* have you been learning English?'

a. 'I'm waiting for a bus.'
   '_____?'

b. 'Tom's saving up to buy a boat.'
   '_____?'

c. 'I'm having driving lessons.'
   '_____?'

d. 'Alice is working in the library.'
   '_____?'

e. 'The Greens are trying to sell their house.'
   '_____?'

Total 5

Exercise 8   Reported statements and questions

Put the following sentences into reported speech.

Examples

'They live in Oxford,' she said.
She said (that) they lived in Oxford.

'Do you live in Oxford?' she asked them.
She asked them if they lived in Oxford.

a. 'Do you often visit your aunt?' she asked him.

   She asked him _____

b. 'I visit her every Sunday,' he said.

   He said that _____

c. 'I took her some flowers for her birthday,' he said.

   He said that _____

d. 'What did you do at the weekend?' he asked her.

   He asked her _____

e. 'I've forgotten,' she said.

   She said that _____

| Total 5 |

Exercise 9   *Had* or *would*?

All the following sentences have **'d** in them.
Write it out in full to show if it is **had** or **would**.

Example
He'd left before I arrived. = **had**

a. I told him that I'*d* like to come.
b. When we'*d* had tea, we went for a walk.
c. Why did you tell her that I'*d* broken the vase?
d. If I had a car, I'*d* drive you there with pleasure.
e. She said that he'*d* just given it to her.

| Total 5 |

Exercise 10   Tenses and verb forms

In the following newspaper article put the verb in brackets in
the correct tense or verb form. Sometimes you will also have
to decide whether the verb is active or passive.

Example
I asked John __***to do***__ *(do) the shopping but he*
__***hasn't done***__ *(not do) it yet.*

£200M Art Stolen

Paintings by Monet, Rembrandt, and Degas
(a) _____ (steal) from the Boston Museum.

   Yesterday afternoon two thieves wearing police uniforms
arrived at the museum and asked the guard (b) _____
(show) them Monet's paintings. They said that they
(c) _____ (receive) a telephone call at the police
station that morning telling them that the paintings were in
danger. The guard immediately let them (d) _____
(see) the paintings. The thieves told him (e) _____
(turn off) the alarm system and then suddenly they made
him (f) _____ (lie) on the ground and they tied his
arms and legs. They worked very quickly and carefully and
when they (g) _____ (collect) the best paintings they
(h) _____ (leave) the museum quietly and calmly
through the front door. The director of the museum, Karen
Haas said:

   'The thieves (i) _____ (take) our best pictures. I
(j) _____ (work) here for 12 years and I can't believe
that this (k) _____ (happen). How did they manage
(l) _____ (take) them so easily? They might
(m) _____ (try) (n) _____ (sell) them to an art
collector in Europe, but this will be difficult because the
paintings are so well known. If they (o) _____ (not
be) so well known, it would (p) _____ (be) easier
(q) _____ (sell) them. We have decided
(r) _____ (employ) more guards, and a new alarm
system (s) _____ already _____ (put) in . I'm
sure the police will find the thieves and our paintings, but
they think it might (t) _____ (take) a long time.'

| Total 20 |

Vocabulary

Exercise 11   Multi-word verbs

Match a line in **A** with a line in **B**.

A	B
I didn't know the word,	but I picked it up quite easily.
I used to enjoy smoking,	I'll look after it.
People say French is difficult,	so I looked it up.
Don't worry about the cat,	but I gave it up.

Total 4

Exercise 12   Prepositions

Put the correct preposition into each gap.

a. I've been reading a story _____ two girls who travelled round the world.

b. I sold my car _____ £2,000.

c. If that machine weren't _____ of order, I'd get you a drink.

d. Do you believe _____ UFOs?

e. He said that she was too young to buy alcohol and that it was _____ the law.

f. Let me pay _____ the drinks.

Total 6

Exercise 13   Words that go together

Match a line in **A** with a line in **B**

A	B	A	B
never	story	narrow	concert
wear	a lift	get	glasses
wait	the truth	sun	in computers
drive	patiently	pop	forecast
tell	weight	rain	path
detective	a uniform	interested	heavily
lose	carefully	weather	ready
give someone	mind		

Total 15

Score

Exercise 1 _____ out of 10
Exercise 2 _____ out of 5
Exercise 3 _____ out of 5
Exercise 4 _____ out of 5
Exercise 5 _____ out of 5
Exercise 6 _____ out of 10
Exercise 7 _____ out of 5
Exercise 8 _____ out of 5
Exercise 9 _____ out of 5
Exercise 10 _____ out of 20
Exercise 11 _____ out of 4
Exercise 12 _____ out of 6
Exercise 13 _____ out of 15

Total _____

100

Percentage Total [/ %]

TEST BOOKLET KEY

Headway Pre-Intermediate Tests

Test One   Units 1–5

Exercise 1

a. When did you start learning English?
b. How often does she play tennis?
c. What do you like doing at the weekend?
d. What would you like to do this weekend?
e. Why haven't you got a dictionary?
f. How much sugar did you put in my coffee?
g. What were you doing when John phoned?
h. Who is going to make the sandwiches?
i. Does your mother enjoy listening to the radio?
j. Where did Anna live when she was a child?

Exercise 2

a. Where do Mr and Mrs Ramsey come from?
b. Where do they live?
c. How old is Xavier?
d. Does he have/Has he got any brothers or sisters?
e. Have Mr and Mrs Ramsey got/Do Mr and Mrs Ramsey have any children?
f. What does Xavier do/What's Xavier's job?
g. Where did he go on holiday last year?
h. How long did Mr and Mrs Ramsey stay in Scotland?
i. Where are they going on holiday next year?
j. Where is Xavier going on holiday next year?

Exercise 3

a. Do you know
b. met
c. was working
d. Does he still live
e. lives
f. has got
g. is working
h. to invite
i. come
j. to see
k. saw
l. was teaching
m. had
n. talking
o. to write
p. don't have/haven't got
q. rang
r. am going to ring/will ring
s. 'll come
t. 'll bring

Exercise 4

bought
did
had
heard
left
made
put
spoke
took
wrote

Exercise 5
Uncountable nouns

money
flour
homework
furniture
rice
bread
luggage
meat
music
food

Exercise 6
Correct sentences

a. Is there any milk? I can't see any.
b. There are some potatoes, but only a few.
c. There are a lot of cars parked in the street.
d. Have you got much unemployment in your town?
e. Only a few people believe his story.
f. How much homework do you have tonight?
g. There isn't much rice and there aren't any eggs.
h. There was some snow last winter but not much.
i. How lovely! Somebody gave you some flowers.
j. I didn't go anywhere very interesting for my holiday.

Exercise 7

a. an
b. a
c. the
d. (nothing)
e. the
f. a
g. (nothing)
h. (nothing)
i. the
j. (nothing)

Exercise 8

a. art (The others are to do with learning a language.)
b. village (A village is man-made.)
c. suitcase (The others are everyday objects.)
d. word processor (The others are to do with food.)
e. iron (The others are to do with entertainment.)
f. lamp (The others are to do with cleaning the house.)

g. pillow (The others are clothes.)
h. sock (The others are parts of the body.)
i. customer (The others all give a service to the customer.)
j. yesterday evening (The others refer to the future.)
k. pineapple (The others are vegetables.)
l. pea (The others are fruit.)
m. knife (The others are all for cooking.)
n. peel (The others are ways of cooking.)
o. chemist's (The others sell food.)

Exercise 9

tell a joke
spend money
hard work
chewing gum
wear glasses
take a photograph
standard of living
taxi driver
pay a bill
department store

Test Two   Units 6–10

Exercise 1

a. like	f. was	k. tastier
b. friendlier	g. the	l. latest
c. more	h. as	m. What
d. than	i. most	n. funniest
e. worst	j. as	o. funnier

Exercise 2
Correct sentences

a. I have lived in Chesswood for five years.
b. We moved here after my daughter was born.
c. Before that we lived in London.
d. I have been a teacher since I left university.
e. I went to Bristol University in 1984.
f. We have studied English for three years.
g. I have never been to Russia, but I'd like to.

Exercise 3

a. earns	e. works
b. studied	f. has been
c. found	g. has been
d. has changed	h. spent

Exercise 4

a. have to	f. don't have to
b. shouldn't	g. have to
c. should	h. shouldn't
d. has to	i. don't have to
e. have to	j. have to

Exercise 5

a. If I hear any news, I will phone you.
b. I will pay you back as soon as I can.
c. You will feel better if you stop smoking.
d. Peter will buy a car when he has enough money.
e. I will help you if you have a problem.

Exercise 6

a. I'll call   lunch is ready
b. you are late   I'll go
c. she passes   she'll buy
d. I'll go   I finish
e. my neighbours don't stop   I'll go

Exercise 7

a. He used to go to Bradford School.
b. He used to play football for the school.
c. He used to write songs with a friend called Keith.
d. He used to play with The Forwards.
e. The Forwards used to play in pubs and clubs.
f. In 1981 he had a number one record.
g. He used to go out with a girl called Mandy.
h. The Forwards toured the United States in 1982.
i. Andy went solo in 1984.
j. He played at a pop festival in Los Angeles the following year.

Exercise 8

a. Who are they talking about?
b. Who does Peter work for?
c. Who hit Lilly?
d. What smells awful?
e. Who does Jeremy live with?
f. What are they arguing about?
g. What are you listening to?
h. Who gave you £100?
i. Who told you Ann was getting married?
j. What just crept across the carpet?

Exercise 9

play the drums	departure lounge
alarm clock	sign post
win an award	notice board
part-time work	rush hour
traffic lights	work in shifts

Exercise 10

a. cheque	d. sale
b. read	e. break
c. fare	

Exercise 11

a. only	d. too
b. especially	e. even
c. exactly	

Exercise 12

a. beautiful
b. pleased
c. quiet
d. generous
e. modern
f. poor
g. miserable
h. well-behaved
i. interesting
j. tidy

Test Three   Units 11–15

Exercise 1

brought	brought	let	let
fell	fallen	lost	lost
felt	felt	spoke	spoken
forgot	forgotten	told	told
knew	known	understood	understood

Exercise 2
Correct forms

a. has failed
b. was written
c. were cut down
d. don't grow
e. have been taken

Exercise 3

a. English is spoken all over the world.
b. Nylon has been made since 1932.
c. Why wasn't I invited to Mary's party?
d. When will the new bridge be built?
e. They were asked to design a new car.

Exercise 4

If I lived in Brazil, I'd learn Portuguese.
If I earned more money, I'd save it.
If I knew Maria's address, I'd go to see her.
If I had a dictionary, I'd look up the word.
If I were you, I wouldn't marry George.

Exercise 5

a. Jane would be happier if she had a more interesting job.
b. Her boss might give her a pay rise next month.
c. If she had a car, she wouldn't go to work by bus.
d. If she didn't live above a restaurant, she would find it easier to sleep.
e. She might go and live with her friend Wendy.

Exercise 6
Correct sentences

a. I saw her five minutes ago.
b. We've been here since last Saturday.
c. How long have you known Wendy?
d. We haven't made coffee yet.
e. He has been waiting to see the doctor since nine o'clock.
f. When did you buy your new car?
g. Mary isn't home. She's gone to work.
h. I've been running in the park, so I'm tired.

i. I've run round the park three times.
j. They've already had their dinner.

Exercise 7

a. How long have you been waiting for a bus?
b. How long has he been saving up to buy a boat?
c. How long have you been having driving lessons?
d. How long has she been working in the library?
e. How long have they been trying to sell their house?

Exercise 8

a. She asked him if he often visited his aunt.
b. He said that he visited her every Sunday.
c. He said that he'd taken her some flowers for her birthday.
d. He asked her what she'd done at the weekend.
e. She said that she'd forgotten.

Exercise 9

a. would
b. had
c. had
d. would
e. had

Exercise 10

a. have been stolen
b. to show
c. had received
d. see
e. to turn off
f. lie
g. had collected
h. left
i. have taken
j. have worked/have been working
k. has happened
l. to take
m. try
n. to sell
o. weren't
p. be
q. to sell
r. to employ
s. has already been put
t. take

Exercise 11

I didn't know the word, so I looked it up.
I used to enjoy smoking, but I gave it up.
People say French is difficult, but I picked it up quite easily.
Don't worry about the cat. I'll look after it.

Exercise 12

a. about
b. for
c. out
d. in
e. against
f. for

Exercise 13

never mind	narrow path
wear a uniform	get ready
wait patiently	sunglasses
drive carefully	pop concert
tell the truth	rain heavily
detective story	interested in computers
lose weight	weather forecast
give someone a lift	